EVOLVE
OR DIE

Hard-Won Lessons from a Hockey Life

John Shannon

PUBLISHED BY SIMON & SCHUSTER

New York   London   Toronto   Sydney   New Delhi

Simon & Schuster Canada
A Division of Simon & Schuster, Inc.
166 King Street East, Suite 300
Toronto, Ontario M5A 1J3

This Simon & Schuster Canada edition October 2022

SIMON & SCHUSTER CANADA and colophon are trademarks of Simon & Schuster, Inc.

For information about special discounts for bulk purchases,
please contact Simon & Schuster Special Sales at
1-800-268-3216 or CustomerService@simonandschuster.ca.

Manufactured in the United States of America

1   3   5   7   9   10   8   6   4   2

Library and Archives Canada Cataloguing in Publication
Title: Evolve or die : hard-won lessons from a hockey life / John Shannon.
Names: Shannon, John, 1956- author.
Identifiers: Canadiana (print) 2022021221X | Canadiana (ebook) 20220212228
| ISBN 9781982169015 (hardcover) | ISBN 9781982169022 (ebook)
Subjects: LCSH: Shannon, John, 1956—Anecdotes. | LCSH: Hockey—
Anecdotes. | LCSH: National Hockey League—Anecdotes. | LCSH: Hockey night
in Canada (Television program)—History. | LCSH: Hockey—Canada—History.
| LCSH: Sportscasters—Canada—Biography. | LCGFT: Autobiographies.
Classification: LCC GV848.5 .S525 2022 | DDC 796.962/092—dc23

ISBN 978-1-9821-6901-5
ISBN 978-1-9821-6902-2 (ebook)

To Mickee, Jake, and Maja, who sacrificed much more than I ever did for me to play in the sandbox.

"As you wish."

CONTENTS

INTRODUCTION

FOR THE RECORD, I HAVE NEVER WORKED A SINGLE DAY OF MY ADULT LIFE.
Since the mid-1970s I have played in radio, television, and sports—
and been paid for it. Quite frankly, it has been a dream come true. Never
good enough to play the actual sports, I always was proud to go to the
"championship" most years. That's what it was all about. To be in the
pressure of the moment with millions watching and, hopefully, enjoying
the product. And knowing when the television show should not over-
shadow the actual event.

The media business of radio, television, and digital is not that difficult, really. We tend to make it difficult. It is the ability with words,
pictures, and graphics to tell a story. A story to make the audience gasp,
laugh, or cry. It's called the "wow" factor. I truly believe the philosophy
that I have used in my work is simpler than most. Show the viewer
"how" and tell them "why." A commonsense approach, almost like a
fairy tale.

1

"Once upon a time . . . the Good Prince rode in on a white stallion . . . And they lived happily ever after."

In the sports television world, you have the challenge of telling that story in fifteen seconds, three minutes, fifteen minutes, or even the duration of a game. Every aspect of doing it right has a beginning, middle, and end. Once you grasp that simple concept, surviving in media becomes thriving in media.

"Once upon a time" becomes the close-up of the superstar centre. "The Good Prince" becomes the replay of his spectacular goal. And "happily ever after" becomes the celebration on the bench and the cheers of the home team crowd.

In televising the game of hockey, you have to know how to do that for one play, one period, one game, and perhaps a whole playoff series. It is that storytelling that was engrained in all of us at *Hockey Night in Canada*.

Working at *HNIC* meant feeling like a champion. You knew that the first day you started there. And everyone involved taught you that, every day after. A pride in doing it right. Spending hours perfecting the craft.

Our crew was always viewed as the third team in the arena. Our expectations and demands were as important, in our minds, as those of the two teams playing the game. We wore our uniform with pride. We played the game hard. We focused for the whole sixty minutes. And our ability to react to events on and off the ice, to create those "wow" factors, gave the audience a chance to enjoy the event that much more.

I wonder if my biggest strength in my career is that I don't think as an athlete. Too often in television, we say "what's going on in the player's mind" (or in the room or on the bench). That's why we have morphed the broadcast booth into a combination of professional broadcasters paired with former athletes. Some of those athletes, while very good at their jobs, often don't understand who they are talking to. The "whys" of an event are often communicated in such a manner that might be too technical. Not everyone in the audience played the sport they are watching. If you make an explanation too complicated, you aren't doing the job properly.

If you ever hear a doctor speak technically, you may not understand what the diagnosis of your ailment is. If the doctor gives it to you in layman's terms, you have a chance.

In television, the power to be the eyes of a fan anywhere in this country was energizing. Good, quality television is like winning the game. I like—no, I *love* to win.

There are many in the industry who view what we do as an art form. I'm not one of them. I think the business we are in is much more of a conversation. And unlike those in the news industry, we are not deciphering current events or interpreting the latest from world leaders. We are, in fact, playing in the sandbox of life. We are following the exploits of modern-day gladiators. Rationalizing people's passion for one team, or one sport, over another. Putting athletes on pedestals or knocking them off. And as much as the business is driven by technology, it truly is guided by the demand for perfection.

Sure, there were some emotional times, both personally and professionally. Actually, it is better to describe it as professionally personal. And I could be hard on people and hard on myself. Sometimes I crossed the line and paid for it. But it never stopped me from wanting to create great television and tell great stories. It never stopped me from wanting to be the best—and to win.

Technology has changed so much over the years. The digitization of the industry has made life much easier. But people haven't changed, and it's the people who have made our business. Managing people—helping, coaching, and watching them grow—is truly the greatest accomplishment of anyone's career. Hoping they learn from you. Certainly, you learn from them. Wanting to be better and wanting those around you to be better.

And along the way, having some fun. Surely, we have to have fun. That's what I want to tell you about in these pages. The joy inherent in how our business has changed, how watching the game has changed, and some of the great people I've met along the way.

As of this writing, I am sixty-four years old, in my sixth decade of being in broadcasting, and around sports, particularly hockey. It's at this point that my wife, Mickee, interjects, "You haven't been in television sixty years. Since you were four!"

No, I haven't. But my career started in the glory years of Scotty Bowman's Montreal Canadiens in the mid-1970s. Through the Islanders, Oilers, Flames, Penguins, Red Wings, and every other Stanley Cup champion, I have witnessed or commented on six decades of triumphs, tragedies, and turmoil. It has been an unbelievable ride.

Along with all those of my generation, I have been part of the greatest period of technology growth, which is supposed to make our lives better. I was born in an analog world; I now live in a digital one. From copper to coax to fibre, we have witnessed our world get smaller and the pictures get bigger and more vivid. It has been an astonishing ride.

I have made friends for life. And I have met people who have influenced me far more than I have influenced them. Some of those people have changed my life for the better. Some, not so much. I have seen much of the world, through Europe and Asia, because of a career that I never, ever, viewed as a job. It was always an adventure. I've been all over Canada and the United States, too. I used to brag that I could drive east to west and back and be able to always stay with a friend, have a good laugh and a glass of wine, and move on. It has been a joyful ride.

It has carried me through six decades of this business, on both sides of the camera and through multiple networks, the offices of NHL teams, and the league office. In this journey, at times closer to a roller-coaster ride, I have witnessed spectacular athletic events. Historic, iconic sports moments. It has been, and continues to be, a great ride. A ride that has brought me to tears (more of joy than anguish), a ride that has allowed me to puff my chest out and say, "Hey, look at us." A ride alongside the viewers, enjoying some of the greatest games, funniest stories, and passionate visuals of hockey.

Enjoy.

ONE
THE END AND
NEW BEGINNINGS

I WASN'T SURPRISED WHEN THE PHONE RANG IN EARLY JULY 2019. AFTER ALL, MY role at Sportsnet, the network I had called home for ten years, had been diminished over the previous fifteen months. At one point I was involved in radio, the website, junior hockey, the NHL package, and the nightly sports show. In sports vernacular, I was "a five-tool player." There had been nights when I followed a radio spot with one or even two television appearances. It was frenetic, and I loved every minute if it!

Rogers-owned Sportsnet was finishing its fourth year as the national rights holder of NHL games in Canada. The first four seasons had been tumultuous, with management changes and budget reductions almost every season. There was a small core of us who had lived through the changes. We loved the day-to-day challenge of doing games on multiple channels, almost every night of the week. I had been one of the fortunate ones who morphed into a jack-of-all-trades, doing television, radio, and even writing a weekly column for the Sportsnet website. My radio and

TV roles were diverse, from games to sportscasts and other shows to go along with my radio responsibilities on *Prime Time Sports* with Bob Mc-Cown, and simple reports for Rogers radio stations across the country. I believed in my heart that I had made myself versatile enough to be indispensable. That obviously was not the case.

We had just finished the annual free agent show on Sportsnet with a minimal crew of production people and announcers. Along with announcers like Nick Kypreos, Doug MacLean, Elliotte Friedman, and Chris Johnston, we were digging up the latest info and background of the thirty-one teams and their attempts to sign free agent players. The job that day demands persistence and patience, as you pester every general manager, agent, scout, and owner to be the first to get the breaking news of pending player signings. It's challenging, and you can strain friendships and other relationships trying to be first. For the record, over the years I have spent days after the free agent and trade deadline show apologizing to my friends in the game for being such a pain in the ass. Most, if not all, understand.

It was the end of the season and our normal routines were clouded. Rumours were rampant that more cuts would be coming to the company as it tried to adjust its profit margins. It felt like every off-season brought a level of insecurity to our group—every summer, the group got smaller. To this day, I believe Rogers Media always made money; they just wanted to make more. Such is the life, and the demands, of a publicly traded company.

Locked into a battle with Bell Canada, its partner in the ownership of Maple Leaf Sports & Entertainment, or MLSE (Bell and Rogers both own 37.5 percent of the company, while Larry Tanenbaum owns 25 percent and the chairman's title), Rogers constantly was trying to create "synergies" between all of its assets. But it was a company of silos, and the bureaucracy was complex. Old-school Rogers brass wouldn't share with the new executives who largely felt (it seemed to me) that the company was too inefficient. After all, information is power. For that reason, the lack of sharing information, there was a perception that the company was always in flux.

The company had grown in leaps and bounds since Ted Rogers envisioned an organization that owned radio stations, then cable TV. Cable, internet, and cell phones were still the driving force of the company, and the media division, which included radio, TV, specialty television, magazines, and the Toronto Blue Jays Major League Baseball team, was just a very small part of the corporate profits and structure. It was a huge company with thousands of employees from coast to coast. In a country this vast, communication is a challenge that will never be fully solved.

A month before free agency, I was working alongside Bob McCown on his successful afternoon radio show in Toronto, when he told me that he had a meeting the next day with Rick Brace, the president of Rogers Media. This wasn't usual. Bob surmised everything from Rick looking for advice on radio to Rick wanting to extend Bob's contract, which would expire in less than a year. Within twenty-four hours, Bob pulled me aside to say that Brace was buying out the remainder of his contract, and that I should watch my back.

This took me a little by surprise because I felt I was contributing enough on all the platforms to continue. I did regular news hits, radio across the country, *Hockey Central* at noon on radio and television, and was a regular contributor to regional hockey packages in Vancouver, Calgary, and Edmonton (my western roots coming out in spades). I had tried to contribute to the growing digital business on a daily basis, writing columns and detailing the game from a different perspective. Put another way, I was trying to stay relevant.

The tip from Bob was a bit numbing, too, because I had been told a few months earlier by a mutual friend of Brace's that "Rogers has big plans for Shannon." What could that be? More TV? Doubtful. More radio? Possibly. Brace had told me on multiple occasions how much he had enjoyed my banter with McCown. I took him at his word when he complimented me. How silly of me. I have always been a trusting person. I suppose my nature of being direct and honest, and sometimes blunt, was something I projected on others, because I was hearing what I wanted to hear.

Not that Bob exaggerates, but I was always wary when he told me these types of stories. He is a dear friend to this day, and we enjoy great discussions and laughs about all kinds of things: politics, golf, media, Ed Sullivan (I do believe my impression of the New York impresario is better than Bob's, but his Foster Hewitt impression is much better than mine). His warning about the future was filed away, and not taken with the alarm it should have been.

That phone call in early July was from Rogers executive Rob Corte. He was in charge of production at Sportsnet, fifteen years my junior, and very proper. He asked if I could "pop into the office" for a quick discussion. I knew right then and there that I was done. Technically I wasn't going to be fired, but rather, for the second time in my career, my contract would not be renewed.

I might handle it differently outwardly, and I've been accused of being too serious, but you never get use to rejection, even at sixty-two. It had been Corte, two weeks earlier, that told me "everything should work out" when I pressed him at the NHL Draft in Vancouver about the future. It was a draft I was not scheduled to go to, but asked to in order to prepare for upcoming free agency, and Corte agreed. I did do some radio from Vancouver, but not one drop of television for the three days, which did not sit well with me. Such was life, I thought. Again, it should have been a warning bell, but it wasn't.

On my return, I told my wife about Corte's initial reassurances, to which she said, "I will believe it when there's a new contract. If they can get rid of Bob [Cole], they can get rid of you." Longtime announcer Bob Cole—a true legend of the game—had recently been forced into retirement, and that *was* an alarm we all heard. I thanked her for the confidence in me, but in my heart, I knew she was right (as usual). I should never argue with her. She has always had a great sense of these types of situations.

I told Corte, no, I am on the way to Halifax for an event that has been part of my off-season for a decade, the Danny Gallivan Cystic Fibrosis Golf Tournament. Danny had long been dead, but his family and the local community had done a tremendous job in keeping alive the dream of curing CF (cystic fibrosis) by raising awareness and money. I would never miss the event, as long as I am invited. I cut to the point: "Just tell me, Rob."

With that, Corte said that my contract was not being renewed, but he had wanted to tell me in person to shake my hand and say thank you. He assured me it wasn't personal, nor was it performance related—and there would be no formal announcement of my departure.

It was at this point I couldn't resist asking, "Why would you announce my departure? You've never announced my arrival [ten years prior] and never once promoted me—why start now?" I knew it was a cheeky remark, and I was bitter, but I needed to say one thing that made me feel better for at least a few minutes.

Within hours, I was in Halifax, putting on a brave face for the tournament, but I worried about what the future held. The phone call to Mickee went as I expected. She had thought this would happen, but she had my back. She told me we should start planning for the future.

My wife doesn't really like the media business: "You're a bunch of old gossips." Nor did she enjoy hockey anymore. It had become 24/7/365: "Get off your Twitter." But she has stuck through it all. There are days I'm not sure why.

I told a few friends, confidentially, and trusted they wouldn't spread the bad news, but it was hard to maintain composure. I think I did, for the most part. At least, I hope I did.

Even during this turbulent time, I was getting phone calls from people still working at Sportsnet, asking my advice as they were forced to take pay cuts or different assignments. My advice was always the same: "Be patient. Times are changing, and the world will work out in the end for good people." This had always been true in the past. If only I believed my own words for my own situation now.

The news finally came out at the end of August. First on social media, where Steve Simmons, whom I have known for forty years, blurted it out on Twitter, without giving me the courtesy of a phone call. By this time I was at peace with the job I had done for ten years. Ten years of a bonus career, really. Almost a decade to the day that I had agreed to join Sportsnet and the Fan 590. Back in 2009, I had little desire to be on television, and only agreed to it because I was going to get twenty-six weeks of radio, with Bob McCown on *Prime Time Sports,* as a commentator.

My departure as head of broadcasting for the NHL, earlier in 2009, had given me time to think of what and where I wanted to be in the broadcasting business, in the game, and beyond. By July I had received a call from Sportsnet management to come and "talk about announcing." Simple enough, I thought. They wanted me to consult on their stable of announcers to help them grow on the air. That was right up my alley. I had grown weary of the commute to the NHL offices in New York City, and to work from home, in Toronto, was attractive.

The first meeting caught me off guard. Programming vice president David Akande made the pitch for me to join the network *as* an announcer. I was, quite frankly, shocked. As David explained, I would fill a void in the network's coverage of the game. They already had ex-players and an ex-coach. To have someone who had been on the inside of the league office was different, and not something rival TSN had, for that matter. I told him, in no uncertain terms, that I had no desire to be on television. "David, I wouldn't hire me."

But I did explain to him, I had a great deal of interest in going on radio. It was my first love. Always had been, always will be. He asked me to think about it, as I asked him to beef up any radio commitments he could give me, and we agreed to take a couple of weeks.

Ours is a small industry. Akande's boss was Doug Beeforth, who was my college roommate and a former cohort at both *HNIC* and CTV. We had been friends since the mid-1970s at what was then called Ryerson University. As well, I had become great friends with Nelson Millman, who had turned the all-sports radio station in Toronto into a powerful platform, first for Telemedia and then for Rogers. I could see the fingerprints of both on this plan. Beeforth was doing what all good bosses do. He was letting his programming person hire people. Millman was quietly finding a bigger place for me on the radio team. I had confidence in each of them, and therefore had confidence in Akande. Within a month, we structured a deal that was 60 percent radio and 40 percent television, which was to my liking. As the years wore on, my time on radio changed as my television responsibilities, for the most part, grew.

From behind the camera, to being in front. I had always dreamt of being a commentator, but could never really figure out how to get there. What's laughable is I can guarantee that I had more power and influence in broadcasting and in how people watched sports in the first three and a half decades in production and management, but I received far more recognition for being in front of the camera.

After the call from Corte in 2019, and a summer of worry and indecision, the ten years as an announcer had fulfilled a childhood dream, and no one—*no one*—could take that away.

I wasn't alone that summer. Scott Morrison was let go, as were Nick Kypreos, Doug MacLean, my pal Bob McCown, and the Soccer Guys, James Sharman and Craig Forrest. And while Rogers didn't make the announcement, I did. Such is the magic and power of social media. A day after Nick and Doug announced they were gone, in a couple of tweets I said the same:

Too many stories already.
Just to confirm I won't be returning to PrimeTime and HockeyCentral this fall.
Ten great years.
Thanks for listening and watching. Thanks for encouraging and critiquing.

Not going away. Will soon be storytelling somewhere else.
#evolveordie
Good Night. And Good Luck.

Social media is a wondrous thing. And while it has been said before, it must be said again: Twitter is the most antisocial medium ever. Since it arrived, it has given common people (and some not so common) a voice and the ability to spout opinion, humour, hatred, love, compassion, contrition, contradiction, and news.

My philosophy of Twitter is simple. Stick to hockey and hockey news. Don't jump into the world of pop culture and politics. When in doubt, don't. Which is to say, if you have any doubt that what you're saying isn't factual, original, or without controversy, just don't tweet at all. Simple. Effective. And it has served me well.

Oh, I've had my share of replies that aren't heartwarming. But such is life in public. Thick skin is required. It comes with the territory, or as my old friend Don Cherry used to tell me, "It's lonely at the top, John."

But overall, the support I received was so positive. I remember telling friends it was as close as possible to going to you own funeral. It made me appreciate the decade even more. And while I wouldn't wish my summer of uncertainty on anyone, it rekindled my love of the business and my love of hockey. And these positive responses underscored that what we were doing was something worth doing, and doing right.

It allowed me to believe that I still had something to offer. A network. A team. Somewhere. Evolve or die.

TWO
WHERE PASSION BEGINS

THE LOVE OF *HOCKEY NIGHT* CAME EARLY AND EASILY.

It happened in a small town in British Columbia, with one TV channel and a CBC Radio transmitter that was connected through the local railway line. If you drove over the tracks, you heard the CBC, no matter what station the radio was on. Saturday night was the only night when the family ate dinner in front of the TV. Thank God for the invention of the TV table! In the Pacific time zone, 6:00 p.m. became 5:30 became 5:00 as we went from watching a portion of *Hockey Night in Canada* (and praying that there was a fight or two to delay the game) to watching the whole game from either the Forum in Montreal or Maple Leaf Gardens. Joining the game in progress was actually the norm back in the 1950s and '60s. It was done on purpose because the team owners didn't want to jeopardize ticket sales for people staying home to watch the game on TV instead. Over the years, obviously, those fears went away. And by the way, was there ever anything more special than listening to Bill Hewitt and Danny Gallivan call a game?

Play-by-play really had not evolved much from Foster Hewitt's style, invented on radio in the 1920s. The main announcer painted with words a picture of what was occurring on the 200-by-85-feet sheet of ice. More than player identification, it was a description of how the man skated, the way he passed or shot the puck, and the force of players colliding into each other. And, finally, if the puck went in the net. The play-by-play man was given full license to create his own cadence and vocabulary while in the broadcast booth. It became almost as important as the game itself, and these men became stars in their own right.

Bill Hewitt, nasally like his dad, was a meat-and-potatoes guy. Nothing fancy, but effective. Who had the puck, where was the face-off, and "the ice looks fast tonight at the Gardens." Gallivan was an impresario, singing his way through the game like the ringmaster at a circus, colourfully describing why Canadiens almost floated above the ice towards the opposition goal, and eventually another Stanley Cup championship. Hewitt reflected everything about "Hogtown" Toronto and the hard-working Maple Leafs. Gallivan was the international attitude of Montreal and the winning pedigree of Canadiens.

Did you ever notice that Danny never put the word "the" before Canadiens? I'm not sure why he said it that way, and never did ask him, but it was one of his subtle signatures. He also invented words. "Cannonating" and "spinnerama" were part of his lexicon, but to say "Canadiens come up the ice . . ." was something only Danny would do, and did, and could get away with. When I became a broadcaster, I tried my best to use it as a salute to a man who became my friend. I didn't always succeed, but when I did, I chuckled to myself that Danny Gallivan would have been proud of me.

As a kid I would not miss a Saturday night. I just loved to watch and listen to the broadcast, trying to envision myself either sitting at the Forum in Montreal or Maple Leaf Gardens in Toronto, or (even better) in the broadcast gondola in either building. In fact, I would not miss a Sunday night, either. Sunday, you say? No games on TV on Sunday back then, that's true. But there were national radio games on CBC. And they were just as compelling for ten-year-old me. My imagination ran wild—my heroes of hockey in New York City, or Boston, or Chicago. That was special, and something we take for granted now. The world is so connected, countries and people. But in the 1960s, the connections were between cities. But even that was technological magic.

I was, at heart, a Maple Leafs fan in the six-team NHL of the 1960s. Dave Keon, Tim Horton, Frank Mahovlich, Johnny Bower, Allan Stanley, and the legendary coach George "Punch" Imlach. To this day, I remember sitting and watching the Maple Leafs lose 11–0 on a Saturday night to Boston, with Don Simmons in goal. 11–0! I spent the third period curled up on my father's lap, bawling my eyes out. How could they lose 11–0—and to the Bruins? There are some things a seven-year-old just cannot understand.

Fast-forward to 2001 and the invention of Leafs TV, the venture into sports broadcasting that was supposed to be a twenty-four-hour-a-day channel about the hockey team. We didn't have live games to broadcast because the games were already sold to both TSN and Sportsnet, but we did have Maple Leaf Classic games to show. I insisted early on that the Bruins debacle of 1964 go into one of our productions. I was overjoyed to learn we did, in fact, have the kinescope (television that is recorded directly to film) transfer of the game, and waited to see if my emotions would bring me back to that of a child.

One of the reasons the kinescopes were made through the 1960s was so Imlach could have a copy of the game to review. Contractually, each Monday morning, after the film was developed, a copy was sent from the CBC's Jarvis Street studio, in downtown Toronto, to Maple Leaf Gardens, just a short walk of a block and a half. On the Monday following the 11–0 game, Imlach took the film and spliced out all the Bruins' goals to show the players at practice the next day. The only problem was the goals were never reinserted into the original copy of the complete game, which meant the copy we had to show the world on Leafs TV was the whole game minus the goals! It became enough of an anecdote for us to use the footage as it was, and have some fun with it, as with everything at Leafs TV.

The 1960s were a great time to be a hockey fan in Canada. The Maple Leafs would win four Stanley Cups in the decade, and Montreal would win four as well. But my fandom all changed in 1966 when the NHL awarded six new expansion teams, which would double the size of the league and grow the game that we loved. Surely that meant there would be hockey in the West, and in Western Canada in particular. Ultimately, Philadelphia, Pittsburgh, St. Louis, Minneapolis–St. Paul, Los Angeles, and Oakland were selected to join in October 1967. As a British Columbian, I could not understand why Vancouver wasn't awarded a team. Was it the huge sum of $2 million to start a new franchise? Surely someone in Vancouver could afford that? The Pacific Coliseum was soon to be finished and ready for NHL hockey. It was a state-of-the-art arena that held 15,003.

This, my friends, was a travesty.

At least a travesty of provincial proportions, if not the national kind. And at least for me. It appeared that any opposition to a Vancouver franchise hadn't come from Boston or New York or Detroit or Chicago, but rather from Toronto and Montreal, whose clubs were reluctant to share the dollars and exposure that *Hockey Night in Canada* gave them. So it was, in fact, Canadians shutting out Canadians when it came to a team in Vancouver. We already didn't like the East (I believe that was a class in both the second and third grades) but this put it over the top.

I said good-bye to my Leafs and embraced the New York Rangers of Emile Francis, Ed Giacomin, Brad Park, Rod Gilbert, Vic Hadfield, and Jean Ratelle. They were my team now. What made the Rangers special were those Sunday night national radio broadcasts on CBC. Being able to listen to Gallivan or Hewitt and others like Fred Sgambati and Fred Walker do games, every once in a while, from old and new (1968) Madison Square Garden. I loved the sound of the game and the arena on the radio. It was perfect for a kid with a vivid imagination and a passion for the game. Sunday games became outdoor listening in the spring and fall, playing road hockey with my brothers and the neighbours, listening, and re-creating the game being played three thousand miles away. This was heaven.

I didn't turn my back completely on Vancouver pro hockey. The old minor pro league in the West, the original Western Hockey League (WHL), was also enticing. The Vancouver Canucks played the Seattle Totems, Portland Buckaroos, San Diego Gulls, Phoenix Roadrunners, and Salt Lake City Golden Eagles. It was an old man's league. Many of the players in it had already had their chance in the NHL and had been relocated, only to settle into life in minor pro hockey and make almost as much money as they did in the NHL, with some having part-time jobs.

Each team had certain players who became characters in my mind. Seattle had Guyle Fielder. Portland had Andy Hebenton and the Schmautz brothers. Willie O'Ree and Len Ronson played in San Diego, while Larry Lund and the Hucul boys were in Phoenix. In Salt Lake City, Elmer "Moose" Vasko had finished his time with the Blackhawks and became the focus of my youthful attention. Vasko had special status because I had seen him play on television, on *Hockey Night in Canada*, and he was larger than life because of that. The rest were names that my imagination made into heroes and villains. That was the magic of radio!

It's funny how those childhood memories have been engraved in my mind. I still get excited to talk about those teams. And my inner child reappears when I meet one of these guys, who are now well into their seventies or more. I hope my enthusiasm for their careers is as special for them as it is for me. It may sound overly nostalgic, but these heroes of mine played the game with passion, and really not for the money. Few of them became rich on the ice and many of them have battle scars, walking with their careers inflicted in every stride. I so appreciate what they did for my youth, and the entertainment of many adoring fans.

Vancouver did finally get its NHL team in 1970, for the mighty sum of $6 million. But even that was a little tainted. No one in Vancouver would pay that much, so a medical equipment company from Minneapolis bought the franchise. "Bud" Poile was the team's first general manager—yes, that's the father of David Poile, current GM of the Nashville Predators—and hired Hal Laycoe from the hated Portland Buckaroos, of the WHL, as their first coach. I never understood that, but didn't care: my Vancouver Canucks were in the NHL.

It was around this time I started to get interested in broadcasting. I had always loved listening to radio and watching television, and was fascinated by the magic of pictures and sound flying through the air. For many years, the Shannon household only had one channel, the mighty Canadian Broadcasting Corporation. Oh, sure, our little town had cable, which meant you got the CBC and three U.S. networks, but our road wasn't big enough to justify running the lines for just one house. That meant if I wanted to watch ABC, NBC, and CBS, I would have to climb into the attic and move the aerial to see if I could catch a signal through the snow of the TV screen. It's not as if we didn't have enough to do as kids. I just thought it was amazing that we could watch the world in our living room.

On radio, big cities boomed into our little home after dusk. Vancouver, Seattle, Portland, San Francisco, Salt Lake City, and Denver, and if it was perfect weather—not overcast or drizzly—we might hear the sounds of Chick Hearn and the Lakers, Vin Scully and the Dodgers, and Jiggs McDonald with the fledgling Kings. I often fell asleep with the radio blaring some sporting event or rock-and-roll music, with my parents coming into the room to turn off the radio at midnight. At this point, sports were my life and I loved them all. They, in fact, are the framework of my memories as a kid. And they seem to get better every day.

There was 1966, on our annual Easter vacation, this time to San Francisco, and to the horseshoe shape of Candlestick Park to watch the Giants' opening game of that season. The Cubs were the visitors. Leo

Durocher was the Chicago manager. Juan Marichal was on mound and the great Willie Mays in centre field for the Giants. My dad, who loved sports as much as his three boys did, joked, "We have great seats, right behind second base." That meant we were 415 feet from home plate, but only twenty feet every inning from the great Mays. I became a Giants fan that day.

The love of sports came from every member of the family. Mostly it came from my two older brothers, Bob and Ross, who were far better athletes than me, and maybe even more competitive. Our parents also loved the games, but not to the same extent as my siblings. What my parents did—and I am forever grateful for it—was facilitate every whim we had about watching games, going to games, participating in sports—and cheering us on. I don't recall ever not seeing one of my parents, if not both, at any sporting event I was involved in. They made loving sports so easy, so acceptable.

The first pro hockey game I ever saw was in April 1970, again on our annual Easter trip, at the Pacific Coliseum. It was the final regular season game of the old WHL in Vancouver. The hated Portland Buckaroos were in town against the Canucks. What I witnessed that night, along with the other 15,002 fans, has never left me.

We had corner seats about twenty-five rows up, "scout seats" if you will. In the corner right in front of us, I saw Connie "Mad Dog" Madigan butt-end a Canucks forward, Pat Hannigan, in the throat, without being detected by the referee. After going down for a moment, Hannigan bounced up on his skates and chased Madigan, who was the toughest, craziest player I ever saw, to the blue line and proceeded to two-hand him with his stick over the head. What ensued, eight years before the movie *Slap Shot* premiered, was total chaos. But it wasn't over. The Canucks were down 3–1 halfway through the third period. Hannigan was given a ten-minute match penalty, which meant the team would finish the game shorthanded.

This version of Vancouver's team was the best in the league all year, and one of the most prosperous. In fact, they owned a farm team in the American Hockey League, the Rochester Americans. They were so good, the coach, Joe Crozier, had bragged the previous year that his WHL Canucks squad could beat some NHL teams, if anyone would take him up on it. (This was particularly bold since the following preseason the Canucks badly lost two exhibition games to the Los Angeles Kings.)

So in the last regular season game of that season, over the boards jumped the great Andy Bathgate, along with teammates Paul Andrea, Ted McCaskill, Duke Harris, and Len Lunde. They proceeded in the next ten minutes to score three shorthanded goals and win the game. For a thirteen-year-old, I was thrilled for the victory, and knew that this was where I wanted, needed, demanded to spend my life's work. I was hooked.

There was only one problem. I couldn't skate. At that point, our little town didn't even have an arena. But the bigger issue was I had been born with club feet, and after multiple surgeries there was little or no flexion in my ankles. But that wouldn't stop me from loving the game, searching for heroes, talking incessantly about it. I made the decision: if I couldn't play the game, I would talk about it. My career was set. My life as a professional announcer was just a matter of time. At least that's what I thought.

Over the next few years, I tried my hardest to become an announcer. I would practice my play-by-play while mowing the lawn. That came to an end one day when my mother came out to tell me the neighbours had called to say that I was louder than the mower, and could I please stop. I did a twice weekly radio report on high school sports (actually replacing my brother Ross, who had done it for years), talking about the wins, losses, and upcoming events of our local school. I even did play-by-play of basketball, after convincing the coach that it would be best for all involved if I left the team (I wasn't very good) to do the radio. He didn't need convincing.

Along with Hewitt and Gallivan, Jim Robson, who called the Canuck games, quickly joined the voices of my youth. Each became a comforting voice for me, on television or radio, as I began an earnest journey to one day replace them.

With high school graduation looming, my parents announced that I would be moving out of the house the following September. Where will you go? What school will you attend? What will you be doing? My mother wanted me to be a lawyer. My dad wanted me to be happy.

They already knew I had decided to enter the broadcasting world, but the three of us had no clue how and where to go to be trained. After spending a weekend in Vancouver visiting my older brother at the University of British Columbia, and hours reading university catalogues in the UBC library, I finally came up with a short list of where to go. In order to get a degree in broadcasting (my parents said getting a degree was part of the deal), I had decided it had to be one of three places: Syracuse University in Syracuse, New York, for $30,000 a year; Washington State University in Pullman, for $17,000 a year; or Ryerson Polytechnical Institute in Toronto, for $950 a year.

The answer from my dad was simple and decisive: "You're going to love living in Toronto."

But even that wasn't simple. My parents were not pleased that a seventeen-year-old kid would be moving from a town of 1,200 to Canada's largest city. My dad recommended I take a year of university credits in Vancouver at UBC and learn how to live in a big city before I made such a significant move of three thousand miles and three time zones. Ryerson allowed me to defer for a year, and also allowed for academic credits. It was a win-win for me. A year in Vancouver at school, close to my brother Ross, and all the Lions, Canucks, and even the WHA Blazers would be a great way to spend the next ten months.

While school wasn't secondary, it certainly wasn't my primary focus. I tried to join the university radio station, but on my first visit to the place, it appeared fraught with politics and hierarchy. The guys running it were in their fourth and fifth years at school and didn't really have time to help a freshman. They didn't seem to understand that I wanted to be an announcer, right away, without any real training or introduction. And I didn't understand that I had to pay my dues.

But I wasn't staying in Vancouver after that year anyway. I was moving to Toronto. I needed to learn what Toronto was all about. And really, the only way to do that in 1974 was to read newspapers. So every weekday, I would walk to a neighbourhood store and buy the Toronto *Globe and Mail*. This was long before it became a national paper. To me, it *was* Toronto. It spoke Toronto. And I had to understand it, even if it was two days late. Many times, the paper referenced something I knew nothing of, but I said every day that I had to find out how Toronto ticked. What made it special? Who made it special? I didn't want to arrive in Toronto knowing little or nothing of the scene, particularly the sports scene, in the city.

Gordon Sinclair, Trent Frayne, Rex MacLeod, James Christie, and Dick Beddoes taught me about "The Big Smoke," "Hogtown," "Toronto the Good." I knew of Pat Marsden and Bill Stephenson because of CFL football on CTV. And I knew Don Chevrier and Tom McKee on anything the CBC did. My goal was to meet at least some of these people. Little did I know that my life would intersect with many of these gentlemen and I would work for, with, and eventually hire some of them.

But there was one event that happened while I lived in Vancouver that had a lasting effect. It occurred on television, and fittingly on *Hockey Night in Canada*. It included two men I would meet and come to know well, to this day.

On a Wednesday night national broadcast during the 1974–75 hockey season, Dave Hodge, who had replaced Ward Cornell in 1971 as host of the show and was not even thirty yet, interviewed a college student. But it wasn't just any college, and it wasn't just any student.

Doug Beeforth was a second-year student at Ryerson Polytechnic Institute in the Radio and Television Arts program. I sat in front of my twelve-inch black-and-white RCA television transfixed by this interview.

Apparently, Beeforth had done a school project on the "behind the scenes" of what it takes to produce *Hockey Night in Canada*. The producers of the show thought the project was so well done, they ran a segment on that Wednesday night and interviewed its creator. This was amazing to me. It was karma. I was going to Ryerson! I wanted to be on *Hockey Night in Canada*! To this day, I can still see that segment vividly in my mind. It made a huge impact on who I would be.

The following September, I moved with my two suitcases from BC to Toronto. I stayed at a boardinghouse owned by the school. But much of my time was spent in the studios at the school, and eventually at Ryerson's radio station. It was on the first visit to the station, to see if I could do anything, that I met the aforementioned Beeforth, in the lobby of the station. He was now in his final year of school, and I was in my first day. Like I'd seen at UBC, by the time you get close to the end, your school/life experiences appear to put you a decade ahead of a first-year student. Except, Doug was different. When I first saw him, he was talking with another student, a young man named Rick Briggs-Jude, and they were talking sports. I jumped into the conversation with both feet, introducing myself and acknowledging Doug's appearance the previous winter on *HNIC*.

Now, some people will chuckle about these names, because for forty years, Doug, Rick, and I have been often mentioned in the same sentence. Over the years we have lived together (I believe it was seven places in seven years), worked together, laughed and cried together. We have all worked for each other, and hired each other, on occasion. We were all part of Doug's wedding, and Rick's as well. The only reason they weren't part of mine was that Mickee and I eloped to Mexico, and were married in about five minutes by a justice of the peace. But that's another story for a book never to be written.

Beeforth, Briggs-Jude, and I did everything together. We would do Ryerson basketball and football games as announcers, producers, and technical operators. We did OHA Marlboros hockey from Maple Leaf

Gardens, on a deal Doug negotiated with Harold Ballard: we could do the games, as long as we couldn't make money. So the dollars from the advertising we sold were put into buying equipment for the college radio station. We even did a radio version of the Vanier Cup one year. It was Western Ontario vs. Acadia, as I recall, and it was before the advent of wireless microphones, so we spent the day before the game stringing a thousand-foot audio cable from the press box to field level for our field-level reporter. These days might have been the most pure fun we ever had in the business. No bosses. No money. No pressure.

I used my time in school a little differently than most. My university credits from UBC afforded me extra time off and I decided to use the student card as a "ticket" to talk to all the power brokers in sports who were in Toronto. One week, I would phone the CFL office and ask for Jake Gaudaur, the commissioner. Next thing you know, I'm sitting across the desk from the CFL's top guy, asking questions I'm sure he thought were naive and inane. But he gave me the time. I did the same with numerous sports and broadcast people, such as Johnny Esaw of CTV, Bill Stephenson at CFRB, Dick Beddoes at the *Globe and Mail*, and Pat Marsden at CFTO. Being a student gave me a tremendous license to knock on doors and talk to people already in the business. They were all more than willing. After all, I was asking them just to talk about themselves, and how they got to their current position. I wasn't looking for a job, I was looking for guidance and counsel. And who doesn't like talking about themselves and giving advice? I can't tell you how many times over the years I have been in the business that receiving a job or recommendation came down to one of those guys remembering that I was eager, polite, and professional in our first meeting.

It's also one of the reasons why, to this day, I always spend time with aspiring broadcasters when possible. There's always that chance the young guy will be your boss one day. As Johnny Esaw once told me around this time, "You'll meet the same people on the way up as you do on the way down."

The blueprint that Beeforth created in producing a school project on *Hockey Night in Canada* looked pretty foolproof. It had, in fact, gotten him a part-time job on the show. With that in mind, I decided to do my project on someone I had been listening to since I was ten: Jim Robson. Because I wanted to follow Robson around in Toronto, Buffalo, and Vancouver, I needed permission from *Hockey Night in Canada* to do it. I was given that permission on only one condition, that I show them the project when it was complete.

Over the next few months, after contacting Robson, I spent days with Jim with a camera and a tape recorder, following him through his day, on the road with the Canucks when they played the Maple Leafs and the Sabres, and at home in Vancouver on a *HNIC* Saturday when I was on my way home for the Christmas break. For the record, I am a terrible photographer. My vision is so poor, deciding what is in focus and what is not became quite a challenge. Framing and composition were also an issue. I was never going to be mistaken for Yousuf Karsh.

But it opened so many doors—to the *Hockey Night* world, the CBC world, the radio world. Just as Beeforth's production had inspired me to do my own, the project allowed me to meet people in the industry with whom I would have lifelong relationships. Jim Thompson and Michael Lansbury at CBC in Vancouver. John Ashbridge and Dave Rutherford at CKNW radio in Vancouver, and countless people in the *Hockey Night in Canada* family. And of course, Jim Robson himself. What I learned on these three trips—to Maple Leaf Gardens, Buffalo's Memorial Auditorium, and Vancouver's Pacific Coliseum—was that Robson left nothing to chance. His complex preparation of statistics and stories of both teams gave a real glimpse into how much work it would take to be at the top of this profession. Robson wrote microscopically and would fill notepad after notepad as the season progressed. It was his personal NHL journal. I also gained a better understanding of the teamwork it took to put sports television on the air. Twenty-five to thirty people working in unison, supporting each other, with a common goal of creating exciting, entertaining television. After all, it was *Hockey Night in Canada*, and you could see the pride everyone had in being part of the program.

With the project done in early 1977, I did what I was dutifully told to do. I showed it to a few of the people at *Hockey Night*. Bob Gordon, who was the Maple Leafs' regular producer, and Frank Selke Jr., an executive with the Canadian Sports Network (CSN) at the time, were both polite enough to keep their eyes open through the thirty minutes. Eventually, it did exactly what I wanted it to: it got me a job on Wednesdays and Saturdays at Maple Leaf Gardens for *Hockey Night in Canada*.

Early in the 1977–78 season, when the Canucks came to Toronto, I had arranged for Robson to watch my project as well. With an 8:00 p.m. start time, we agreed that we would meet in the TV studio at MLG at 3:00 p.m. to watch it. That worked well for me; my new job started at 5:00 p.m. with a production meeting. Well, three o'clock came and went. No Robson. So did 3:30. And then 4:00 p.m. When I called the hotel, and Robson answered, something was obviously wrong. He had either slept in or forgotten about our prearranged meeting. When he finally arrived, embarrassed and out of breath, I think we were able to watch about fifteen minutes of the show before people started to arrive. Jim apologized profusely, and again after the game that night. And by letter the following week. For forty years, Jim has apologized to me for missing that single meeting almost every time we have connected. And we worked closely together for a decade!

Jim, apology accepted.

The Robson project began my association with one of the iconic brands in Canadian television and sports. What followed, through six decades, was a love affair between me and a television show. Like any relationship, there were ups and downs, ins and outs, and curves galore. But what a journey it was.

THREE
TO WEAR THE BABY BLUE

TO THIS DAY, I REMEMBER WALKING INTO THE *HOCKEY NIGHT IN CANADA* **OFFICES** eager to see if I got a baby blue jacket. I waited three long weeks before the call came to go to a little shop on Yonge Street in Toronto to be measured for it. It was such an important, special moment in my young life. This jacket made you feel bigger, better, and smarter. But more significantly, it meant respect in the hockey world.

I was a runner. A gopher. Essentially, the conduit between the show and the players, checking they were ready for interviews or telling them they'd been selected as one of the three stars of the game. As the bottom rung on the ladder, it was my job to get people anything they needed, even coffee. With all the back-and-forth between the arena and the TV mobile, there was a lot of running, but I loved it. It was this first job that drove me to develop relationships with the players, something I valued for all my career.

The baby blue jacket was an icon in Canadian broadcasting for decades. Wearing the jacket in any arena, in any city, became a calling card. Players would acknowledge you as they walked into the building. Coaches and managers knew that their skills and expertise were going to be on full display across the country. It meant a big name in the game would smile and nod at you, not knowing your name, but knowing you were part of television elite, part of the tradition of *Hockey Night in Canada*. To this day, I never had more fun, joy, or pride than in those years I wore a baby blue *Hockey Night in Canada* blazer.

One of my favourite moments, one that Don Cherry and I still laugh about, occurred in Boston during the 1978 playoffs. The Bruins, whom Cherry was coaching at the time, had won a playoff game against Montreal. My job was to wind through the halls of Boston Garden to Cherry's small office and get the coach to make a postgame appearance with Dave Hodge. The press horde was twenty deep around Cherry, who was standing on the top of his desk to be seen by all. But he saw me, or rather saw my baby blue jacket, and yelled, "Boys, I see there's someone here from *Hockey Night in Canada*. They must need me on television. I have to go on national television!" The reporters parted as Don descended from on top of his desk and walked out of the office with me. Cherry and I giggled all the way back to the makeshift studio at the Garden. He always knew the power of the baby blue.

These jackets meant that much. There was more to it than a simple uniform. I was wearing the same polyester (yup, polyester) blazer that Danny Gallivan, Bill Hewitt, and Dave Hodge wore. In Montreal, we were part of a greater team that included our friends at the show *La Soirée du Hockey*. The legendary René Lecavalier, Gilles Tremblay, and Lionel Duval wore the same baby blues as we did. We felt, in many ways, that we helped unite the country, in English and French, on a singular team in a divisive time.

By the time I joined *Hockey Night* in the mid-1970s, Ralph Mellanby was the executive producer. He's the one who had brought the baby blue jacket to *Hockey Night* a few years before after experimenting with navy blue jackets and even plum-coloured jackets, too. We wore the greatest uniform. On any night in the NHL, we were the third hockey team. The baby blue team. It was great branding, before branding became the norm.

Perhaps the few who wore the jacket were just at the right place at the right time, when dynasties were prevalent in the game. In my time, Scotty Bowman's Canadiens, Al Arbour's Islanders, and Glen Sather's Oilers all did postgame interviews in the dressing room with an announcer wearing baby blue. I suppose it was an association that will forever keep us bonded. And one that fans and viewers expected to see by season's end.

It was a different time in the NHL when I joined *Hockey Night.* The game was moving on from the rough style of the Philadelphia Flyers—the "Broad Street Bullies"—to the fast and skilled teams that Bowman coached in Montreal. Cable TV in Canada meant you could also add the three American networks. Fox was still years from Rupert Murdoch's wallet. Not every sporting event was on television. Wednesdays and Saturdays were sacred hockey nights. And *Hockey Night in Canada* stood above them all. So much so that what the announcers wore on that show became a measure of hockey royalty.

Did I say, "what the announcers wore"? What we *all* wore. That's what made it so special. I was on hockey's greatest team. Its most successful team. We won every year. A team that went to the All-Star game every winter and the Stanley Cup Final every spring. It was my first real job. It was my dream job. I had made it. That jacket was our uniform. We were able to rub shoulders with the game's greatest stars and its most powerful leaders. To walk into an arena or a dressing room without being stopped, and greeted with a nod or a handshake, was glorious.

The pay? Ten dollars a game: cash. But that was far from the greatest reward.

Ralph Mellanby was more than a brand guy. He was "the man." As big as the names of the announcers were, Ralph's was bigger. He thought big. And if you weren't intimidated by him, he made you think and feel big, too. Perhaps it was his time spent working with ABC, and watching the legendary Roone Arledge doing Olympics in Innsbruck (and later work for the American network in Lake Placid and Sarajevo). But Mellanby thought creatively about the game, and all the television aspects. He also knew about hockey, and how it should be played, which was a huge asset to the show.

Ralph was impressive, and had an ego to match. His pals were movers and shakers, in TV and sports, and he made sure we all knew about them. Call it bragging, but he could back up the stories with good television. Mellanby had replaced George Retzlaff as executive producer of the show in the mid-1960s, and while the latter deserved tons of credit for building the foundation of the show, it was Mellanby's vision and editorial insight that yielded the show that people remember.

Hockey Night in Canada was more than just a TV show. It was a way of life. There is nothing else like it. With it came prestige and responsibility. Strangely, even though it was a TV show on CBC, it wasn't really produced by the CBC.

The history of *Hockey Night* goes all the way back to the famous golf outing between advertising executive Jack MacLaren and Maple Leafs owner Conn Smythe. MacLaren needed content for some of his clients. Smythe wanted to broaden the appeal of his team in the market. The two dynamos of their respective worlds needed something from the other. Smythe had the content, MacLaren had the sponsors. By putting Smythe's hockey games on the radio, MacLaren was able to deliver high ratings for his advertising clients. Smythe was able to take the Maple Leaf broadcasts well past Toronto. The marriage first began on radio, then moved to television in 1952.

In the early radio years, the Maple Leafs were at the top of the heap. Only when Frank Selke Sr. moved from the Maple Leafs to be manager of the Montreal Canadiens in 1944 did Canada's other NHL team start to receive true national exposure. Selke, who had worked for Smythe before World War II, and ran the team while Smythe was overseas during the conflict, understood the value of radio and media exposure and demanded that his team share national airtime with his old boss. Hence, outside of Quebec and southern Ontario, hockey fans heard and later saw both the Maple Leafs and Canadiens on an alternating basis.

Hockey Night in Canada had been conservative and methodical for two decades. The commentary was rather sedate and calming, with very little opinion. The camera angles were traditional, and there had been no desire to change over the years. Mellanby took chances and created the show that the rest of us have subsequently adapted. He used his connections with networks in the United States to advantage—people like Arledge at ABC and Scotty Connal at NBC—to make the show look "bigger." Sports television in the United States had bigger budgets, and far more viewers. Mellanby was able to transform the show by comparing how the Americans built intermission content and expanded game coverage, and by using some Canadian ingenuity to build the *Hockey Night* style. His demand for excellence made the show stand well above any others without making it less Canadian.

Mellanby created "layers" on the show, introducing more music, geographic scenes of cities, and short animations that linked the program to the commercial. He added "sizzle" to *HNIC* without compromising its innate style. Player profiles and improved editorial content, with people like Bob Goldham, Howie Meeker, and Don Cherry, made the show feel more dynamic. These changes compelled viewers to stay around and watch the intermission content, which drove advertising rates up. If the game lacked energy or was otherwise uninteresting, viewers would still watch the intermission. Many times, he would say, "We can't program the game better, but we sure can program the intermissions better." All the while, he worked to maintain the smaller budgets. Mellanby was a master of creating content at ten cents on the dollar.

If you could look beyond his arrogance, you saw his brilliance and you learned from him. He was the best. In my opinion, he should be in the Hockey Hall of Fame, as a builder. In fact, early in 2002, I wrote a letter of nomination for Ralph to be considered for the Hall.

Part of the process is that a member of the selection committee must actually put the person's name up for consideration. At the time, Frank Selke Jr., the former Oakland Seals manager and a longtime *Hockey Night in Canada* executive, was on the selection committee and agreed to put Ralph's name forward, if I would write the letter of nomination. That was easy for me. Mellanby, who had left the show in 1985, had been the executive producer longer than any of us. It was the right thing to do. He had been the most influential television exec in hockey for more than two decades. I took weeks to craft the letter and assemble the enclosed research material, which listed all of Ralph's awards and acknowledgements. I was proud of the document.

On the morning I was to deliver the letter by hand to Jim Gregory, who was the chair of the Hall's selection committee, I opened up the *Globe and Mail* newspaper, as I usually did, to read Bill Houston's "Truth and Rumours" media column, only to find paragraph after paragraph of an interview Bill had done with Ralph over the past weekend. In the article, Mellanby spared no words in criticizing the NHL, the quality of play, the quality of television, and the commissioner, Gary Bettman (who, for no reason I know of, had become a focus of many of Mellanby's tirades over the previous few years). Mellanby, who loved to be quoted in the paper, was making it clear that he did not like the NHL, and its leadership at the time. I had just finished the column, wondering what Ralph's agenda was, when the phone rang. It was Frank Selke:

FS: Johnny, my boy.

JS: Hi, Frank.

FS: You read Houston this morning?

JS: Yes, just finished it.

FS: Have you sent Ralph's nomination into Jim yet?

JS: No. I was going to walk it over this morning.

FS: Good. Well, don't send it. I can't nominate him after that article.

With that, I put Ralph's letter in a file, and never sent it. Without someone on the committee to put him forward, the letter would do no good. It really was a shame. He was the greatest hockey producer and executive producer ever. He taught creativity and he taught loyalty. That loyalty would be challenged a great many times in the years to come.

When you worked on *Hockey Night in Canada*, you viewed the world of sports television differently. By the late 1970s, after a decade of Mellanby's influence, *HNIC* had become the standard that sports were measured against, in Canada, for sure, and at times in the United States. *Monday Night Football* was in its infancy in the United States. Cable TV sports were still a few years away. So when you worked for *Hockey Night* you had swagger. Mellanby had swagger. We all did. You were different than the people that worked at CBC or CTV Sports. You worked on *the* show. Some called it confidence, others called it cockiness, but nothing could touch what *Hockey Night* or its sister show in French, *La Soirée du Hockey*, did in the Canadian TV world. At that time, we were the only group that produced NHL games in Canada. We were truly a band of brothers. We all felt that way. Other than a handful of Vancouver Canucks games in the early 1980s that were produced by the team-owned television station, our dominance as *the* producer of record would continue for almost another decade.

In many ways, it was the golden era of *HNIC*. Our jackets were identifiable in every NHL rink, in Canada and the United States. Our influence on the game was extensive. The league office was in constant communication with our group on issues of game scheduling, broadcast protocols, and game presentation. People in strong hockey markets like Boston and Detroit could actually watch *HNIC* on their cable packages. American audiences learned to appreciate our style of coverage, and the detail and passion we carried into every broadcast.

Of course, I didn't stay at *Hockey Night* forever, and by the time I returned to the show in 1994, the baby blue had been replaced. Perhaps for the better, as our business had become more splintered and sophisticated. By that time there were at least three different networks and an independent production company producing hockey games across the country. Gone were the days of one small group of Canadians producing every game, and on-air uniforms had been replaced by well-tailored suits. But there isn't a Saturday that I don't think about the days and power of the baby blue.

The *Hockey Night* philosophy was more than "look good, feel good." It was about the style of production. And so much had to do with the pride that every person took on being on the show. The tender, loving care of every technician, who believed in *Hockey Night* as much as we all did. Audio engineers understood the importance of the mix of microphones between the announcers and the ice effects. There really was a difference between how a *Hockey Night* game used to sound versus other productions of the time. While many believe that hearing the ice effects—skates, sticks, pucks, posts, and glass—are most important, we felt that the sound of the crowd was just as important. That "mix" of all the arena sounds gave *Hockey Night* games a special feel that reflected not only the action of the game, but also the bigness of the event.

It is something that many have come to appreciate even more in the past few seasons of NHL hockey as the league and its broadcasters were forced to cover games in the pandemic "bubbles" in Canada, and during the shortened fifty-six-game schedule of 2021, when crowd noise was piped into empty arenas. People yearned for the crowd sound and began to understand that the off-ice sounds were just as important as those inside the glass.

The roar of the crowd, the oohs and ahhs, combined with the sticks, skates, and other sounds were rarely duplicated anywhere else because we were the only group producing games at that time. Even though there was no competition yet, we would try to learn from other networks doing other sports. I think most of us studied very closely how CBS and NBC covered the NFL. We always took note of how the American TV networks covered the NHL. All the while, we knew that we did it better. It was one of our many "secret sauces" that we carried from arena to arena.

In the years since, many of those philosophies moved from network to network, as we all moved from network to network. But the love of the jacket, the memories that it elicits, and the innovation it symbolizes puts a lump in my throat every time.

Just as I did when I wore it, I feel taller, walk straighter, and smile wider.

FOUR
THE TWO-HEADED MONSTER

PERHAPS IT WAS A PRECURSOR OF THINGS TO COME, BUT 1984 WAS ONE STRANGE year for me. There were highs and lows and for the first time in my career I faced an indecisiveness about what my path should be. I was at an age, twenty-seven, where I wanted more. More money, more power, more recognition. It was the classic trifecta of a young professional not being satisfied with the status quo. In the end, I recoiled from a chance for all of that for the familiar comfort of *Hockey Night in Canada*. I had clamoured for change, and then it scared me so much, I couldn't handle it. This was the year I tried to evolve and it almost killed me.

It was a big year in hockey. I had been stationed in the West (Calgary became home) for four years, producing games for the four western-based teams: Winnipeg, Calgary, Edmonton, and Vancouver. I got to watch the Edmonton Oilers build what would become a dynasty in the 1980s, and in 1984 they won their first Stanley Cup against the defending champions, the New York Islanders. The Islanders had nearly won the Stanley

Cup five straight seasons, a feat that only Montreal had done, in the late 1950s. Another championship would have put the already great Islanders team on an even higher pedestal. But that wasn't the story.

Bob Cole's famous line "There's a new bunch on the block . . . the Edmonton Oilers by name" became the iconic words that Oilers fans and the players remember to this day. It endeared Cole to the organization forever. Then the party began. I was planning to return home to Calgary late in the day after Game 5. Season done, let my summer begin. But we kept having fun, day after day. In fact, it was a full week of celebrations, big and small, that made the time unforgettable. It was the first Stanley Cup for the Oilers, but winning championships had become common in Edmonton. The CFL Eskimos had just finished a five-year term as Grey Cup champions. The city knew how to celebrate.

I actually moved out of the hotel to stay with friends for the week, thinking it would be difficult to justify an extra week of room charges when the games had finished six days earlier. I was staying with John and Blythe Wells in suburban Edmonton. John was our Edmonton host and would soon be on his way to host the Olympic Games in Los Angeles, where he did a brilliant job for the CBC. In many ways, as good as he was for *Hockey Night in Canada* in Edmonton and with as strong a relationship as he had with the Oilers, his on-air duties in Los Angeles put him on the national map. So much so, he received an offer to join the soon-to-be-launched TSN as its number one anchor. It was a tough decision for John and his family, but it was the right thing. In fact, hockey in the West would lose another announcer to TSN, too. Jim Van Horne was our host for regional games in Calgary. He would also accept a job offer to join the fledgling cable sports network. We had two very large holes to fill before the NHL season would begin again in October.

During the previous NHL season, I had made numerous trips from west to east, to produce both regional and national games for *Hockey Night in Canada*. It was always a way for our operation to stay on the same page from an editorial and production point of view. Too many times—and we saw this with both CBC Sports and CTV Sports—the production philosophy between the two parts of the country were different, and it was reflected on the air. Perhaps the style difference was reflected in the teams we covered. The Oilers and Flames, for example, were filled with bright, young stars. Our coverage of the game had to reflect what these young stars were doing on the ice. We needed to show not just where the puck was going, but also where the player was going. These isolated replays changed the pattern of game coverage. They made storytelling better. They made the players bigger stars. The number of times we saw Wayne Gretzky or Mark Messier away from the puck gave the viewer more understanding of those players' skills. When the camera stayed with Lanny McDonald, rather than following the puck, we learned to appreciate his passion for scoring—how he read the play and how he played without the puck, all the while supporting his teammates—as well as his strength at shooting. It gave the television viewer a chance to see what the in-arena spectator saw all the time: action away from the puck.

The differences created friction internally at both networks. There was a group of us at *Hockey Night* that wanted to avoid that. What was good in Calgary had to work in Toronto or Montreal. It was difficult to maintain, but we certainly tried. Weekly conference calls helped, but they weren't enough. Allowing other producers to come west, and me to go east, made the most sense. To some extent, it worked.

On one of those trips early in the season, I received a call from a friend, Michael Lansbury, who had been at the CBC but was now working on a project for Labatt Brewing Company. At this time, breweries were the driving force behind most, if not all, pro sports in our country. Molson was the driver in the hockey world, Carling O'Keefe had been a big part of the Canadian Football League and international hockey, and Labatt had been instrumental in bringing the Blue Jays to Toronto in 1977. While their investment in hockey was limited to some non-NHL events, Labatt was now investigating creating an all-sports cable television network, to mirror what ESPN had done five years earlier in the United States.

Lansbury and former head of CBC Sports John Hudson were set up in offices at First Canadian Place in Toronto, under the banner of the "Action Canada Sports Network." Michael and I had known each other for a decade, meeting first at CBC in Vancouver, when as a college student I was observing the production of *HNIC* at the Pacific Coliseum. Lansbury was working for Jim Thompson, who was a rising star within the CBC system, and in those days would produce and direct *Hockey Night*'s four regional broadcasts of the Canucks in British Columbia. When Thompson was moved to Toronto to run CBC *Sports Weekend*, Lansbury followed. Our friendship flourished.

Before my move to Western Canada, and in my early years as a producer for *HNIC*, Michael would often direct some of the shows I was assigned. While we were quite different in our approach to work and life—he was a free spirit, I was more buttoned down—we got along famously. So while visiting with Lansbury and Hudson, their new venture came up and they asked if I had any interest in it. It would mean moving away from hockey, but it was intriguing. There was no real job discussed, but it was clear they wanted me to consider returning to Toronto to work with them.

While I continued to produce games for *HNIC*, thoughts of the new network lingered, and were then fueled by infighting at *Hockey Night*. A few years earlier, the company had decided to break the executive producer's job into two pieces. While Ralph Mellanby would continue to run the flagship show, *Hockey Night in Canada*, and everyone in baby blue blazers, the non-network regional packages and everything else would be handled now by Don Wallace. It created some interesting dynamics amongst the staff. You see, if I produced a game on a Tuesday in Edmonton between the Canucks and the Oilers, I reported to Wallace. If I did the same two teams on the Saturday, I reported to Mellanby.

While Ralph had a bigger-than-life personality, Don was much more pragmatic. He had worked his way through numerous television jobs before landing a position at CSN. His style, it seemed to me at least, was more "folksy" than Ralph's. He was always affable, always willing to have fun. My introduction to and acceptance by Don came from my ability to remember statistics and know the most trivial events of the NHL. He liked that. It was a strength he didn't have, so it made sense for him to keep me around. For my first two years on the job, we travelled extensively, Don as the game producer, me as his jack-of-all-trades. In those early years, we got along very well. However, that began to change in the early 1980s.

The company had created a two-headed monster that could be confusing to those of us who worked for both men. Mellanby and Wallace did not see the game the same way, nor did they like or respect each other that much.

Making matters worse for me, I was working in the West, and the issues were being played out in Toronto. At times it made my life easier, because what I didn't know about wouldn't interfere in my day-to-day work, allowing me to do my own thing. At other times I was asked to align myself with one or the other men and their vision for the shows. It was not healthy. My time in the West had allowed me to develop my own production style. We did a different style of replays based on the stars we had to cover. We had created a stronger bond with the hockey clubs in the West, which enhanced our ability to tell stories about the players, on and off the ice, as well as be much more reflective of the cities and the fans who followed the teams. Understanding the people of the city, their passions, was key to our success. We produced hockey for Western Canadians. We made them feel that we understood what they wanted.

Meanwhile, H. E. "Ted" Hough, the president of CSN, which produced *Hockey Night*, had grown weary of the power that Mellanby could wield with the network, staff, league, and sponsors. He was, after all, a "star" even if he wasn't on the air. Ralph talked a big game, and usually could deliver. This drove Hough nuts. In Hough's opinion, Mellanby's bravado and brand were conflicting with the brand of the show. Nothing was to be bigger than *Hockey Night in Canada*.

On the other side, Don Wallace had been hired by Hough in the mid-1970s as a producer, to work in Montreal. He had done a very good job nurturing relationships with the hockey club there, and in the always fragile relationship between the CBC and its French-language counterpart, the Société Radio-Canada (SRC) in Quebec. There is little doubt that Hough saw Wallace as a possible replacement for Mellanby, if and when the mercurial Ralph quit, was lured away, or was fired.

Each of them tried to put his own fingerprints on the product, and at times it became uncomfortable for the game producers to do their jobs. It was probably toughest on the guys in the East, particularly Toronto, where both Wallace and Mellanby lived and rarely left. But even in the West it became a bit of a juggling act. No better example was a Saturday night in Edmonton during that 1983–84 season.

I was in my regular producer's chair in the CBC mobile at Northlands Coliseum. Mellanby was in the greenroom at Maple Leaf Gardens, and Wallace was in our control room at the Forum in Montreal. As was customary at the time, in order to link games up as they ended, there was a scheduled conference call about thirty minutes before the *Hockey Night in Canada* broadcast ended. On a regular Saturday night, it was uncanny how closely all these games came to an end at around the same time. However, Wallace's Montreal game was ending at least fifteen minutes before the call was to begin (sports don't care about schedules and time slots). This meant we had to quickly coordinate the Montreal game and the Edmonton game, in order for Canadiens viewers to see the conclusion of the Edmonton broadcast before joining the complete network together.

Confusing, right? Not really. You remember that famous line about the three most important things about opening a successful restaurant? The answer is location, location, location. Well in television, the three most important things about a successful broadcast are transmission, transmission, transmission. Or simply the ability to move pictures and sound from one location to another. If you know how to do that, everything else is easy.

On this particular Saturday night, it was obvious that the "join in progress" for viewers of the Montreal game was going to happen much earlier than normal. It also meant that we in Edmonton would have to use all the in-game commercials before any "joins" could occur. We know before each broadcast how many minutes of commercials we have to fit in. The commercials for the game in Montreal had all already run, and we weren't about to give the advertisers any bonus airtime, perhaps up to two additional minutes of commercials. That meant we would be cramming in two or three thirty-second commercials (because that's how long they used to be in hockey on TV) in a short period of time.

By rule, they could air on a penalty being called, but not during the power play, and you couldn't run them right after a goal. Both reasons not to go to commercial were put in place to ensure that television would not be able to dictate the flow and momentum of a game. You wouldn't want either team claiming the other had received an unfair advantage by getting time to rest at an important moment. Going to commercial on icings was always good, as were any opportunities that were dictated by both teams chasing their lines. Remember, these were the days of long shifts by players. Some of them were up to two and a half minutes long, or in the case of Wayne Gretzky, more than three minutes. As per the norm, our production crew was monitoring the events in Montreal and was preparing for the early join, when the phone rang in the TV mobile. It was Wallace in Montreal:

DW: Johnny, I have one fifteen left in our game . . . going to join you!

Immediately another phone line rang: it was Mellanby in Toronto. The Oilers had iced the puck and we were going to commercial.

JS: Just a minute, Don . . . commercial in seven, six, five, four, three, two, one . . . Let me put you on hold for a second.
RM: John, it's Ralph. Montreal is going to join soon . . . you'll be getting a call from—
JS: Just a minute, Ralph, let me put you on hold.

And with that, the Edmonton truck was on the verge of being in complete control—and I had put both my bosses on hold! I turned to our production group, including director Larry Brown, and smiled. "Folks," I said, "Mellanby is on hold, Wallace is on hold—that, ladies and gentlemen, is power!"

Everyone giggled, and we continued on our way. I assured Mellanby that all was in good order, and that Wallace and I could navigate the process from that point until the conference call opened up.

But to me it was symbolic of a rather uncomfortable leadership issue at the country's greatest sports program.

In order to keep Don appeased, he was brought back to Toronto and, at some point, had to be given some additional responsibilities in preparation for the future. The second executive producer was that appeasement. Mellanby ran *Hockey Night* and Wallace ran everything else. The "two-headed monster" became more of a competition than it did a struggle of philosophy. *Hockey Night in Canada* had bigger budgets, and a much broader philosophy of talking to all Canadians. Our regional, midweek shows were more specific to the teams and markets they were covering with a fraction of the resources, like cameras and replay machines. The thought process was not always the same on a midweek show as it was on Saturdays. These were not insurmountable issues, but they were at times uncomfortable, very uncomfortable. That made the idea of a start-up network much more attractive.

By season's end, the Labatt-owned Action Canada Sports Network had changed its name to The Sports Network, or TSN. John Hudson's role in the project was now being played by Gordon Craig, yet another former CBC Sports legend, who was best known for building the world-class host broadcast unit at the Montreal Olympic Games. (A host broadcaster provides all of the audio and video feeds from each Olympic venue to any broadcaster around the world who can then customize it for their own use. It's a huge responsibility and privilege.) Craig would be the president of TSN, with Lansbury at his side, while

Hudson continued to manage all of Labatt's live sports television, such as Blue Jays baseball.

I had met Gordon on a few occasions over the previous five or six years, but did not know him well. My biggest memory of him was from April 1981 in Calgary. Craig was the lead member of a management team that took position when our union technical crew went on strike during a Stanley Cup playoff game in Calgary. He was authoritative and efficient and commanded great respect. He was also part of the CBC management that had always been angered that CBC's number one program was actually produced by an outside company.

Hockey Night in Canada was produced by a subsidiary of MacLaren Advertising, because the agency delivered all the sponsors of the show—for years it was Imperial Oil, then Molson Brewery, Ford, General Electric, and more. It was almost a classic case of the content between commercials. And the relationship between MacLaren (through Canadian Sports Network, CSN) and the CBC Sports department was strained, to say the least. In fact, in the early 1970s at Maple Leaf Gardens, in the viewing room off the studio, there was at one point a velvet rope separating the CSN management group from the CBC group. CSN's power was based on the ability to be the middleman between the league and the network, and its ability through its parent company to deliver most, if not all, of the sponsors. Also, the revenue that hockey generated for the network was so large, CBC had no choice but to allow an outside production group to manage the product. It drove many at the CBC crazy.

The prospect of joining Craig and Lansbury at the new venture was exciting. But I had trepidations. It was out of my comfort zone, beyond the hockey world. And there was another hesitation. I had been a Molson guy from the first day I walked into the *HNIC* office. We were trained that Molson was good, and the others weren't. It was an amazing level of brand loyalty that pervaded our whole group. To move to a Labatt-owned company, TSN, would be such a change. It sounds so irrational that we felt that way, but we did. Our loyalty to the brewery was unwavering.

So when Lansbury offered me the number two production job on the network, I was dumbfounded. It was almost double the money I was making, and it meant a return to Toronto. As a young guy in the industry, it was mind-boggling to think that I could make such a big move. I was comfortable in my life in Alberta. The teams that I followed were the best in the NHL. Alberta was a fantastic place to live. In the three previous seasons, I had produced part of the Stanley Cup Final in the West. The All-Star Game was coming to Calgary. Quite frankly, my career was in a very good place. It was not the time to leave.

As the NHL season ended, John Wells was on the verge of leaving for TSN. Jim Van Horne had accepted a position at the new channel, as well. My friends, people who had helped me cope with those first four years in Calgary, were deserting me. I was happy for them. But I wasn't looking forward to putting an "under construction" sign up for hockey broadcasting in Western Canada.

As had been tradition, I spent some time in June in Toronto visiting friends and starting the planning for the fall. This was the first year that *Hockey Night* would actually have some network competition in Canada, as it was announced that CTV would, in fact, carry some regular season games and a portion of the Stanley Cup playoffs. That announcement alone sent our offices into a tizzy—it was a long summer of litigation in Chicago about whether or not the NHL had the right to sell off some of the games without CSN's right to match.

No matter what the courts said, we had to plan to have direct competition for the first time. It was under this veil of competition that we as a group came up with the slogan "The Tradition Continues." After all, our show had been on the air on television since 1952. We *owned* Saturday nights. We were the leader in producing hockey on television. We believed that we had a "secret sauce" for producing the game. No one could touch us.

Hockey Night in Canada, in its arrogant style, was above everyone. I was certainly a part of that. After all, that was all I had ever known, and it was tough to beat. I have often joked that I started at the top and worked my way down.

It was on this June trip to Toronto that I first got a sense of my value to the company as well. Following one of our planning sessions, I was walking to the elevator with Ron Simpson, who had joined the company from the ad agency side as a senior marketing executive. He had long been part of the Molson account for MacLaren. He was now being groomed to be part of the business side of CSN, and to protect the Molson brand on hockey. The conversation on the way to the ground floor turned to the future. I had not mentioned any of my TSN discussions to anyone. Still, it became very evident that my name had come up. Ron started to ask me what my long-term plan was.

RS: What do you think about executive producer?

JS: What do you mean? That's Ralph's job.

RS: It is. But Ralph won't be executive producer forever. If you ask me, we should be grooming you to be the next executive producer.

I was shocked. I had never given any thought to being the executive producer of *Hockey Night in Canada*. I was twenty-seven. I was having too much fun producing. I lived out of the spotlight, away from the corporate world of the ad agency or the network. In fact, I did almost anything I wanted to do, within reason. And I was in the hotbed of hockey, Alberta! Why would I even think about it? Conversation over. Never to be discussed again.

Knowing what was coming down the pike, with the challenges of bringing in new people and a competing network, I turned down TSN, and my friend Lansbury. It had been a huge boost to my ego that someone was coming after me, but in June 1984, I wasn't ready.

Then—I truly don't know what changed, but by July, after some rest and relaxation, and getting out of the limelight of Toronto, I was ready to make the move. Michael had been very smart in how he left it with me. He said that he wouldn't fill the job until he knew for sure I wouldn't come. Even though I had told him I wasn't coming, he didn't believe me. Three weeks after my first rebuff of the offer, I called him back to say I had reconsidered. I would take the job and be in Toronto the following week.

There are parts of that summer that I actually can't remember. After the decision to move to TSN, it became a bit of a blur. I am not a very good note taker. I only remember phoning Ted Hough, who was in Chicago at the time to attend the court case about the CTV package, and telling him I was leaving. I told him the terms of my deal, and that I would be sending an official letter in the next few days. He tried to talk me out of it. He offered me even more money, a car, and a vice presidency in the company. But I had given Lansbury my word. I was going to TSN.

This is the part that nearly killed me. I lasted two days at TSN. Two long, excruciating days. Within an hour of being in the new, under-construction offices on Leslie Street, I knew I didn't belong. Perhaps it was that Labatt vs. Molson rivalry, or maybe it was the workload that came with starting a network from scratch, but I knew almost immediately that I didn't fit in.

How could I get myself out of this?

I did the only thing I knew to do: I told the truth. I spent the morning of the third day at TSN with Lansbury. I poured my heart out. I told him, in very simple terms, that I wasn't going to be happy at TSN. Michael took it as a friend, not a business associate. He saw it in my face. He knew I needed out, and understood. His boss, Gordon Craig, was not as sympathetic at the time, but I really didn't care. I needed to go home. Home to Calgary. Home to *Hockey Night in Canada*.

I did so with a raise, a car, and a vice presidency.

Make no mistake about it, though: I was embarrassed. Not for letting the people at TSN down, but for myself. I had always prided myself on being decisive. Making a decision and living with it.

I had waffled on the offer. Waffled on changing my mind. I had proved to be all too human, and it drove me crazy. I hated those six weeks, and still bristle when I think about what transpired. But I also knew I made the right decision to return where I fit. Funny thing was, it had happened so quickly—leaving, coming back—that many people never knew I had gone. I was pleased about that.

I spent the remainder of that summer trying to rebuild our local show in Calgary and helping find a replacement for Wells in Edmonton. The job in Edmonton was the easy one. Chris Cuthbert had become one of the best young announcers in the country. In early 1983, we launched a commercial-free hockey package on one of Canada's first ever-cable channels, Super Channel, owned by the same people who owned the Oilers' rights in Edmonton. We had to produce a three-hour program with absolutely no commercials. To start with a blank slate—for graphics, features, animations, and philosophy—was thrilling. It was also totally exhausting. There was no downtime, and I was always concerned whether the pictures and sound we were creating were getting on the air and making sense. Cuthbert was the show's host; he was joined by Jim Hughson (who had recently replaced Bill Hewitt as the regional voice of the Toronto Maple Leafs) and initially with Gary Dornhoefer or later John Davidson. The package was under the supervision of Don Wallace as part of the "two-headed monster." Because it involved extra travel, Wallace wanted little or nothing to do with the show. So being in Edmonton for half the schedule, it was on me to build it. It also gave me a chance to work with two of the best young announcers in the game in Hughson and Cuthbert. We were all about the same age and shared many of the same thoughts about how the game should be covered.

Hughson was such an interesting story. I met Jim during the 1981–82 season, while producing Canucks games for *HNIC*. Hughson was the backup play-by-play voice of the Canucks on CKNW radio in Vancouver. When Jim Robson moved to television, Hughson would do play-by-play. Our first meeting was at a morning skate at the Pacific Coliseum. I was in the traditional garb of a *Hockey Night* employee on game day: shirt and tie, blazer, grey slacks. Hughson was wearing torn blue jean cutoffs, with an old T-shirt, sporting a Fu Manchu moustache and long hair. He was the prototypical radio guy. I was the straitlaced television guy. But we got along.

At one point early in the playoffs that year, I asked Jim for a tape of his work. I wanted to marry his radio call to our video and see if it translated. While we were set for announcers in the West, we were struggling in Toronto. In the preseason of 1981, the legendary voice of the Maple Leafs, Bill Hewitt, had a mysterious breakdown on the air and was replaced during the game. He never returned. For the whole season, a small group of announcers, including Danny Gallivan and Dave Hodge, rotated through the job. As a company, we needed to find a full-time replacement for Hewitt. Cuthbert was on the list and, based on our marriage of Jim's radio call to our TV pictures, so was Hughson.

Eventually, Hughson got the job full-time and moved from Vancouver. Cuthbert, who was living in Montreal and was the voice of the CFL team there, was pegged for the next job in the CSN/*HNIC* family. After the Super Channel experiment, the first opportunity to put Cuthbert into the mix was when John Wells left. Our relationship with the CBC had improved greatly in the past few years, basically on the success of the Oilers, so Wallace and I recommended that Chris replace Wells as the CBC sports anchor in Edmonton, and we would use him on *Hockey Night* as both a host and a play-by-play announcer. It was a seamless and logical transition, and years later, with Cuthbert's talent and greatness, it proved to be an amazing move. His work has put him high on the list of the greatest sports broadcasters in this country.

I was more hands-on in hiring the replacement for Jim Van Horne in Calgary. As a "TV-aholic" I watched anything and everything when I had downtime. That included the local news on the station halfway between Calgary and Edmonton, CKRD in Red Deer, Alberta. For the whole year prior to 1984, I had been amused and entertained by the weatherman on the evening news. He basically had a six- or seven-minute segment to talk about the unpredictable weather patterns that haunt central Alberta, but he barely did the weather. His weather board was always filled with silly little graphics or sports logos, for all the teams in the province.

What he did do, while mentioning the weather, was ad-lib his way through stories that would make people smile. He was brilliant. He had an immediate relationship with the viewer; you could see it a mile away. By the time Van Horne left, I knew in my heart that the Red Deer weatherman would be the host of Flames hockey.

That man was Ron MacLean.

We went through the charade of auditioning nine people for the job in Calgary, but we had already decided that Ron was our man. I actually got in trouble with the management of the local station because I told Ron not to be concerned with the auditions; he would be getting the job no matter what. I also suggested to Ron what his first salary should be, which was $15,000 more than the station manager wanted to pay. It was the best money they ever spent on an announcer. MacLean was raw, but like Cuthbert, you could see his greatness.

So, after a summer of indecision and rebuilding our announcer teams, 1984 appeared to be ending without a hitch—until the announcement early in the regular season that Ralph Mellanby was stepping down as executive producer of *Hockey Night in Canada*. Mellanby was going to take on the lead production job for the host broadcaster of Calgary's 1988 Olympic Winter Games. It was amazing that one of my bosses was actually going to move to Calgary in an ever-changing broadcast world. A Toronto guy coming to Calgary? Wonders never cease. In reality, the lure of running broadcast production at the Olympics obviously excited Ralph. It gave him a new challenge, one that *Hockey Night* couldn't provide. Mellanby would run *HNIC* through the 1984–85 season as the search for his replacement would begin in earnest.

To most of us, it was obvious that Don Wallace would replace Ralph. After all, he was half of the two-headed monster that we had learned to tolerate for three seasons. My relationship with Don was strong. He had always relied on me for insight on the West and there was a mutual respect between us. The idea of Wallace running *Hockey Night* gave me a ton of assurance that my voice and philosophy would be heard. After all, I thought, we were friends.

That all changed one day in December 1984. As was the tradition, I would travel east to Toronto for the annual company Christmas party. All was proceeding according to plan when I received a note before leaving Calgary that Don would meet me at the airport. That would be nice of him, to pick me up from my flight before the party that night. It was always great to see him. We had had many laughs since I joined the company seven years earlier and began my career travelling the continent with Don on various productions. I had always been a bit of a sounding board for Don, particularly when it came to Mellanby, whose style was different than Don's. Ralph was always in your face. Up-front. Brutally honest. Don was a low-key, backroom operator who had been blessed by Ted Hough as the future of the company. They were oil and water. Nitro and glycerine. Mellanby was far more creative, and knew it. Wallace had an ability to work better with the teams and the rights holders.

As I left baggage claim, I saw Don in the distance. There was no smile, just a nod and a handshake. He suggested we go up a level, into a restaurant for a cup of coffee. What followed put us on a collision course and changed everything for me at *Hockey Night*.

DW: Good flight?

JS: Yup, fine. What's up?

DW: Listen, this Ralph thing—the executive producer job—you want it? I hear you want it.

JS: Quite frankly, I haven't given it much thought, Don.

DW: That's not what I hear. I keep getting told you want it and are lobbying for it.

JS: Bullshit. I haven't talked to anyone about it.

DW: Because if you want a fight for it, I'll give you a fight!

JS: I don't know what you're talking about, but I can't believe you're saying that.

DW: So you haven't applied for it?

JS: No.

DW: Okay then.

With that, the conversation ended. I could only think that this man across the table, whom I had confided in and cajoled with for the past few years, was putting our friendship to the test. No, in fact, he had quickly and succinctly destroyed it in one short conversation.

I went to the hotel, to shower and get ready for the Christmas party, where I would watch this man politick his way through the evening. I wanted to get on a plane back to Calgary, without going to the event. And I should have.

Before the evening started, I confided in a friend about the day's events. He found it hard to believe. I challenged him to watch it all unfold at the soirée and then make a decision. Throughout the night, Wallace tried time and again to engage with me as if nothing had happened. I did as little as possible to respond, without being impolite. It was obvious that he was trying to mask our confrontation. I returned to Calgary the next day, ready to envelop myself in my western world, Mellanby's final season as the boss, and try to figure out who was friend or who was foe.

In the end, 1984 wasn't a turning point in my career, but it was a fork in the road. I knew I had to choose the right path to help stabilize my career. I wasn't ready to face the challenge of a new network when my love of *Hockey Night* still burned. But my passion for Saturday nights would have to be reformulated because I knew in my heart that my loyalty would not be reciprocated. I was going to be viewed not as a co-worker, but rather as a rival. I had returned west in the summer thinking my career would forever be at *Hockey Night in Canada*, but now those thoughts started to waver.

FIVE
STANDING UP FOR YOURSELF

HOCKEY, LIKE BROADCASTING, ATTRACTS SOME BIG PERSONALITIES. THESE ARE high-pressure businesses, with big moments that everyone wants to get right. Over my career I've earned a reputation for bluntness—it's often the best way to get something done, in my experience. However, that trait has nearly landed me in hot water many times. And some other times, it has dropped me right into it!

I started to get some time in the producer's chair early in my career. I was proving myself to all the senior people, like Mellanby and Wallace, that I could do anything they threw my way. Such was the life of an associate producer for *HNIC* in those days. There was tons of travel and long workdays in and around the arena. And I loved it.

In this spring of 1979, just before four World Hockey Association (WHA) teams joined the NHL, the Stanley Cup Final featured the Montreal Canadiens. They were attempting to win their fourth consecutive Cup with Scotty Bowman as head coach. Their opponents were the New

York Rangers, coached by Fred Shero, who was in his first year with the team after successfully helming the Philadelphia Flyers to two championships in the mid-1970s. While the New York team shocked the hockey world by winning the first game of the series, Bowman's team won four straight games to claim yet another title.

The Final series was smack in the middle of a federal election campaign in Canada. That meant that political figures were always trying to create "photo ops" at events with a large audience. In our country, there was no better place to do that than in the hockey hotbed, and political hotbed, of Montreal. However, as *Hockey Night in Canada* was seen on the CBC, there were specific rules in place for the public broadcaster that would prevent any type of one-sided reporting or coverage. For instance, if we saw the prime minister on television, then the opposition leader would and could demand equal time. With that in mind, *HNIC* executive producer Ralph Mellanby warned me of the ramifications:

> RM: Listen, kid, I'm hearing [Prime Minister Pierre] Trudeau is
> going to show up tonight, and sit close to the Montreal bench. If
> that happens, and the Habs win the Cup tonight, you know he's
> going to want to go in the room after the game.
> JS: What do you want me to do?
> RM: He can't be on camera. I don't care what you do, or how you do
> it, just make sure he's not seen on TV. This is the most important
> thing you'll do tonight.

I wasn't producing the actual broadcast, but I was in charge of coordinating the staging and execution of the interviews that Dick Irvin would be doing in the Montreal dressing room after the game. With Ralph's warning, I was hoping to avoid my own execution if I screwed up!

Just as scripted, following a rousing rendition of "O Canada" by Roger Doucet, on cue the prime minister of Canada, Pierre Elliott Trudeau, glided through an exit to the left of the home team bench, just a few feet from the players. The crowd of more than seventeen thousand rose as one. This, after all, is the liberal bastion of Montreal, and Trudeau was a Montrealer. Trudeau's arrival could not be seen on television. The standing ovation could be heard on television, but not seen. As I recall, the announcers were not even permitted to explain why the ovation occurred. The elections law trumped even *Hockey Night in Canada.*

After the Cup had been presented, I was escorted into the very small weight room at the back of the Canadiens' dressing room where we would do all of our interviews. Dick Irvin arrived from the broadcast booth, where Danny Gallivan would call the last few seconds alone. Dick, too, reminded me about the potential of the prime minister crashing the party on television. We were aware that that could happen. What we would do, if he did show, was another story.

As the players, all in various stages of disrobing, showed up to talk with Dick about the victory, the pending departure of Bowman as coach, and the greatness of their dynasty, some movement caught the corner of my eye. It was, in fact, Prime Minister Trudeau and his contingent. Security at the Forum had allowed him to access the dressing room through a back door that led directly to the weight room first. The only way the PM could get through to the players' area was to walk behind Dick and whoever he was interviewing. The moment of truth was upon us.

Trudeau's security detail was starting to move towards passing Dick when I, in my famous baby blue jacket, sprang into action. There I was, now standing directly in the way of the country's leader, four security people, as well as a Trudeau aide, telling them they couldn't pass. The only thing I could think to do at the time was tell the truth. So I did.

I informed Mr. Trudeau that, as he knew, the rules of election coverage on the CBC prohibited the network from showing him on TV without showing Joe Clark (the man who was leading the Progressive Conservative Party). But I did have a compromise.

JS: Mr. Prime Minister, if you have to pass, the only way you can do
it is if you duck underneath the camera lens or crawl on the floor.

With that, several grown men and women crawled in front of Dick
Irvin, and whoever he was talking to, so as not to be seen. Amongst the
group was the Right Honourable Pierre Elliott Trudeau. Trudeau, himself, understood the situation. The only way for him to get in to see the
team was to crawl, and crawl he did. No anger. No chagrin. Just crawl. To
this day, I still remember seeing the look on Dick Irvin's face: pure amazement, and a bit of shock.

Going off the air that night, Dick turned to me and asked if I really
made the PM crawl.

JS: Yup. I had no choice.
DI: You're good.

From that day forward, Dick has always called me "Boss."

Of course, bluntness isn't always met with such acceptance or understanding. At twenty-seven years of age, I was riding high. I was living
in Alberta, producing more hockey games than anyone else in the NHL
production business. Living in Calgary, my responsibilities were to plan
television broadcasts for the Calgary Flames, Edmonton Oilers, Winnipeg Jets, and Vancouver Canucks, in addition to my similar responsibilities on *Hockey Night in Canada* every Saturday night. I'm not sure there
were enough days in a week to do it all, but I had fun doing it. Travelling North America, living life, working with friends. Absolutely nothing
could have been better. I suppose that, like many athletes of that age, I
thought I was invincible.

In May 1984, one of the teams I regularly produced won their first
Stanley Cup. The Edmonton Oilers was the brightest, fastest, youngest,
coolest team in the NHL. It was a team that featured seven future Hockey

Hall of Fame players on the roster, including Wayne Gretzky and Mark Messier. They played the game with swagger, reflecting the personality of their coach and general manager, Glen Sather.

Over the first four seasons I was around his hockey club, Glen and I were hardly amicable. There is little doubt he was in charge on the ice, behind the bench, and yes, even with certain aspects of our broadcast. And he heard and saw everything! Or had people that did.

I learned that early, in just my second season of producing Oilers hockey, in 1981, when we hired three university students to do a fan poll outside the arena in Edmonton. The poll was simply a quick way to create interaction with the fans and viewers—some inexpensive, easy content. It was not supposed to be confrontational or controversial, merely entertaining. This was long before the internet allowed for instant polling, and doing it ourselves was much cheaper than hiring a company to do telephone polling. And it hardly needed to be scientific.

As I recall, there were three questions:

1. Will the Oilers make the playoffs this season?
2. Should Mark Messier [who had just two goals in the first twenty games of the season] be sent to the minors?
3. Should Glen Sather give up the coach's job, just to manage the team?

All good questions, I thought. All timely. Certainly questions 2 and 3 were watercooler talk in Edmonton those days. And they would garner some reaction from our audience. Unfortunately, the poll garnered a rather prickly reaction from the organization.

About fifteen minutes before airtime, just as warm-ups finished, I received a tap on my shoulder as I sat in position in the television mobile. It was Oilers assistant general manager Bruce MacGregor. He told me that Glen wanted to see me—right now. Peculiar, I thought, but nevertheless I followed Bruce to Glen's office, where the coach and GM had a copy of the poll we were running outside the arena. I wasn't the only one who could be blunt.

> GS: What the fuck is this?
>
> JS: Oh that, it's our fan poll.
>
> GS: Who do you think you are, asking these questions?
>
> JS: What do you mean?
>
> GS: Why are you asking the fans what I should do with Messier, and with my job? Who the fuck do you think you are?
>
> JS: Glen, we were just having some fun. These are topics people are talking about, and we wanted to address them.
>
> GS: Oh, you wanted to address them, did you? Maybe I should address with your boss when you should get fired?

I melted. This was very early in my time in Edmonton. Sather could be intimidating. And on this night he certainly was. He spent the next five minutes in my face, dressing me down. The one-sided conversation was so loud, his players heard every word in the dressing room next door.

I left his office as the team left their room. Four or five of them saw me and asked if I was all right. Most were my age or younger, and most, I suspect, had seen some of this from him, and felt my pain.

The poll results never ran.

I didn't sleep that night. Not one bit. The following morning, I phoned my direct report at Canadian Sports Network, Don Wallace, to tell him the story. He had already heard. There would be a face-to-face meeting between Wallace, Sather, and myself in Montreal the following week. One way or the other, I was being called on the carpet. Apparently, the team had interpreted my actions as criticism, as opposed to creating compelling content. In the meantime, I had two more Oilers games to produce. Eggshells.

The meeting in Montreal was short and humiliating. I had to apologize for my actions and promise that something like this would never occur again. It was almost like Wallace and Sather were going through a hazing exercise. It was totally choreographed. They had conspired to put me in my place. The two had a previous experience in Montreal, where they both had lived: Sather as a player, Wallace as the TV producer. With Glen as the bad guy and Don as my perceived ally, they both made it clear that what I had done was not acceptable. For Wallace's part, I still trusted him. At this point, I still thought he had my back and had saved my job in Edmonton. With my tail fully between my legs, I tried to compose myself for the next few weeks.

Slowly, very slowly, I began to feel normal again, and not fearful of losing my job, although Sather was rather frosty towards me for some time. He knew he had pushed me into submission. He also knew my bosses really didn't have my back. He would push me at every opportunity.

But by 1984, as the Oilers approached their first Cup victory, my relationship with Sather had improved. During that Stanley Cup run, the Oilers defeated Calgary in a seven-game series that truly ignited the Battle of Alberta. Between Games 1 and 2 of the series, I was walking through the bowels of Edmonton's Northlands Coliseum, only to hear my name being bellowed out—it was Sather:

GS: Hey, Shannon . . . Shannon!

JS: Yes, sir.

GS: That camera between the benches—every time I'm on the camera, I'm swearing. Why do you always have the camera on me when I'm swearing?

JS: Maybe you swear too much.

GS: My mother gave me shit this morning. She saw me on television, saying I'm always swearing.

JS: We don't show you just swearing. We simply don't know when you're going to swear.

GS: Don't put me on camera then. It makes my mom mad!

JS: We can't do that. Maybe you have to stop swearing.

GS: No, don't put me on camera. Or maybe we should move that camera.

JS: Glen, why don't you just fuck off! Stop fucking swearing, and your mom won't be mad.

Then I caught myself. Did I just say that? *Really?* One look at Sather and, yes, I had said it, for sure. I had told Glen Sather where to go. No one around, not a soul to witness it. Once again, my brain went into overdrive, wondering if this was the straw that broke the camel's back. For an instant, I stood there, alone. Sather, twenty feet away, also paused.

And then he laughed! Almost as if to acknowledge that I was right. This moment began the next phase of our relationship, one of mutual respect. I was finally in a position to push back, and I had. It was almost as if he was testing me, just one last time. If I had backed down, he would have kept on pushing.

I never did I have an issue with Glen again. In fact, I would say that Glen, and his wife, Anne, became friends. In later years, with my time at the NHL, we shared a few dinners near the Sather home on the Upper East Side in New York. We would even spend time watching the late NHL games in their penthouse, talking about the game we both loved. Every once in a while, I reflect back on how the relationship started and marvel at how far we've come.

Sometimes doing the right thing comes with consequences. That's life. But there were times when my bluntness didn't help matters. At the end of 1984, I hadn't been sure about my future with *Hockey Night*. But it would take two more years for that uncertainty to be born out.

The night of April 30, 1986, was special for me. A career-changing night. For the fans of the Calgary Flames and the Edmonton Oilers, it was a historic Game 7 of the Smythe Division Final. The Oilers were the best team in hockey that year. The Flames were second best. These two towns, these two teams, were and remain the bitterest of rivals.

For the first portion of my career, based in the West, I spent my life juggling flights between Calgary and Edmonton (with a trip or two to Winnipeg and Vancouver thrown in for good measure). On any given Wednesday it was a treat to watch Wayne Gretzky, Mark Messier, Jari Kurri, Paul Coffey, Glenn Anderson, and the rest of the gang. Thursday meant that the same team that lost in Edmonton traipsed down Highway 2 to be beaten by the Flames, led by Paul Reinhart, Kent Nilsson, Willi Plett, Al MacInnis, and Jim Peplinski.

A few years later it was Craig Simpson, Adam Graves, Marty McSorley, and Esa Tikkanen up north, and the likes of Hakan Loob, Gary Roberts, Joe Nieuwendyk, and Doug Gilmour in the south. Playing in Wild Rose Country was pure horror for most teams.

We used to dub those road trips as being "Ambushed on the Alberta Trail." The Flames had great teams, no doubt about it. But there was only one problem: they weren't as good as the teams in Edmonton. Even when the Flames were on a roll, we joked that they were still the "second-best team in Alberta." Every year from 1983 to 1989, one of those two teams played in the Stanley Cup championship.

In 1984, the two teams played a seven-game series that Edmonton won on the way to their first Stanley Cup. Two years later, with the rivalry at a fever pitch, it was a series of a lifetime. Another seven games. And a finish to that last game of the series that changed so much for a few of us.

The game itself is now part of hockey lore, not just in Alberta, but throughout hockey fandom. With the score tied at 2, the game's emotion and momentum swung with every line rush, every hit, every penalty, and every broken play. The Oilers, defending Stanley Cup champions, had fought back from a 2–0 deficit to tie the game, and like most games at Northlands Coliseum you felt that the greatness of that team would win out, and be that much closer to a third consecutive Stanley Cup championship.

On the other bench, a master motivator, Coach Bob Johnson, had convinced all those around him that his cast of superstars had enough to dethrone the champions. Johnson did everything he could to create a winning attitude. He could motivate, he would strategize, he would call on luck and every superstition possible. That series, rather than watch most of the warm-up, he and his coaching staff would walk the concourse and talk. He would also go out that morning and buy new ties for his staff and himself. No such thing as a lucky tie, but a new tie for every game would do the trick.

With fifteen minutes to play in the third, young Oiler defenceman Steve Smith had the puck behind his own net, and with little pressure from the Flames' forwards elected to pass the puck up the ice. Except the puck hit the left pad of his own goaltender, Grant Fuhr, and bounced into the net. A pure fluke. Except this fluke, eventually credited to Flames forward Perry Berezan, who had dumped the puck into the Oilers' zone, became the game-winning goal in the deciding game of the series. Pure heartbreak for Smith, his teammates, and Oilers fans. Pure exhilaration for the Flames and their fans. Because of the rivalry, it will live forever.

From a television perspective it was what sports was all about: ecstasy. Calamity. Happiness. Sadness. By coincidence, we had been able to convince the powers that be to add a camera to our coverage that year. We had worked closely with the Oilers' ticket department to buy four seats, so as not to block any fans. We put it along the right goal line, at ice level, a perfect angle for a replay of the Smith bank shot. Even the TV guys needed some luck sometimes. Hockey fans remember this moment well, but this is where it gets interesting for me.

As the game ended, a shocked sold-out crowd at the Coliseum sat in disbelief as the Flames rushed towards rookie goaltender Mike Vernon, and pure pandemonium broke loose on the ice—it was fantastic television. It took more than four minutes for the emotions to subside and the traditional team handshakes to begin. Only one problem: we were supposed to be off the air in seven minutes, and we still had two minutes of commercials to run. Our script assistant, Liz Kjellbotten, was in constant communication with master control in Toronto. While she appeared calm, you could sense she was getting grief from the other end of the phone to hurry up and get off the air.

But we couldn't go off the air just yet. We weren't going to commercial during the handshakes, and that would take three minutes. In my opinion, this was an important milestone for hockey, certainly hockey in Alberta and between the two best teams in the game. There was no way we—*I*—would go off the air without hearing from both teams. We owed it to the fans. The purpose of my move to Alberta six years earlier had been to give the teams and their fans better service and coverage than a producer based in and commuting from Toronto could. There was no way I could let this moment be compromised by Toronto now.

By the time the commercial was inserted, we were over our allotted time. Liz was receiving a lot of grief from Toronto Master. She told me, with tears rolling down her face, that we were in trouble.

At twenty-nine years of age, feeling full of myself (rightly or wrongly), I said to her, "Liz, this isn't on you. Don't worry. We will be fine, we have to do this. This is on me. If you live by the sword, you die by the sword." I was maybe not as reassuring as I could have been, but there's that bluntness again.

So, we stayed on the air and delayed the national news in the east region, and an in-progress episode of *Star Trek* in the West, to show a tearful Lanny McDonald outside his room and a somber Glen Sather outside his. It had to be done.

After the game, nothing was said right away. Not by my bosses, not by the announcers. In the meantime, this same crew had to prepare to depart early the next day for St. Louis, to cover the Flames' next opponent. It was life in the playoffs: game ends and "where do we go next"? It was one of the most exciting parts of the job, and never got old.

In this case, a small group of us travelled from Edmonton to St. Louis via Denver. The emotions of the night, the controversial show ending, had drained me. I hadn't slept well after the game, knowing I was truly in trouble. I sat alone for most of the half-filled flight, listening to Don Wittman and Gary Dornhoefer giggle over their perpetual game of cards and the fact that they were working the next round of the Stanley Cup playoffs (which meant more money). At one point, Dornhoefer sneaked up behind my seat and proceeded to reach under my chair and slap butter all over my shoes. The proverbial "shoe check." The butter could have been there for twenty or thirty minutes before these two howling hyenas yelled out "Shoe check!" and I noticed. I was not amused, but I tried to smile my way through the incident.

As we travelled to our St. Louis hotel, I mentioned to both announcers that I was going to be facing some difficult times and might be a little quiet for the next few days. They didn't understand or believe it. Within two minutes of checking into my room, the phone was ringing. It was the president of our company, Ted Hough. He was not happy. I had embarrassed the company and jeopardized the relationship with the CBC by my "antics." I believe I was calm in responding, explaining my position (which, by the way, he understood), but still, I had to be punished. He needed to show the network and the company that I could be controlled.

TH: So, John, listen, I've decided to suspend you for two games.

JS: But, Ted, I'm already in St. Louis.

TH: I understand. So I'm going to let you choose which two games they are. But you have to be suspended.

JS: Ted, this is stupid. We are in a competitive business now [with CTV also carrying games]. We need our best people working. It doesn't make any sense.

TH: John, I know it's tough, but you need to be punished and I'm doing you a favour. Pick two games.

JS: This is silly.

TH (getting angrier): *Pick* two games.

JS: Fine, I choose next November seventh and fourteenth.

TH: *These* playoffs!

JS: That's not what you said . . .

TH: That's it! You're suspended for tomorrow night and Game Two!
(click)

News travelled quickly, as a substitute producer showed up. Both Don Wittman and Flames general manager Cliff Fletcher phoned Hough and network executives to convince them of their poor decision, but the deed was done. So I sat out the first two games of the series in St. Louis, but stayed to watch the games, and even sat in the booth with Don and Gary and helped a bit with some statistics. By Game 3, I was back in the saddle, but knew nothing would ever be the same.

Within four weeks I was given my notice that my contract would not be renewed, as the company (CSN) was being sold to Ohlmeyer Communications. But it was obvious: I was that guy in the West that the suits couldn't control. I was done.

Well, almost done. I was handed my notice by then executive producer Don Wallace on the day before Game 1 of the Stanley Cup Final, between the Canadiens and the Flames. He was the same guy who had challenged me to a "fight" the previous year for the job. This was the best way for him to get rid of the competition. It was a Stanley Cup Final, by the way, for which I had been scheduled to produce Games 1, 2, 5, and 7: the games in Calgary. For hockey history buffs, this was the series featuring Patrick Roy at one end and Mike Vernon at the other. It also featured the fastest overtime goal in Stanley Cup history, which was nine seconds into extra time by the Canadiens' Brian Skrudland in Game 2.

I held on to the news until after that Game 2 at the Saddledome, and called an all-crew meeting following the dramatic and speedy Skrudland goal. I told the group that I was being let go by the company, but hoped to be able to produce Games 5 and 7 in Calgary when the series returned from Montreal. Some in the room were shocked; others were not. Whether it was my demeanor for two games, or leaked information from the company, the reaction was subdued.

Within minutes of the meeting, I had Flames general manager Cliff Fletcher inviting me to fly with the team to Montreal, and to enjoy the time with one of the teams I had been producing since their arrival from Atlanta (the franchise began as the Atlanta Flames but was sold in 1980). I was in no mood to go on a trip and be around tons of my peers and answer too many questions. For the past four days, I had been working on sheer adrenaline. Internally, I was wondering if my short career was over. Externally, I tried to maintain a stoic, mature attitude. I must admit that sometimes it didn't work that well.

The series returned to Calgary for Game 5, which Montreal won, along with the series and the Stanley Cup. What followed was a night that those in attendance will never forget. At least that's what they tell me.

I had worn the baby blue for ten years. Wore it so proudly. On this night, I wouldn't wear it to the game. I posed for pictures, which was a *HNIC* tradition, with everyone adorned in their *Hockey Night* blazers, me in grey. But I did bring the blue blazer to the postgame event. It was hardly a celebration, and it certainly wasn't a wake. Call it a punctuation mark on a brief career at that point. The climax of the night, in my favourite watering hole in Calgary, was stabbing the back of my blazer with a giant butcher knife, as I stood on the bar in front of a standing-room-only crowd, knife in hand. Network executives, league executives, team executives were all in the room. It was as crazy a night as I'm sure the Canadiens were having as they flew home to Montreal. The logo on my jacket was dipped in Sambuca and set on fire and finally the tattered jacket was hung in the ceiling in honour of my tenure with the show. It remained there until the bar closed for good. Where it is now is anyone's guess.

I spent the next few days in shock. The *Calgary Herald* had a small story under the headline of "Shannon Axed," which hung in my office for years as a reminder of my actions, and that perhaps I should mute some of my bluntness. There were times I regretted the original sin of staying on the air too long, but then I shake my head. I did the proper thing for the hockey fans in Calgary and Edmonton. And if I couldn't do the job properly, maybe I shouldn't be doing it at all.

It should be noted that the following year, someone at the CBC or *Hockey Night* had the wisdom to change the original off-air rule. A series-ending game would take eleven minutes to get off the air. Those four extra minutes would help any producer to tell a story, but came a year too late to save my tenure at *HNIC*—for now.

SIX
THE LEARNING CURVE

IT IS IMPORTANT TO UNDERSTAND HOW SMALL THE INDUSTRY WAS, AND PROBABLY still is, in Canada. With TSN joining the fray in September 1984, there were now four major places to work in sports television in Canada. You could ply your trade with CBC, CTV, Canadian Sports Network, and the fledging TSN. I had turned down a chance to work at TSN two years earlier, and they held a grudge. I had departed TSN after two days and they were, understandably, not thrilled with me. I had been let go by CSN. That left just one place to work: CTV. They weren't hiring.

CTV did have the Olympic Winter Games coming up, and I was to be in charge of the hockey venue, but that was in February 1988, and only for seventeen days. There was nothing else on the horizon. Something had to give—and it did. Timing is everything.

It was a revelation that summer, 1986, that I no longer had the door-opening power of that baby blue jacket. I could no longer walk into a room and gain the instant credibility that accompanied those four simple words: *Hockey Night in Canada.* I was embarrassed by my fall, but I also knew that I had to take steps in making myself more marketable. I had to swallow my pride, make phone calls, write letters. I needed to reach out constantly to the powers that be, and say, "I'm a good producer, a quality team player, and I can make your network better." I had to learn to sell myself. It was the only way I would be able to stay in the business, and eventually thrive. I didn't have an assistant to write those letters anymore. I didn't have anyone to help me in the edit suite, building examples of my work. I was on my own. If I wanted to continue to produce television sports, I needed to sell the only product I had: myself. I needed to become a businessman.

On my way out of *Hockey Night,* I spent a week composing thank-you notes for more than one hundred people, each note customized. I thanked people for their patience, persistence, and friendship in my time at *HNIC.* I also vowed that I would never miss a Stanley Cup playoff, and fully expected to be in the chair for the playoffs in 1987. I truly believed in my ability, but had no idea how I would accomplish this prediction. There was no doubt in my mind that the powers that be had made a terrible mistake. And while I knew I wasn't going back, I was driven to make sure those involved knew they had made a mistake.

The response to my demise around the hockey world kept me thinking positively about the future. The letters and phone calls from almost every team, and many high-profile hockey people, were heartwarming. They didn't pay any bills, but they were nice to receive. As buoying as they were, I feel that much of that summer was spent under the covers in bed. Trying to find a job in hockey, when you've been dismissed by the one place who produces most of the game can be a challenge. Life became a blur. There was a series of commercials for the St. Louis Blues that I produced, and a small package of college football games that my old college roommate Rick Briggs-Jude, at TSN, threw me over the autumn.

Bill Torrey, then the general manager of the New York Islanders, phoned almost every Thursday morning. I had befriended Torrey during the Islanders' Stanley Cup run in the early 1980s. He had become a really good ally and someone I could call about absolutely everything. He would call to simply ask how I was doing, to invite me to New York, and to reassure me, "Things are going to happen, just you wait and see." Torrey remained a friend until his passing in 2018.

As the leaves began to turn in Calgary and the hockey season was about to start, I received a surprise phone call from my friend Dan Kelly. He was under contract to be the play-by-play announcer for the second national package in Canada, which had been on CTV for the past two seasons. But CTV was walking away from the package because it wasn't helping their prime-time ratings. During the regular season, the only Canadian team they could televise was the Quebec Nordiques; all the others were controlled by Molson. It was only during the playoffs that CTV could broadcast other Canadian team games, and even then they were limited to specific teams and had to allow *Hockey Night in Canada* to broadcast locally. It was a tremendously convoluted contract that didn't make any sense for CTV. It only made sense because Carling O'Keefe Breweries controlled the broadcast rights to some NHL games and half the Stanley Cup playoffs. Yet another "Battle of the Breweries." This was at a time when some NHL owners were not happy that one of their partners (the Montreal Canadiens) actually had control of the league product in Canada. Combine that with Carling's investment in the Nordiques NHL team and you had a real internal power struggle for Canadian network television.

To simplify things, Canadian Sports Network was a front for Molson and the CBC, through MacLaren Advertising. CSN would use brewery money to buy the national rights for games to be placed on CBC. They were to be produced by CSN and sold by the CBC (after Molson took its share of the commercial inventory). This was a win, win, win. In addition to *Hockey Night*, in those days CSN would also purchase the local rights to the games for the Maple Leafs, Jets, Flames, Oilers, and

Canucks, as well as the brewery-owned Canadiens. Those games were sold regionally to television stations in the respective markets across the country. But truthfully, only one group of people produced all of the hockey in Canada, for decades. It protected all the partners from hostile bids from other breweries and networks. Moreover, the powers at CSN had always been able to "grandfather" a right-to-match clause in the contract, which made it almost impossible for someone else to take over the vaunted Saturday night national package. This made CSN/*HNIC* a powerful player in television sports in Canada and a huge voice in the NHL world. That's what really drove some of the American-based owners crazy.

Ed Snider in Philadelphia, Bill Wirtz in Chicago, Jeremy Jacobs in Boston: all felt they weren't getting enough in rights fees for the product their teams (and their partners) were delivering to *Hockey Night in Canada.* Under the guidance of Marcel Aubut, the Nordiques' owner who fronted the group for the American owners, and Gil Stein, the NHL's general counsel, they sold a second national package to Carling O'Keefe to place on CTV as direct competition to the CBC show. But because the games placed on CTV didn't have as much Canadian content, CTV walked away after two seasons.

There was only one employee left under the Carling banner, Dan Kelly, whose contract was guaranteed by the brewery. So Dan became the person the brewery leaned on to rebuild the production package. That was the gist of Dan's phone call to me that October. He was going to be doing the games, and he wanted to know if I would produce them. It wouldn't start until the spring, but it was a job in hockey, both regular season and playoffs, and half of the Stanley Cup Final.

I was in. Timing, it seems, was everything. CTV's loss was my gain.

With CTV out, Carling had been able to secure airtime with Canada's third network, Global Television Network, to carry the games. Global, in turn, would build a network across the country to carry the games where they didn't have a signal. I couldn't have been happier. Even though I was months away from doing games again, I was back. Only, I couldn't tell anyone yet.

In 1986, Calgary was a vibrant, happening city to be living in. In addition to the Flames and the CFL Stampeders, the city was ramping up for the Olympic Winter Games, which would take place in less than two years. My old boss Ralph Mellanby, and my old college roommate, Doug Beeforth (who left *HNIC* just weeks after I was fired), were both in Calgary as the production masterminds for the host broadcaster for the Olympic Winter Games. There was plenty of project work, and socializing, over the winter to keep me busy and in a positive place. Quite frankly, I didn't miss *Hockey Night* as much as I thought I would, because I was so busy. The Flames hockey team, in particular Cliff Fletcher and Al Coates, the team's president and GM and vice president of communications, respectively, treated me like family. I produced season-in-review videos for the club recounting their journey to the Stanley Cup Final, and also produced a couple of major in-game events for the club. Life was pretty darn good.

As an aside, it was Coates who came up with the "C of Red" slogan that the team still uses today. He mentioned it to *HNIC* play-by-play man Don Wittman and me during the second-round series against Edmonton in April 1986, and Wittman "just happened" to mention how great it would be to see people wear red at the Saddledome when the series moved to Calgary. Not that we were taking sides, trying to help promote the Flames. We weren't. It just happened. Thirty-five years later, people are still wearing red to the games.

So as 1986 came to an end, I didn't smother myself under the covers nearly as much, and truly did see a bright 1987 in my future. At the age of thirty, I was well on my way to reinventing myself for the first time. It wouldn't be the last.

In addition to walking away from the NHL, the CTV network also walked away from the Canadian Football League. Their last Grey Cup game was the Edmonton Eskimos vs. the Hamilton Tiger-Cats in

November 1986. (For the record, Harold Ballard's Tiger-Cats upset the Eskimos for the championship.) That left the CFL without one of its two broadcast partners. The CBC would maintain its role, but it left a giant hole (more than half the schedule) in the broadcast landscape for the league.

My love of the CFL was deep. When I was growing up in rural British Columbia, the Vancouver CFL team was a huge part of my childhood. In fact, I dare to say it was much more influential on my youth than the NHL. The Lions were our team. I knew the roster better than I knew my own family. The CFL was truly in a glory period. Every team had stars, and star quarterbacks, to be specific. Great players on other teams were villains. Heck, legendary media people in other towns played the villain, too. Being a Canadian Football fan in those days was all-encompassing. Grey Cup Saturday, then Grey Cup Sunday was a national celebration. And for me, what made the CFL so much more influential than hockey was the fact that I could actually walk into Empire Stadium and watch them live. I could only watch the NHL on television.

The commissioner of the CFL at the time was Calgary lawyer and former player Doug Mitchell. I had had some contact with Doug and his wife, Lois (who in a later life became the lieutenant governor of Alberta), when the Flames arrived in Calgary. Doug was the lawyer for some of the ownership group of the Flames. Every once in a while we would cross paths commuting between Calgary and Edmonton, or in a social setting in the neighbourhood we shared. He had hired Ron Simpson away from CSN to be his number one marketing guy. That's the same Ron Simpson who had suggested to me, in the summer of 1984, that I should probably be trained as the next executive producer of *Hockey Night in Canada*, just in case Ralph Mellanby left. Both Mitchell and Simpson were put in a very difficult position in early 1987, in trying to recoup at least some of the television rights money that CTV used to pay. Simpson was very familiar with the independent stations across Canada, from his days in the hockey world. We had been able to put NHL games on TV, away from the conventional networks, with great success. Toronto/Hamilton, Winnipeg, Edmonton, Calgary, Ottawa, and Vancouver all had these types of stations that would carry games. At a certain point early in that year, it was the CFL's only option to get the volume of games they needed to get on the air.

Some preliminary calls from the CFL's Toronto Bay Street office made it sound like producing their own package was being contemplated. Except they didn't have any idea how to produce the game, hire the personnel to do it, and run the commercials. Simpson's strengths from the ad world, and his contacts, made selling the commercials relatively easy. Having a plan to broadcast the games was simple, as well. Knowing how to execute the plan, outside the norms of a network, would be a challenge. Simpson and the commissioner really didn't know what to do.

I spent most of January 1987 in stealth mode: working from home, planning, plotting, and creating some documents that would allow easy execution of a production plan for both hockey (which I knew I was doing) and football (which I was hoping I was doing). I would write down the names of people who might want to help on the football or hockey side or both. The only real problem was that I couldn't tell anyone about either. I was sworn to secrecy until contracts were signed and every option was properly explored. It was an amazingly exciting time. While there wasn't a ton of money coming in, there was enough with small contracts (TSN, Olympics, Flames) for me to lead a comfortable life. But that would change quickly.

In fact, one night in February, I happened to host Ralph Mellanby and Doug Beeforth and his wife, Carol, at my house to watch the NHL All-Stars face the Soviet National Team in Rendez-vous '87 in Quebec City. Originally intended to be on CTV, it actually appeared on CBC, but not as part of *Hockey Night in Canada*. This was due to the brewery war between Molson (*HNIC*) and Carling O'Keefe, who at that time owned the Nordiques. *Hockey Night* personnel did not work that series, but CBC Sports people did. Strange and confusing, I know. But true. On this night, with the wine and beer flowing, the barbecue smouldering, my old boss Ralph, who was now living in Calgary working the Olympics, announced that his brother Jim, a longtime Global Television Network producer/director, was going to be in charge of the soon-to-be-announced Carling O'Keefe package for that network.

I was stunned. But I couldn't say anything.

I couldn't tell Ralph that I had already agreed to terms on a deal that would make me in charge of that package. And that I was soon going to be on a plane to Toronto, to spend most of the spring there, in building the package. Ralph was very proud and happy for his brother, as he should be. And when Ralph gets on one of these rolls, it's best to just let him speak. So I did.

Two weeks later, with hockey deal in hand, I sat at home alone watching *Hockey Night in Canada*. This is the show that had set me adrift eight months earlier, and, truthfully, had created a great deal of internal bitterness in me, which I had not been able to express. There sitting directly behind the Maple Leafs' bench was my old boss, Ted Hough. Hough had come out of the advertising business and positioned himself for two decades as one of hockey's most powerful players that no one knew. This was the day of the backroom deal, the quiet negotiation, and Hough did it better than most. His time was coming to an end at CSN/Ohlmeyer, but he was still around doing some backroom deals. So it was in utter amazement that I sat in my chair, as the camera revealed the person sitting beside Ted. It was the commissioner of the CFL, Doug Mitchell. Every hair on my head stood up. My face, I'm sure, was ruby red. My paranoia got the best of me. I was being usurped! The company that turfed me was now in competition with me for the CFL contract. There I was, 2,500 miles away, with no way of knowing what the hell was going on between the two.

It was driving me crazy. I didn't sleep at all on Saturday. Or Sunday. In the days before email and cell phones, business had to wait until Monday to be resolved. This did not help my mental state for forty-eight hours. These people were standing in my way again! Could I not be rid of them? What could I do to fix it? Get on a plane? I might have to.

The Monday phone call was brief, but satisfying. Hough had indeed invited Mitchell to watch the game from the first row of the Golds, and put him on television, in order to discuss the Molson-owned company producing the games for the league. But according to one person, Mitchell was already convinced he had a better option at his disposal for production, and a competing beer sponsor.

My fears were put to rest. I could sleep again.

I soon had a two-year deal to produce hockey and a four-year deal for football. I had learned how to be a one-person business—and market myself. I was becoming, in some fashion, my own brand.

SEVEN
PEOPLE WHO MAKE
A DIFFERENCE

AS IMPORTANT AS LEARNING TO SELL MYSELF WAS, THERE'S MUCH MORE TO THRIV-ing in a competitive and passionate industry. Many people at *Hockey Night* and beyond made an impression on me. Four, in particular, have had long-lasting influences on my career and how I approach the broadcast world. From each I learned something valuable about the business, about people, about friendship. Those gentlemen are Dan Kelly, Bob Cole, Dave Hodge, and John Davidson. All were consummate professionals. All were very demanding of themselves (or me). All took me under their wings to make me better. One taught me to be reflective, and not too big to say you're sorry. Another showed me how to strive for perfection in every performance, while another showed me how well-focused passion made our jobs easier and more enjoyable to do. Finally, the fourth taught me the value of a solid work ethic.

Our friendships survived the ups and downs of a fragile, ego-driven industry. Even though our business relationships changed over time, eventually our friendships flourished. I had gone from underling, to equal, to boss, and was fortunate that throughout the process, all could be called friends.

Dan Kelly was the voice of the St. Louis Blues. He was also the voice of the NHL when CBS tried to make hockey a national game in the United States. He was Canadian, from Ottawa, and spent a brief time on *Hockey Night* in the mid to late 1960s. His play-by-play style was outstanding and translated well from radio to television. His sense of anticipation was second to none. His ability to always make sure of player identification, along with puck location, puts him in the discussion of the game's greatest announcers. With such great focus comes the demand for perfection. Perfection of his own delivery and perfection of those around him. I worked alongside Dan for close to fourteen years and viewed him as a friend and mentor until his passing in 1989.

I was fortunate to work at *Hockey Night* through my last two years of university in 1977 and 1978, basically going to school Monday through Thursday and working on productions over the weekend. On any given Friday, I would travel to an NHL city to work on our American version of the show with Dan as our play-by-play announcer. That came with the strenuous duty of going to dinner with Dan and talking hockey from A to Z. I lived for my Friday nights. Although they weren't without their abuses:

DK: Well, kid, what do you want to drink?

JS: I'll have milk, Dan.

DK: Milk? *Milk?* We are at the most expensive steak house in New York, and you want fucking milk?

JS: That's right, Dan.

DK: It's more expensive here than Scotch!

JS: Milk, please, Dan.

DK *(to the waiter)*: I'll have a B & B on the rocks . . . and give the kid a milk.

Then we would talk about hockey, life, what I wanted to do for the rest of my career. It was better than any broadcast class I could have taken.

Dan could be tough, though. You could ill afford to make a mistake on a piece of information with Dan, or give him an incorrect statistic or time on the clock.

"Listen, kid, all you have to do is get it right. If you don't get it right, I can't trust you. If I can't trust you, I don't know why you're here."

I believed him. I never wanted to let Dan down. As hard as he could be on me, he only wanted one thing: a good broadcast. That was the ultimate team goal. He made me want to be better, every show. At the conclusion of the 1979 Stanley Cup Final, Dan and I ended up at the Alpine Steakhouse on St. Catharines Street in Montreal. The Canadiens had just defeated the Rangers in five games for their fourth straight championship, Scotty Bowman's last in Montreal. It had to be three in the morning, and Dan was listening more than he was talking as I told him what I wanted to do in my career. The people at *Hockey Night* were imploring me to work behind the scenes, eventually as a game producer. I still had the dream of following in the footsteps of people like Dan and Jim Robson. Dan listened, and he replied with one simple sentence.

"Whatever you do, just be happy."

He taught me well. There are two other instances in our time together that have been branded into my brain. The first, in March 1981, in Boston, nearly drove us apart forever. The second, in May 1987, drew us closer.

The Edmonton Oilers were making a late drive to the playoffs in 1981; on this particular Saturday they were the matinee opponent of the Boston Bruins at the old Garden. We were starting to see hints of the greatness of the Oilers that would win five Stanley Cups in the decade. In addition to future Hall of Famers Wayne Gretzky, Mark Messier, Glenn Anderson, Jari Kurri, and Paul Coffey, the team featured a rookie goaltender, Andy Moog, who was making his first mark in the NHL, and the former iron man of the NHL, centre Garry Unger. Unger's consecutive-game streak had ended in Atlanta the previous season at 914 games, with a large amount of the streak occurring while he played for the Blues, where Dan was the voice of the team.

By this time in my career, I had moved from associate producer to producer (having produced my first final the previous season) and was now confident, cocky, and full of everything else you could think of.

At some point in the second period, we took a shot of Unger, who played sparingly for Glen Sather's Oilers, but it was the perfect time for Dan to extoll the virtues of a veteran player he knew tons about:

JS *(to Dan in his earpiece)*: Here's Unger, Dan.

DK: And there's Garry Unger, the NHL's iron man . . . nine hundred and fourteen games, Detroit, St. Louis, Atlanta . . .

JS *(to Dan in his earpiece)*: Don't forget Toronto.

At that point Dan became flustered, and tripped on a few words before finishing his thought, at which point I knew I had broken his train of thought, which was not a good thing. Fast-forward to the next commercial break:

FLOOR DIRECTOR *(nervously)*: Uh, could you open Dan's mic, please?

JS: Hey, Dan, what's up?

DK: If you want to do the play-by-play, you can come up here and do it. Otherwise, don't talk to me.

JS: But Dan, you know that Unger's streak started in Toronto.

DK: I don't give a shit.

JS: Let's talk after the game.

Needless to say, the rest of the show was "pins and needles" for everyone. We did everything we needed to do to tell the stories and get off the air, but there was some uneasiness throughout the rest of the broadcast, and very little interaction between the TV truck and the play-by-play man.

Not twenty seconds after we were off the air, I was walking out of the mobile control room, only to be confronted by Mr. Dan Kelly. His face was completely red, from anger and running from the broadcast booth all the way to our location on Causeway Street, outside Boston Garden.

Dan was livid. He viewed my interruption as the worst act of treason a producer could do to an announcer. For fifteen minutes he went up one side of me and down the other, in front of every passerby and most people who had been inside the arena watching the game. Apparently, my protestations of accuracy were incorrect to Dan on this occasion. But by the end of the argument Dan did not get what he expected from me: an apology. It did not come. The last I saw of Dan that day—and for the next seven months—was him turning on his heels and walking down the alley beside the Garden to his rental car, in which I was supposed to ride with him back to the hotel. I took a cab.

On my return to the office on Monday, Dan had expounded to my superiors how out of line I was, and that if I didn't apologize, I should never, ever work in the industry again. It was not a fun few days.

Well, I still didn't apologize. Certainly not right away, and not as Dan had expected. The following October, with a new season upon us, saw the Blues play a preseason game in Edmonton. I happened to be in Edmonton for the game, as was Dan. I noticed him across the media room, and thought I should say hello, and I'm glad I did:

JS: Hello, Dan, how are you?

DK: You were wrong, you know? You shouldn't have talked in my ear.

JS: I know, Dan, but I wanted you to be right.

DK: Apology accepted.

We went on for the next eight years as the best of friends, confidants, and supporters. A pure hockey TV bromance.

As the years went by, our paths crossed a great deal. Canada Cups, Olympics, Stanley Cup playoffs. I mentioned earlier that in 1987, Dan was the voice of Carling O'Keefe hockey in Canada, which had been on CTV for the past few seasons. CTV elected not to carry the games that spring, and the brewery did a deal with the Global Television Network. I was no longer at *Hockey Night in Canada* and was looking for work. Dan, who had called every week that I was out of work, insisted to the network that I should be the lead producer for the playoff games the network would carry. No ifs, ands, or buts—I was the guy. To work with Dan again was a real treat, a true honour. Our crew of Kelly, John Davidson, and Dave Hodge was arguably the best broadcast crew in Canadian TV history. All three were at the top of their game.

As we got to a conference final game in Detroit, as is the tradition, you have to plan for events that might not occur. The most important one is overtime, and the intermissions between the actual game action. On this night, the game went not to one overtime, but two extra periods of play, which meant two additional intermissions to plan. I had noticed that Mike Bossy, the former Islander great, was in Joe Louis Arena broadcasting for our French-language partner, TVA. In my infinite wisdom, I thought having Bossy, the Islander, would be great if he was interviewed by Davidson, the Ranger. After all, JD had beaten Bossy's team in the playoffs eight years earlier. It was going to be fun. And it was. It went off without a hitch, the game continued and (eventually) ended in the second overtime, and a good night was had by all.

Except, one person was not happy: Dan.

As we prepared for a two-day break between games (which meant a long night of laughter and drinking), Dan had a quick postgame bite and went to bed. He was heading back to St. Louis for the off day to see his wife, Fran, and his family. At about 2:30 in the morning, I walked into my hotel room and heard the phone ringing. Who would be calling me at this time of night?

> DK: You know I'm really pissed at you.
> JS: What? Why? We had a great show.
> DK: I should have been the one interviewing Bossy. I'm the professional broadcaster up there. It should have been me.

Memories of our seven-month stalemate of 1981 flashed through my mind.

> JS: Well, Dan, here was my reasoning. We've heard you for more than four periods already, and I felt you needed a rest to be great for overtime, and I love the Ranger/Islander idea for JD and Mike. And, quite frankly, it's my decision.
> DK: Well, you were wrong! (click)

So there I was, years later in the same pickle, with a man I adored and respected. By now I was a family friend. I couldn't believe we would have to go through it again. Except, this time it ended differently.

Not three hours later, the phone rang again. I was still awake, worried about my relationship with the great Dan Kelly. Dan was already at Detroit Metro Airport for his flight.

> JS: Hello.
> DK: Yeah, it's Dan.
> JS: Hi, Dan.
> DK: You were right. (click)

With a full day off, I slept like a baby.

We worked again together twice in 1988: at the Olympic Winter

Games in Calgary, where he was CTV's play-by-play man for hockey and I was in charge of the hockey venue for the host broadcaster, and then again for the Stanley Cup playoffs. Not long after we completed those playoffs, Dan started having terrible back pains. Within a year, he had passed away. He was just fifty-two! He had accomplished so much in our business and made an impact on generations of hockey fans in both countries.

In fall 1988, he accomplished something that I think we would all love to do. He worked alongside his son John in the Blues' broadcast booth. He and John joined the pantheon of broadcast and sports families, like the Bucks and the Hewitts in our business, and the Howes on the ice. Through it all, Dan was a family man, truly dedicated to his wife, Fran, and their children. Prior to his passing, I phoned to tell him I was getting married and to say how much he meant to me. His advice, just as it was a decade earlier, was "to be happy" with my married life.

In January 1989, the Blues and the National Hockey League honoured Dan with a huge event, a dinner in downtown St. Louis. More than a thousand people showed up to pay tribute to Dan, with just one person not in attendance: Dan. His health had deteriorated to the point he couldn't leave the hospital. Jack Buck was the MC. Bob Costas spoke, as did Don Cherry. It was a night to remember.

On the afternoon of the event, I had made the decision to go to the hospital to visit Dan. There was no guarantee I could get into the room, but I had to try. In the lobby of the hotel, one of Dan's oldest friends and a great broadcaster in his own right, Pat Marsden, mentioned to me that he had seen Dan the day before, and he was heartbroken at Dan's state. He suggested I shouldn't go and see Dan—better that I remember the always cherubic Kelly. A few minutes later I chatted with former coach turned broadcaster Gary Green, who had had the same conversation with Marsden. As much as we knew that Pat might be right, in our hearts we knew we had to go see Dan. Well, the word spread. Twenty minutes later, Dave Hodge said he wanted to go, and just after that, Flames GM Cliff

Fletcher was on board, too. So it was the four of us going to visit Dan in a hospital in suburban St. Louis.

The half-hour drive was filled with a combination of trepidation and laughter. We all had our favourite Dan stories and impressions. Three of us had worked TV with Dan. Cliff went all the way back to 1968 with the Blues, when Dan arrived in the Midwest from Ottawa. Once at the hospital, we had to convince our way onto the cancer ward and into the room. After checking with Dan himself, the nurses relented and allowed us in. Sitting up, in hospital whites, with little hair left on his head, was Dan. While he was a little pale, and a little gaunt, it was him. In his hand, for all the world to see, was a lit Marlboro cigarette.

"If I'm going to go out, I'm going to do it my way."

We sat, we laughed, we cried. We said good-bye. Less than a month later, Dan died of lung cancer.

Like Kelly, I met Bob Cole as a teenager working for *Hockey Night in Canada*. Dan and Bob had similar work ethics, and similar demands to be great. I have known Bob for well over forty years, longer than any of the cohorts he worked alongside on *HNIC* at his departure. Our time together goes from the Super Series to Stanley Cups, from Olympics to fish and chips on the South Shore. To call his 2019 removal the end of an era might be one of the great understatements of all time.

His voice. His style. His passion. Bob and all his traits transcend generations. Grandparents, parents, and children have all heard the voice of Bob Cole tell stories on Saturday nights.

No one in our business, in front of the camera, in the booth, or behind the scenes, had a better flair for the dramatic than Bob Cole. His sense of "moment" has been brilliant. There are many stories his broadcast partners tell of receiving the "Heisman" from Bob as he orchestrated from the booth, putting a hand up dictating when the next words should be spoken. He treats the event like that of a great conductor of a symphony orchestra. His sense of anticipation reveals a tremendous understanding and knowledge of the game of hockey. With a simple change in tone or a quick phrase—"Watch out!" . . . "Here THEY come!" . . . "Oh baby!"— the delivery forces you to look up from whatever you are doing and move to the edge of your seat. Not big words, but emphatic ones. His sense of anticipation separates Cole from most others, and puts him on a level with the greatest: Gallivan, Hewitt, Kelly.

If he conducts from the booth, his voice is that of a great entertainer. He knows that a big goal in the first minute of the first period is important, but not as important as one in the third. Like many of the Broadway plays Bob loves to attend, he knows that the end of Scene 1 is not as important as the show finale, so he will use his voice accordingly. No one in the game has a better sense of drama. His sense of moment is impeccable. He understands that in the biggest events, on the biggest stage, maybe it's important to say *nothing*. Bob shouldn't be in a textbook; he is the textbook.

In this day and age of play-by-play announcers and coloured charts with every small detail on every player, Bob is a minimalist. A piece of cardboard, maybe a flip chart, with both teams and the lines for the night. That's it. And it's a lineup Bob has been able to procure on the morning of the game in a very private moment with each of the head coaches. A moment that almost every coach in the NHL will take to talk to the legend. Even if, at a morning press conference, the coach tells the media horde that certain players are questionable or will be a game-time decision, he will have told Bob Cole his complete lineup and starting goaltender. That's because he trusts that Bob won't be sharing it with the other team or tweeting it out, or blabbing it to writers. Cole will be taking the information back to his room, just to study the lines and ensure proper pronunciation of every player's name.

It is that loyalty and privacy and attention to detail that makes Bob so special. He has built friendships over the years because managers, coaches, and players appreciate his passion for the game and his direct, simple approach. We've all seen examples of that. Wayne Gretzky's farewell game at Madison Square Garden, when Bob and Wayne had a private moment, a handshake and a hug, prior to the game. Pre- and postgame moments with Sidney Crosby and Connor McDavid, who as players know what Bob means to the game.

Cole was, is, and will always be revered in hockey circles as one of a kind, and treated accordingly. What makes those moments even more wonderful is that Bob never takes it for granted. He is in awe of it all. He's honoured to have called Jean Béliveau's only overtime goal. He will chuckle like a child when he realizes that the greats of the game want to meet him, to shake his hand and say hello.

Bob does everything with passion. He's passionate about his family, and curling, and Newfoundland, and golf, and hockey—and doing it right. Doing it all right.

Bob Cole loves Frank Sinatra and the New York Yankees. And he loved being a part of *Hockey Night in Canada*. To this day, I don't believe I've ever seen Bob without his favourite piece of jewelry: a *Hockey Night in Canada* ring. He wears it with the same pride a championship player wears his Stanley Cup ring.

My lasting memory of Bob is a simple conversation we had in April 1999, the week that Wayne Gretzky decided to retire.

JS: Listen, Bob, that Toronto-Montreal game you're supposed to do on Saturday—I'm going to pull you off it . . .

BC: *What?*

JS: Yes, it's not that important.

BC: Not that important? It's Toronto against Montreal. The last game of the season. I always do the last game of the season. No, boy, I have to do that game!

JS: I know, Bob, but I'd rather have you ready for the next day. In New York.

BC: What's happening there?

JS: Wayne's going to retire. It's going to be his last game. He will announce it tomorrow. And you have to be in New York for Sunday afternoon. We can't risk travel issues.

BC: So I'm not working on Saturday.

JS: Nope, but you will work Sunday at MSG.

BC: For Wayne.

JS: Yes, for Wayne.

BC: Okay, I guess that's the right thing to do.

Well, it was the right thing to do. Bob rose to the occasion and was his brilliant self, creating a bond between the viewer and Gretzky like no one else could. The day started for him with that private moment with No. 99 in the hall outside the Rangers' dressing room, and ended with some great words, as only Bob could elicit.

"It's okay, Wayne, we all have a tear. You deserve it."

On that Sunday, Bob knew when to speak, and when to be quiet. As the faithful at MSG chanted Gretzky's name, Bob stayed quiet. He understood the moment better than anyone.

"I don't believe a soul has left this building, they are all standing . . . they want to see him again . . . and again . . . and he has obliged them . . . as always."

"He's as perfect as anybody would ever hope to be . . . Great for the game. Good-bye, Wayne . . . and thank you for all those great moments."

No one, absolutely no one, not the great Danny Gallivan or the equally great Dan Kelly, had the dramatic flair for an event like Bob. Both Danny and Dan are at the top of the list of the game's greatest. They were pure announcers. Their roots in radio came through, even on television. While Bob Cole's roots were there, too, he could marry words to pictures better than anyone. He understood the moment visually, as much as he did audibly. He was pure television royalty. I learned from Bob just how special it was to work for *Hockey Night in Canada.* His passion for the show and game allowed me to be as passionate, too. His drive for greatness allowed me to strive for the same greatness.

Kelly and Cole were constants for many years. But Dave Hodge was different. He didn't think as an announcer; he thought as a producer. That could be a good or a bad thing.

Not only did we spend most Wednesdays and most Saturdays together, but we spent many hours at a Toronto radio station, CFRB. Hodge was the nightly sports announcer. I was a lowly newsroom assistant. I was working at the station while I attended university in the mid-1970s. That didn't stop us from connecting. We spent many nights in the sports office, well after the 11 p.m. sports report, telling stories (that was Dave's part) and listening (that was my part). When we first met, he was in his sixth season as host of *Hockey Night*. In that time, he had changed the editorial tone of the show. Having replaced Ward Cornell for the 1971–72 season as the Toronto host, Hodge was a bit of a phenom. Just twenty-six, Dave had finished a year of play-by-play with the Buffalo Sabres. In addition to his radio commitments at CFRB, there was little doubt he had a bright future.

Dave was a star. He was the face of Saturday night. For a long time *Hockey Night* had for the most part been a voice of the establishment: the teams, the owners, the league. Hodge very much changed that. He expected honesty. He demanded journalism. He assumed access. And he prepared. Long before computerized stats, Hodge compiled his own on a daily basis, through the morning newspaper. Marking goals, assist, points, goals-against average—everything. All in longhand.

Dave knew everything there was about hockey. He knew stats, people, and trends. His analytical mind appeared to never stop. And with his knowledge came opinion. I've always maintained that Dave was too smart to just be in sports broadcasting. He should have been in politics, or at the very least a lawyer.

When you worked alongside Dave Hodge, the expectation—his and yours—was to be perfect, exact, and correct. There were times it was exhilarating, and times it was embarrassing. The one thing you could not do was let Dave (and therefore the show) down. His demand for perfection rubbed off on me. As did his level of preparation.

You could see Dave's mind at work, thinking of the next question, trying to raise the sports broadcasting business to a craft. Dave was the ultimate craftsman. A wordsmith. He personified storytelling the way that *Hockey Night in Canada* had always espoused to anyone that would listen, that it was supposed to be the ultimate storytelling show.

Early in my career as a producer, in our game day production meeting, I had not thought through the complete intermission content. In our lexicon, "I left a blank." Well, in no uncertain terms, this was a message to Hodge that I wasn't fully prepared for the meeting, the game, the show. While not angry, he was totally pragmatic about the show plan. He wasn't condescending, but he put out the vibe that if John Shannon wasn't going to be ready to produce, then Dave Hodge would be. After I left *HNIC* in 2000, Ron MacLean said the same thing to me about why he had become more involved in the editorial side of the show. If the producers didn't have good ideas, MacLean would have his own.

Hodge made the producer prepare better. He also made the producer justify. It was one thing to have a plan. It was another thing to have a quality plan. Dave's favourite question in production meetings was simple, and to the point: "Why?"

The response "Because I'm the producer" wasn't the correct answer. Don't get me wrong, Hodge was fun. He loved the broadcast business and he loved hockey. His dry sense of humour came through to those of us close to him. He just wanted to be great every day. I believe that helped me grow as a broadcaster.

No one ever worked harder or delivered more than Hodge. He did it with such an on-air ease, he became the standard by which sports announcers in Canada were measured. That was until February 1987, a night where the national audience watching the Maple Leafs game was not allowed to join the conclusion of the regional game from Montreal. The night of the famous pen flip. Hodge's closing remarks:

> That's the way things go today in sports on this network . . . and the Flyers and the Canadiens have us in suspense and will remain that way until we can find out somehow who won this game . . . or who's responsible for the way we do things here . . . Good night for *Hockey Night in Canada*.

I was in Calgary that night, just a regular *HNIC* viewer. I had already agreed to terms to produce the competing NHL show on Global. I sat in stunned silence in my house, knowing full well that leadership of Canadian Sports Network (*HNIC's* parent company) and CBC Sports would not be pleased with Dave's closing remarks. This had, in fact, been the second time on this given Saturday that the viewer had been robbed of the conclusion of a sports event on CBC. Earlier that day, the network cut away from the semifinal of the Canadian curling championship, the Brier. Needless to say, Hodge was displeased in the afternoon, long before the *Hockey Night* debacle occurred.

I found out later that Don MacPherson, the head of CBC Sports, was in Banff, Alberta, at the Olympic Broadcasters Conference, preparing for the upcoming games to be held in Calgary the following year. On this Saturday, executives from around the world were together watching *Hockey Night in Canada*, the CBC's flagship show. When Hodge uttered his famous words and flipped his little black pen, it was an international embarrassment for MacPherson, in front of his peers. Some teased him, some admonished him. All were in agreement that something had to happen to Hodge. He never again hosted *Hockey Night in Canada*.

I was at home, about twenty minutes after the event, when my phone rang. It was a familiar voice: "Got a job for me?"

Hodge had packed his briefcase, put on his overcoat, and departed the hockey studio at Maple Leaf Gardens, without saying a word to anyone.

He had walked from 60 Carlton Street to the Harbour Castle hotel on the lakeshore, where he called me.

The following Monday, I contacted the senior management group at Global to discuss Saturday's events and the possibility of having Dave Hodge, the number one host of *Hockey Night in Canada*, join Dan Kelly and John Davidson on our broadcast crew. They were in disbelief that Hodge would be available. As the week went on, and the following Saturday *HNIC* went on with no Hodge, it became apparent that we could, in fact, have Hodge on our show. Great PR and great for credibility. Hodge was ours. And remember about that mix of professional and personal? The sense of satisfaction for me, to have Hodge join our show, was exhilarating. I was now able to extend an offering of employment to the man who taught me so much about preparation and integrity (it wouldn't be the last time, either). It was a moment of pride.

John Davidson was not a classically trained announcer. He was supposed to be the jock in the booth. Eventually, he proved to be the best analyst the game has ever heard.

My first personal encounter with John was in the shower, at the Montreal Forum. Before your mind is completely in the gutter, let me explain. JD, as nearly everyone calls him, was the New York Rangers' star goalie and had led them to a Cinderella appearance in the 1979 Stanley Cup Final, against Scotty Bowman's Canadiens—what would be their fourth consecutive Stanley Cup championship. Davidson's team would win the first game of the series in Montreal, before losing the next four games, and thus the series, to one of the greatest teams ever assembled. Following the game, and our extended coverage of the winning team's celebration, I had been asked to get an interview with John for an upcoming trip of NHL players and *Hockey Night* announcers to the Yukon. It wasn't the most opportune time—after all, he had just lost in the Stanley Cup Final. And in the old Forum, the visitors' room was small, steamy, and hot.

Davidson was nowhere to be found. There were tons of reporters still milling about the room, in full sweat, talking to the remaining Ranger players. Also, the trainers and support staff were gathering up equipment, sweaters, and towels in an attempt to get quickly to the charter flight returning to New York in a few hours. Exasperated, I finally asked the trainer where Davidson was, and yes, he was still in the shower. The trainer told John I was waiting, and I could hear the big goalie tell the trainer in the background, "Tell him to come back here."

So I did. The Montreal Forum was built in the 1920s and remodeled in the late 1960s. Some parts of the remodel were better than others. The dressing room was a honeycomb of small, dank rooms with little or no air circulation. When the steam from the showers started, it blew through the whole room, raising the temperature twenty degrees Fahrenheit. I was already hot, sweaty, and wet from the celebration in the Canadiens' room. But I had to get this interview with Davidson.

There he was, water pouring down his back, naked, with at least six or seven welts on his arms and upper chest from stopping pucks in the playoffs for the past two months. And there I was, clad in my *Hockey Night in Canada* baby blue polyester jacket. Tie askew, hair soaked, glasses steaming up and tape recorder in hand.

JD: Hey, how you doing?

JS: Great, John. Sorry to bother you, but I need this interview to promote the summer trip to the Yukon.

JD: Oh yeah. Let's do it. Fire away.

JS: Right now?

JD: Yeah, that's okay, isn't it?

Davidson had just lost the Stanley Cup Final. He was obviously in a bit of pain. But he had a smile on his face and wanted to help.

I proceeded to interview John, while he continued to shower. My right arm reached through the spray of the water, as he leaned forward, letting the water fall down over him, shielding the microphone with his body. To this day, I remember walking out with the interview done and the right side of my clothes completely soaked. We have joked about this night many times over the years, over a glass of wine or two. The friendship that began then has endured more than forty years.

In 1984, John agreed to return to his hometown of Calgary to work for *Hockey Night in Canada* and the regional games in the West. He instantly became a star. He made the game fun. He had excitement in his voice. He broke down the game for the viewers better than anyone. He was a natural. But he worked at it. Every night at the Davidson house, from 5 p.m. Mountain time on, John, with his yellow legal pad in front of him, watched as much hockey as he could. This was before NHL Centre Ice or multiple cable channels. John installed a rather subtle ten-foot satellite dish in his backyard to watch every game, and indeed he spent every night at home watching games, scouting teams, analyzing other broadcasters—trying to get better. He quickly became the best in the game, purely because of his work ethic.

I should know. I was at the house, a lot. Invariably, on an office night, the phone would ring.

JD: Hey, big boy, what are you doing?

JS: Just finishing some game planning for the trip.

JD: When you finish, come by the house. Diana's made too much dinner, and we can watch some hockey.

On most quiet nights, I did just that. I wasn't married at the time, but I was as committed to my craft as John, so it became part of our weekly routine. Much to the chagrin (I'm sure) of John's wife, Diana. After a while (and this went on for two years) it became a scene out of *Seinfeld*:

JS: Hi, Di.

DIANA: Hello . . . Shhhhhannnnon.

To this day, that is how she greets me. I have never forgotten the hospitality of both of them through their time in Calgary, the birth of their daughters, the return to New York, and the ensuing trips to St. Louis and Columbus before returning to New York. Truly, they are two of the most wonderful people to have as friends.

Those nights watching games created a bond. We talked constantly through the night, discussing game production, what was right and what was wrong about the game and/or the broadcast. It was a master class in sports broadcasting.

We would sit and predict what replays would or should come up at the whistle. We spoke incessantly about how to manage the number of words to be used in analyzing a play, and how to speak proper English. Every now and then, there would be a eureka moment, when we both noticed a play or a player's reaction away from the puck and yelled at the television that "there better be a replay on this," and when there wasn't, we shared a disgust that a key story was being missed.

So much of the game could be broken down without using X's and O's, by instead telling a story about a player and *why* he did what he did with a simple replay sequence. Davidson embraced this philosophy, and for the remainder of his broadcast career was at the top of the pyramid.

I would like to think that John taught me hockey and I taught him broadcasting, but it was closer to John teaching me to be a sponge about information and content. John's infectious enthusiasm about the hockey world and the broadcast business made learning easy. Anyone who came in contact with him became better at their jobs. He made me a better producer.

Our friendship was deep, from those days in Calgary, through our time at Olympics and in New York. But it took a hit in 2011 when John moved to St. Louis to be the president of hockey operations. I was in my twilight career, on the air with Sportsnet. We had always been open with our discussions and rarely (if ever) compromised our friendship for putting information on the public airways. We truly could trust each other.

On one occasion, though, it didn't work that way, or at least not the way I wanted it to work.

In November 2011, JD's Blues were struggling. For weeks, my cohorts at Sportsnet had been telling me that the Blues were going to fire their young head coach, Davis Payne. JD, in our thrice-weekly conversations, never mentioned that hiring Ken Hitchcock was in the works. Because of our friendship, I would never ask him. This was early in the Twitter world, and early in my time as a so-called insider. Getting the scoop was key to all of our success. Needless to say, I did not get the inside story on the hiring of Ken Hitchcock, and I was sour. Over the next few days, I absorbed the wrath of my workmates on my inability to get the story—given in jest, I'm sure. But the failure really bothered me. I was trying to create a new role in my career, in my fifties. I needed all the help I could get. The next few conversations with Davidson were abrupt, businesslike, and hardly friendly. Then, one day, driving home, my phone rang:

JD: Hey, big boy.

JS: Hi, John.

JD: I get the sense you're mad at me. Why would that be?

JS: Well, I guess it's because you didn't tell me about Hitch.

JD: I couldn't. We had had too many leaks, and I had already given
  everyone shit for the leaks, so I couldn't be that guy.

JS: But you know how competitive things are . . .

JD: But, John, I can't worry about that. This is a tough business and
  I can't be concerned about you and your stories.

It was ironic, really, because twenty years earlier, John had been one of the originals on *Hockey Night*'s "Satellite Hot Stove" segment and getting the stories right—and first—was part of his job description. But things changed, just as jobs changed. I should have known better.

We obviously had differing opinions on the topic, but I had made a huge mistake. I had asked one of my closest friends to compromise his principles over business, simply to make me look good. I realized only after months of feeling sour that what I had expected from him wasn't fair. While John and I are still close, it was an episode in our relationship that I am not proud of. It took a couple of years to rebuild the trust and honesty that we had had.

In retrospect, it put to a test the friendship and respect we had since those early days in Calgary. His desire to be the best had always been matched by my desire to make him the best. His thorough research was always followed by a question from me, on how to best tell the story on the air. We understood each other. We always knew where the other stood. The work ethic that fueled us both for years was challenged. I made a mistake. Lesson learned.

EIGHT
NEVER FORGET OR FORGIVE

I'VE BEEN FORTUNATE TO WORK WITH, AND BEFRIEND, SOME OF THE MOST PAS-
sionate and dedicated people to ever call or produce a game. A career
in such a competitive industry—make that several if you count the different sports involved—means working shoulder to shoulder with some
big personalities. Even the kindest, most generous people feel the strain
and pressure of a long season and high stakes. The point is, we all have
bad days or moments. Some you ignore, some you forgive, some require
apologies. But there are times when forgiveness is not what's called for.

Early in my career, I was in awe of many of the NHL greats I got to
work with. There was a Saturday afternoon with Jacques Plante in Boston. Plante had come in from his home in Switzerland to work a Bruins
game, much to the chagrin of Coach Harry Sinden, who had not forgiven
Plante for bailing on the Bruins after just ten games a few seasons earlier.
He actually refused the Hall of Fame goaltender a media pass for the Saturday matinee at the Garden and made us buy Plante a ticket just to get

him into the game. Nothing seemed to faze the five-time Vezina Trophy winner, though. Plante was his own man, did things his way, and moved on. Still, it was a mistake to try him as an analyst. All he could talk about was goaltending, and he didn't seem to like the two guys between the pipes in the game that day.

It was always important (and still is) to understand that the two dimensions we see or read about in athletes can in no way reflect the actual person. Most are as complex, insecure, overbearing, or shy as the rest of us. But many have been protected, advised, and guided through their work lives since they were teenagers. It was not uncommon for pro athletes to not know how to rent a car at the airport. Why would they know? Every time they had travelled, it was on an airplane with forty other people and then onto a chartered bus. They were told when to leave, when to eat, when to skate, when to sleep. Their job was to play the game. They lived, in so many ways, in a bubble of pro sports, long before the COVID bubble became part of our lexicon.

And then there was Bobby Hull.

For most of my childhood, Hull was different than most NHL players. He had taken the mantle as the game's best goal scorer from Maurice "Rocket" Richard, who had retired in 1960. Hull was "The Golden Jet." He had it all: unbelievable talent, beautiful skating, a Herculean physique, magnetic smile, incredible shot. He was one of the greatest players ever to lace up.

He was also well spoken, and an ad agency's dream. So it was no surprise that my boss, Ralph Mellanby, decided to recruit Hull to be an occasional announcer for *Hockey Night in Canada*, once his playing career ended with the Hartford Whalers in the 1979–80 season.

Mellanby loved his superstars. We were always experimenting, particularly in the playoffs, with players who Ralph thought might be good announcers or ratings grabbers. One year it was Glenn "Chico" Resch, who had become a bit of a character with the Islanders. Bobby Orr took a stab at the broadcast business, including the Challenge Cup of 1979, but didn't find it to his liking. In one playoff we tried both Herb Brooks and Wayne Gretzky as studio analysts. Brooks was fresh from coaching his Lake Placid Olympic victory and Gretzky had just finished his first season in the NHL.

In many ways, Ralph always viewed himself in the same breath as the greats of the game. After all, he had become a bit of a public figure in Canada and the hockey world as the visionary of the game's premier television show. Hiring Hull fit into Mellanby's playbook. Remember, the NHL had added four more Canadian teams by 1981. Quebec, Winnipeg, and Edmonton had come from the World Hockey Association two seasons earlier. A Calgary-based ownership group had purchased the Atlanta Flames in 1980 and moved the team to the Stampede City. In twenty-four short months, we had gone from three Canadian-based teams to seven. That meant a ton more work for people like me (as a producer) and the demand for more on-air personalities.

Beyond play-by-play announcers, *Hockey Night* employed Dick Irvin in Montreal, Brian McFarlane in Toronto, and Gary Dornhoefer and Gerry Pinder as colour commentators. As a group, with Mellanby's blessing, we were always on the lookout for additional talent because of the increased workload, particularly in Western Canada. We had recently moved Howie Meeker from the studio to the booth to occasionally do colour, but that wasn't Howie's strength. In addition to *Hockey Night in Canada*, we also produced regional broadcasts in Toronto, Winnipeg, Edmonton, and Calgary, and a portion of the Vancouver broadcasts. At this time, as a group, we were the only company in the country producing NHL games for television. It wasn't uncommon to be in an arena in the United States on a Monday, Winnipeg on Tuesday, Edmonton on Wednesday, and Calgary on Thursday, before preparing for *Hockey Night in Canada* on Saturday—and doing it all over again the next week. If you loved travel, television, and hockey, it was nirvana!

But it wasn't perfect. Sometimes the best of intentions don't result in a successful broadcast or broadcaster. For me that was the case with "The

Golden Jet." It was early in the 1981–82 season and I was set to produce the Hartford Whalers against the Vancouver Canucks in the Pacific
Coliseum. Our host was local CBC legend Steve Armitage. Play-by-play
would be handled by Jim Robson, and Hull was to do the colour. It was
a rather simple show. It was to be seen regionally, just in the province of
British Columbia.

These were special shows for me. Working with Robson, whom I
listened to for years, was always an honour. Delivering in Vancouver, not
250 miles from where I grew up, was energizing. I always wanted these
games to be extra good.

When it came to Hull's role, I had already been warned by my peers
in the East about his work ethic and lack of focus. The week before, he
had worked in Montreal with Danny Gallivan and Dick Irvin, and if not
for Dick's tremendous ability to be inclusive, Hull would probably have
not lasted another week. Dick gave him pertinent information, asked him
relevant questions, and basically spoon-fed Hull everything he needed to
get through the broadcast. The highlight for most of our crew was Hull's
analysis of one particular replay when he said, "Larry Robinson knocked
him on his ass." In this decade, many wouldn't flinch at that description, although I wouldn't recommend it to budding analysts. However,
in 1981, that was as close to blasphemy as one could get on *Hockey Night
in Canada*.

Hull was raw, but the boss believed he deserved another chance. He
was assigned to the Whalers game in Vancouver because Hartford was the
last team he played for in the NHL. Plus it was a small audience, so even
if he was bad, the damage would be minimal.

Arriving late on Friday night from an eastern road trip, I got an earful
from our travelling group that "Bobby Hawk" (as he liked to be called)
was the life of the party on Friday night. He was affable and approachable, and always willing to have a conversation with any fans who recognized him. It was the Hull I had heard about through my youth.

However, there was one thing that kind of disturbed me. At the end of the evening, Hull was still a little hungry for a late-night snack. But rather than going to his room at the Hotel Vancouver and ordering something, Hull elected to wander the floors of the hotel, picking uneaten food off the service trays that had been put out in the hall. This became known as "Bobby Hull Room Service."

I met Bobby for the first time at our regularly scheduled Saturday morning breakfast meeting. He was pleasant but appeared distracted. Apparently he had booked himself for an autograph session in suburban Vancouver for the afternoon for a new hockey stick company he was working with. This was not greeted by the producer (me) warmly.

How could Hull be booked on the afternoon of a game, when he should be researching and preparing for the broadcast? As an announcer, Hull should have been poring over the teams' player guides for stories and statistics. He should use the time to talk to the coaches involved, just to understand what their thinking was going into the game. He needed to know the strengths and weaknesses of each and every player on both rosters. And he needed to rest.

Unlike a player, when you broadcast a game, you don't do a sixty-second shift and then go to the bench. Announcers are "on" for every shift, every moment, from puck drop to buzzer. It is physically and mentally draining. That actually surprises some former players when they get in the business. Obviously, Hull thought he was different. Or he didn't think at all. Did he understand it was a five o'clock start time?

At any rate, we stumbled through breakfast, agreeing that Hull would appear in the opening segment of the show with Steve Armitage to discuss the Whalers. The talking points were simple.

1. Ron Francis, the team's number one draft pick, was off to an excellent start in his rookie season. Tons of pressure on an eighteen-year-old to lead a team that had lost veterans like Gordie Howe, Dave Keon, and others, since they joined the NHL from the WHA.

2. Pierre Larouche had been acquired from Pittsburgh, and Hartford finally had a bona fide fifty-goal scorer to help Francis lead this team. Larouche always played the game with a smile on his face, and had excellent stick-handling skills.

That was it. That's all Hull had to say, even if it was verbatim. Armitage would lead Hull to each player, and we only needed a minute of content. Our goal was to give him some profile at the beginning of the show, and to give the viewers a couple of players to watch as the night went on. We would tape the opening at the beginning of the team warm-ups at 4:30. That meant everyone had to be in position by 4:20. Simple.

Well, 4:20, and then 4:40, came and went, with no Hull in sight. He wasn't even in the building. By 4:45, and with warm-ups ending, I wasn't even sure he was going to be at the arena for the game. I prepared Armitage and Robson for the possibility of a two-man show. With ten minutes before airtime, Hull finally appeared. He was ready to tape. Only one problem. "Uh . . . what am I talking about?" He hadn't listened to a single thing at the morning meeting.

The look on Steve Armitage's face was priceless. We were ten minutes to air and, realistically, if we were to videotape the opening, we only had one crack at it. With what had gone on with the late arrival, I did not trust Hull to be ready to go live. But this is when the "Bobby Hawk" magic appeared. I quickly recapped what Hull was to know about both Ron Francis and Pierre Larouche, and told the floor director to instruct our director, Larry Brown, to roll and record. Less than two minutes later, Hull put that glint in his eye and his legendary smile to work. He repeated, verbatim, what I had told him about the two young Whalers stars.

He was spot-on perfect. Smooth, professional, warm. Hull was *very* good. We did the opening in one take and quickly went our separate ways: Hull to the broadcast booth to join Robson, Steve to the studio to voice any highlights, and me to the television mobile. I sat in my chair as the *Hockey Night in Canada* theme began blaring through the speakers, and the show was on the air!

Following the national anthems and the drop of the puck, the Canucks went to work against the Whalers and scored early in the first period. Robson was his usual steady self.

JR: [Ivan] Boldirev shoots, and scores. Vancouver leads 1–0!

What followed has been engrained in my brain for four decades. This was, after all, *Hockey Night in Canada*, the best hockey broadcast in the world. Every person on the crew, from the maintenance man to the cameramen, from the replay operators to the production staff, had dreamt of working on this show for their entire careers. The only person who didn't have that aspiration was Robert Marvin Hull. As one friend said to me later, Bobby wanted to work for the post office, because this one he mailed in.

BH: Oh, what a great goal . . . 7 passed it to 21, who gave it to 9 . . . who put it in the net.

There was no *why*. There was no *how*. Damn it, there wasn't even a *who*! I was stunned. I believe I froze, not knowing what to say or what to do. It was at this point that our director, Larry Brown, turned to me.

LB: Did you hear that?
JS: Uh, yup.
LB: What are you going to do about it?
JS: I'm not sure right now.

At the same time, I could see Armitage in the studio on a monitor, just to my right. He had that same look now that he'd had about ten minutes before game time. It was pure panic. I'm sure I had the same look. We were four minutes into a game, with a mere two hours and twenty-five minutes to go. And one of our broadcasters had no clue who was playing.

If we were to salvage this show, Robson and Armitage would have to be on their games. And my knowledge of the NHL and its players would be put to the test. For the rest of the night, I talked incessantly into Hull's ear.

> JS: Bobby, on the whistle, we are going to talk about Ivan Hlinka.
> He's a big Czech centre that came over after a great career in
> Europe to make his mark in the NHL. You know, he reminds me
> of your old teammate Phil Esposito—big lanky player, with a big
> blade, great passer, can just sit in the slot and fire the puck.
> BH: There's Ivan Hlinka. He's a big centre. Reminds me of my old
> teammate, Phil Esposito—big lanky player, with a big blade . . .

You get the idea. It was one of the most exhausting nights of my life. From my lips, to Hull's ear, and on the air. I suppose it was a great audition for me as an analyst, but I still had my regular job as the producer to do, in addition to feeding Bobby Hawk every single tidbit, all night long. By game's end, I was drained physically and emotionally. I couldn't even tell you the score of the game; it had been that taxing.

Hull offered nothing. Not once. It had been one of the most frustrating nights ever. After the game, when Hull showed up outside the mobile, I couldn't hold anything back.

I told him he had been so selfish, so unprepared, so reckless, so disrespectful not just of me, but everyone on the show and the baby blue jacket he was wearing. In no uncertain terms, this would be the last and only time we would work together. He was an embarrassment. Walking away, I wondered how in the world anyone could be that cavalier about the job.

I knew that Hull was not pleased with my lecture. After all, he was a legend, a member of the Hockey Hall of Fame. I was a twenty-five-year-old kid and thought I knew everything about hockey, and in particular, hockey on television. Needless to say, after the game, we went our separate ways: me to the hotel, Hull into the crowd of adoring fans.

The following Monday, I received an early morning call from Ralph Mellanby. He was not amused. He had just finished a call with Hull, who recounted his side of the story, and how insensitive I had been postgame. Ralph, it seemed, felt I had been unfair to Hull. I hadn't been supportive enough of the rookie announcer.

Ralph loved being around the royalty of hockey, and obviously Hull was exactly that. But that didn't make him untouchable off the ice. In fact, I suspect that people around Bobby Hawk had enabled him to act less than responsible away from the game because of his greatness on the ice. Ralph believed in Hull, as a star. As the junior producer in the *HNIC* system, I was probably not supposed to challenge Ralph's authority and judgement. But by this time, it was personal. After all, as the youngest producer in the system, I was the one who made the commitment to move to Western Canada. I was actually producing more games than most of my Toronto colleagues combined. Also, I was feeling relatively confident at the time (probably cocky to most people).

Bobby, I explained in a rather animated rant, was not the team player that Ralph had always espoused for the rest of us on the *Hockey Night* team. He was late, lazy, and uninformed. It had created a very difficult situation, not just for me, but for the entire crew in Vancouver on Saturday. If Hull was to continue on the show, it was strongly recommended that it be in the East, where Ralph could work much closer with the superstar. In making my point, I told my boss that I would prefer never to work with Hull again.

Hull's tenure on our show lasted just a few weeks more. What had been reported to Ralph on that Monday appeared to be much more accurate after other producers had similar experiences with him on ensuing shows. I never did work with Hull again. In fact, I never spoke to him again. I have never regretted that decision.

• • •

There's another story worth repeating. This one began in my first year as a production assistant on *Hockey Night* in 1977 and concluded when I became the executive producer of the show in 1994. Seventeen years is a long time to carry a grudge, but that is, in fact, what I did.

The production assistant, or runner, on the show was the first line of contact between the producer and the players. That first job was, in many ways, the most fun you could have. In this entry-level position, you spent much of your time around the dressing room, creating relationships with the teams and bouncing between the arena, the studio, and the television mobile. You only got ten dollars a game, but it came with a *Hockey Night* jacket. It was a dream job.

On this night, the show's producer, Bob Gordon, had instructed me to meet Maple Leafs goaltender Mike Palmateer before he got into the dressing room and ask him to make a detour into our small studio across the hall for a quick interview. It wasn't normal to talk to goaltenders on the day of the game, but Bob was sure that Mike was different than most, and it would make for great television. Palmateer had become a hero in hockey-starved Toronto, finally solidifying the team's goaltending. His acrobatic style and diminutive size made him a fan favourite. The fact that he was a Toronto native made him even more popular.

Plus he was on a team that was very television-savvy. Darryl Sittler and Lanny McDonald had multiple national television commercials, and Dave "Tiger" Williams was at his peak as a character, playing for Toronto. This team was winning, the city loved them, and they drove ratings on television.

But for the most part, they remained regular people, always willing to say hello or do anything we requested. However, Tiger did start to ask if the game was regional or national in coverage. A national game meant friends and family at home in Saskatchewan would be able to see him. It wasn't as important for him to do interviews for games that were relegated to just southern Ontario.

Parked outside the Maple Leafs room, I watched as the players straggled in between 4 and 5 p.m. for the 8 p.m. start. Most did not recognize me as a person but they did recognize my *Hockey Night in Canada* blazer and they were polite. Both Sittler and McDonald acknowledged me. Williams called me by name. For a twenty-year-old, this was heady stuff. I noticed Palmateer walking around the gold seats at the Gardens, entering the bowl from the Zamboni entrance, walking around the curve of the glass, behind the team bench and into the hallway to get to the room. This is where I was waiting.

JS: Hi, Mike, I was wondering if you wouldn't mind coming over to
the studio and—
MP: Fuck off, kid.

With that, he opened the door to the dressing room, never to be seen again until warm-up.

I had one job and screwed it up. Bob Gordon would be pissed. Dave Hodge would be, too. *HNIC* would be missing a key element in the opening of the show. This was not a banner moment for young John. On top of all that, Mike Palmateer, two years older than me, had told me to fuck off. Not a great day.

Seventeen years later, in October or November of 1994, the NHL was in the midst of a labour dispute. In Gary Bettman's third year as commissioner, he was taking on Bob Goodenow and the NHL Players' Association (NHLPA) in negotiations for a new collective bargaining agreement. It was ugly. And we wouldn't have hockey until January.

I had returned to the show in September of that year, with a clear mandate from the CBC to remake the show. We were, eventually, going to a doubleheader format that would require more than twice the resources and creativity of the old show. These early days on the job were to reestablish relationships around the NHL and learn how the CBC and its production and technical resources worked. Not very exciting stuff, but as we waited, it was very important in growing the show.

Then, one day, the phone rang. Out of the blue, it was Mike Palmateer.

MP: Hello. John Shannon, please.

JS: Speaking.

MP: John, this is Mike Palmateer.

JS: Hello, Mike.

MP: John, I'm living in Florida, selling real estate. I've been told I have a bit of the gift for the gab. And I'm thinking of moving back to Toronto and would like to get into television. I think I'd be very good on TV, and *Hockey Night in Canada.*

JS: Mike, I'm going to tell you the same thing you told me, the last time we spoke . . .

MP: What's that?

JS: Fuck off!

With that, I slammed down the phone. Seventeen years of angst, gone! It wasn't and isn't one of my proudest moments. I had always been told to forgive and forget. But this one—I just couldn't resist.

Over the years, I have used the story to remind young players, whether they be in junior hockey or prospects at NHL camps, how to talk to others. And what the ramifications of your actions might be. I have also had tons of people within the game—players, coaches, managers—ask me, "Did you really tell Mike Palmateer to fuck off?" I sheepishly confirm the story. The reaction is always the same:

"Holy shit, that's great!"

I'm not sure it is or was great. But it left a lasting mark on me on how to treat people.

I'm not the only one to ever open my mouth without thinking, not by a long shot (some might suggest I still do it). The circumstances of this story, though, are unique.

From my first departure from *Hockey Night in Canada* in the summer of 1986, I had been able to carve out a successful career producing NHL games for Carling O'Keefe and Global Television, and the Canadian Football League. I wasn't bound by any office, or office politics. For the most part, I was able to work from home in Calgary, a quarter of a century before the whole pandemic world realized that working from home was actually possible and enjoyable. The Global NHL hockey package was followed by a similar contract in the United States for the American TV rights holder SportsChannel America, which allowed me to continue to produce the biggest games in the NHL, now for a U.S. audience. I was working side by side with many of the people I had worked with at *Hockey Night*. No, it wasn't uncomfortable—it was just a fact of life in the small community of hockey television. Friends helping friends.

As the SportsChannel contract was winding down, I received an opportunity to move my family and myself to the United States, as the producer of the regional package for the Minnesota North Stars. The team had been purchased by a Calgary businessman, Norm Green, who professed his desire to re-create the same warm, storytelling bond between his team and the viewers in the Twin Cities. I had known Green since my arrival in Calgary in 1980, where he was a minority owner of the NHL Flames. I thought I knew him well. Obviously, not well enough. It was a year to remember, to say the least.

Green loved being an NHL owner. Being a part owner of the Flames had a tremendous amount of glamour to it in Calgary. You were part of an elite group. Even within the hockey world, being in the ownership group of a Canadian franchise, especially a successful one, had its perks. Quite frankly, in the decade that the Flames had been in Calgary, there were few bad days. They were always in the playoffs, hosting All-Star games, played in a new arena, an Olympic host city, and two Stanley Cup Finals—and your name was on the Stanley Cup. Nothing went wrong with the Flaming "C."

The next step? Own your own team. That's what Green did. He left the security of being one of six owners of the Flames to be the proprietor of the Minnesota North Stars. The North Stars were part of the original 1967 NHL expansion and by the late 1980s had become a bit of a challenge for more than one ownership group. In his first year as sole owner, Green's team limped into the playoffs, and then astonished the hockey world by advancing through three rounds, against three better teams (Chicago, St. Louis, Edmonton) to play Pittsburgh for the Stanley Cup. Pittsburgh won the series in six games, but Green became something of a folk hero for hockey fans in the Twin Cities.

In the summer of 1991, Green got even more ambitious about his product in the Minnesota hockey market. He wanted to re-create some of the magic that *Hockey Night in Canada* had made for his previous team in Calgary. He hired me to build *Hockey Night in Minnesota*. My wife, Mickee, and I were the proud parents of a one-year-old boy, but we relished the challenge of moving to the United States. For the summer, I commuted between Calgary and Bloomington, Minnesota, where the arena was located. Throughout that period, I had unbelievable access to Green, who, as the owner, treated me very well. I felt that I had risen to a new level. At one point he sent me, with the team's lawyer, to represent the club at an NHL Board of Governors meeting in Toronto. Very heady stuff. I couldn't believe my luck. I was getting a great deal of respect from a very special man. But then again, we hadn't played any games yet.

For this season, I hired Dave Hodge to be the play-by-play man for the Minnesota North Stars.

Hiring Hodge was an easy sell to Norm. Dave *was Hockey Night in Canada*—or had been until he was let go over the infamous "pen flip" incident. Regardless, he fit exactly what the owner wanted for the product. We added Joe Micheletti, a former St. Louis Blues player and, more important, a native Minnesotan and former captain of Herb Brooks's Minnesota Golden Gophers college hockey team. Micheletti was Minnesota royalty. My connection with Joe goes back to Dan Kelly. Joe had briefly been Dan's radio analyst. We met in Calgary one night before a game, with Dan making the introduction: "This is John Shannon, Joe. Send him a tape of the game. He'll make you better." Despite that introduction, Joe and I became friends. I convinced him to leave the investment world he was working in to join Dave and me for *Hockey Night in Minnesota.*

This should be where the story blossoms into three people, sharing the same desires and goals, creating great television to critical acclaim, and they live happily ever after. That is far from what happened. By November 2, 1991, I knew we were in trouble.

Just a few games into the season, the North Stars were scheduled to play the Penguins in Pittsburgh—the first meeting since the previous Stanley Cup Final. It was Halloween night, in fact. October 31. We had planned quality features on the stars of the previous playoffs and musical bumpers to build the rivalry. It was a production well planned and well executed—except for one key thing.

Pittsburgh mauled the North Stars. The final score was 8–1. The Penguins' big boys had come to play. Mario Lemieux, Mark Recchi, Jaromir Jagr, Kevin Stevens, Joe Mullen—all scored. There was no doubt who the better team was. The only highlight of the night for the North Stars came at the end of the third period, when Derian Hatcher scored. To say it was humiliating would have been kind.

There's nothing we could have done about the score. But our problem on television? Apparently, we had mentioned the score too many times. We had shown too many replays of Pittsburgh scoring. We were *very* positive about the Penguins. We, the messengers, were being shot.

Meanwhile, Minneapolis–St. Paul was in the midst of a blizzard that left thirty-seven inches of snow on the ground. We were forced to stay in Pittsburgh for the night, and take a barrage of phone calls on how we screwed up. My family had been in the Twin Cities for less than a month. We had moved lock, stock, and barrel to a new city where Mickee couldn't even get the car out of the driveway. Things weren't going very well.

On our return to the Met Center on Friday, there were more meetings and phone calls about our approach to the game. For Dave and Joe, it must have been confusing. We had hired them on the premise of creating "network quality" television for the local market. It took only four games for the owner to criticize. It was supremely frustrating, and embarrassing.

Saturday was a home game against the archrival Chicago Blackhawks. The blizzard was not going to stop fifteen thousand North Stars fans from showing up. But it almost stopped our show from getting on the air. Road travel was so treacherous that our mobile control room was late arriving for the show that night. All the mobile doors and locks were frozen. We only obtained power forty-five minutes before airtime. The stress and strain of the last two days, combined with the equipment issues, put everyone on edge.

As we finally got on the air, a huge black cloud was lifted. Live television can be such an adrenaline rush. We had not been able to build many graphics, or features, or roll-ins, but at that point we were thrilled to just have pictures and sound. Then, not long into the game, the phone rang:

NG: John . . . Norman.

JS: Hi, Norm, how are you? Great game, isn't it?

NG: John, I'm listening to the announcers and they aren't very positive again. I thought we had solved that problem.

JS: Yes, we have, Norm. Not to worry.

NG: Thanks, John, okay.

Near the end of the first period, it was the owner on the phone, once more.

NG: John . . . Norman.

JS: Yes, Norm.

NG: Did you talk to the announcers? What did they say?

JS: I think Dave and Joe understand what's going on. The game is so good, it's easy to be positive.

NG: Yes, it is. But they better improve, or we will have to make changes.

What changes? Between periods? I began to dread the rest of the night. With that I turned to the director and said, "The owner's not happy."

Not twenty minutes later, in the second period, after the North Stars' Dave Gagner tied the game at 1, the phone rang again.

NG: John . . . Norman.

JS: Yes, Norm.

NG: The announcers are *not* being very nice about our team and our building. They don't like our new uniforms! Please fix it—and fix it now!

Again I turn to the director. This time I asked him if the game was any good. He responded that it was a great game and the crowd was into it.

On the intercom to the announcers, I reinforced how good the game was, and how great the crowd was, and that we were going to show them having fun. Both Dave and Joe complied, on the air, with similar comments. We had a good thing going. Then the phone rang again.

NG: If you don't fix this right now, you are all fucking fired! This is an embarrassment. I don't know why I brought you in. This is awful.

It was at this point that I might have appeared rattled. I knew in my heart that my decision to leave Canada, to invite friends to join me, was a mistake. It was an awful feeling. I had moved my wife and my child into a hostile situation.

Also, I was confused. The game itself was electric; the crowd was wild. Dave Hodge and Joe Micheletti were very good in explaining the how, what, and why of two rivals. It was truly an unforgettable night, in so many ways.

We survived the remainder of the second period, and the second intermission. The phone was quiet—until five minutes into the third period.

NG: John . . . Norman.

JS: Yes, Norm.

NG: I . . . uh . . . well, what I mean to say is . . . Kelly and I are in
    Palm Springs . . . and uh, well . . . we are watching on the satellite.

JS: Oh? Yes.

NG: Well . . . uh . . . we are watching the Chicago broadcast. So
    never mind. (click)

With that, the threats, the controversy, the scandal was averted. The owner did not recognize his own announcers, or his own show with North Stars graphics. He had been listening to Pat Foley and Dale Tallon—who were paid by the Blackhawks to cheer for the Blackhawks and hate the opposition. Hodge and Micheletti had delivered a network-quality broadcast. It's a shame Norm never saw it.

Hodge and Micheletti never knew at the time that Norm had phoned the truck no fewer than five times and threatened to fire us all between periods. As a producer, it was my job to be the buffer, to allow the announcers to do the job to the best of their abilities, oblivious of outside influences. It's my belief that that's what a good producer does. As I had been taught by the best, I should protect my teammates at all costs.

Our regular postgame session in the Met Center's Founders Club was a little more colourful that night. Dave, Joe, and Executive Vice President John Thomas heard the account of the telephone affair with Norm, blow by blow. We all laughed—to the point of crying. But inside, we knew we were done, less than a month into *Hockey Night in Minnesota*.

Within a week, our story grew into an urban myth throughout the

NHL broadcast community. Soon after, some of the story appeared in Red Fisher's Saturday hockey column in the *Montreal Gazette*.

It was the first indication, to me at least, that this owner was somewhat impetuous. Would he fly off the handle again? Would he phone to apologize the next time? This was not the way to produce television. I knew in my heart that it was the beginning of the end, again. We were four weeks into a hockey season, and the interference was already beginning.

Oh, by the way: North Stars 4, Blackhawks 3.

NINE
WORKING MY WAY BACK
TO *HOCKEY NIGHT*

WE LABOURED THROUGH THE REST OF THE SEASON IN MINNESOTA. AND DESPITE
the loyalty of Hodge and Micheletti, we knew our time wasn't going to
last long. Following the team's loss in the first round of the playoffs, I
was summoned to the office. Even my wife knew the end had come,
when she gave the sage advice "Take some boxes."

Being dismissed in April 1992 by the North Stars meant that for the
first time since 1977, I might not be involved in the NHL. Work was
not really an issue—there were other sports and events to produce—but
working in hockey was going to be a problem. I always viewed myself as
a hockey producer. My calling card was hockey producer. I had been involved in the NHL for almost fifteen years by then and had worked every
Stanley Cup playoffs all that time. To be outside of the circle really hurt.
Not that anyone would know, but I was frustrated beyond belief. My goal
now, in addition to putting food on our table, was to get my family and
me back within the NHL world. I didn't have a plan, but I had a goal.

Our Minnesota experience had been a disaster professionally (but not critically), and remarkable on a personal front. We loved the lifestyle living in West Bloomington, with a big house close to a lake. Great neighbours. Tough to beat. As a place to live, the twin cities of Minneapolis and St. Paul will always have a special place for my wife and me. Despite mosquitos the size of condors, and the winter weather, I would move back to Minnesota anytime.

Returning to Canada, and Toronto, for an Olympic assignment, was special for me. I had left in 1980 to run *HNIC* in the West, and returning twelve years later, married and with a child, felt like the next step in a natural progression. But this return did not include producing or being involved in the NHL and hockey. I had produced some games for NBC, and the 1993 All-Star Game in Montreal, but I was no longer involved in producing hockey games on a regular basis. And as much as I loved my Lillehammer Olympic experience, it drove me crazy not to be in the middle of the hockey action. My wife, Mickee, was adamant that I couldn't sulk around the house anymore, pretending to be happy for my friends who were still working on *Hockey Night* or on broadcasts in the United States.

In the spring of 1994, after the Olympics and the birth of our second child, a girl, Maja, I spent every waking hour on the phone trying to find a landing spot in the game. I also watched every game on every night of the Stanley Cup playoffs. By the time the Rangers-Canucks series had concluded, my enthusiasm to return to the hockey world was at an all-time high. I was able to finagle a ticket to the NHL Awards, which gave me some much-needed face time with the brass of all the teams, networks, and the league. I'm not sure it made a difference, but it was a much-needed "fix" for my NHL addiction.

I thought I had an NHL job twenty months earlier. After being fired in April 1992 by Norm Green and the Minnesota North Stars, I was preparing with CTV for the Summer Olympics in Barcelona, Spain. At the same time, the New York Rangers and the MSG Network were making changes in their production team. John Davidson and I had been friends for years and had worked together many times. John made a huge effort with Mike McCarthy, who was running MSG Network, to give me a chance. In July of that year, McCarthy and I met in Toronto. A one-hour breakfast interview started well and got better. We sat in a hotel restaurant through the breakfast sitting, then the lunch sitting, and as they were about to reset the tables for the dinner session, we laughed at how long we had spent together. McCarthy's vision and my vision of television production were so similar, we had instant chemistry. We ended up dealing in such detail, it became more of a think tank, rather than an interview. By meeting's end, we had agreed in principle on a three-year deal at great money that would allow my family to continue to live in Minnesota and me to commute to the job in New York City or wherever the Rangers were playing. Remaining in the United States, and particularly in the Twin Cities, was a priority for our family. Mickee had great new friends in the neighbourhood, and we loved what the area had to offer us. All that was needed was executive approval in New York and I would know the deal was official within twenty-four hours.

Returning home that night, my wife and I were relieved to know we probably wouldn't have to move, and I was back in the NHL. To be reconnected with Davidson was a plus, and to produce games for a team that I once cheered for as a child in the greatest city in the world, and the electricity of Madison Square Garden, was exciting. I couldn't wait for the next season. It was the best sleep we had in months. But it lasted only one night.

The next morning, I picked up *USA Today* to read that MSG Network had signed a $500 million deal to cover the New York Yankees. Within ten minutes the phone rang. It was McCarthy. I heard it in his voice. It was not the voice of promise and confidence I had heard for hours the day before. It was a voice of resignation. While we were at that lunch, ownerships of both groups got together. The Yankees and MSG made a ten-year commitment to be business partners. But it cost a ton of production dollars on other sports. Rangers hockey was one of them. My deal was gone. McCarthy apologized profusely, but there was no chance of doing anything. I couldn't compete with the New York Yankees. We were back at the drawing board.

Quickly thereafter, I began negotiations with TSN to return to Canada to produce a new nightly sports show that was modeled on Ted Koppel's *Nightline* on ABC, except it didn't deal with hostage crises or government scandals—it was purely sports. In fact, we even convinced TSN to hire Dave Hodge as the face and anchor of the new prime-time show. Due to my travelling to Spain for the Olympics and not being located in Toronto, my deal to join TSN wasn't slated to start until October 1992. It gave us some quality "down" time in Minnesota and our home province of British Columbia.

Barcelona was a tremendous experience. As a city, it was gorgeous. Hot, but gorgeous. Those Olympics had a ton of great stories. The original Dream Team was there, so every basketball game was an event. Mark Tewksbury's gold medal in the pool was a particularly proud moment for Canada, but those games were hardly significant for our country. It was a real joy to produce other sports and it opened my eyes to the planning and preparation it takes to work the Olympics. However, we did it live to Canada, which meant getting on the air at 2 a.m. Barcelona time.

Our host for the show was Rod Black, one of the most affable, open-minded people I have ever worked with. Athletes and broadcast people love Rod. His friendships are many and deep. But he is, and continues to be, a big, lovable child. It's one of his greatest attributes. In Spain, as our first prime-time show ended at 5 a.m. local time, Rod strapped on his Rollerblades, said good-bye, and started to skate back to our hotel from the International Broadcast Centre (IBC). I was not amused.

JS: What the fuck are you doing?
RB: Going back to the hotel.
JS: You're what? Rollerblading?

RB: Yeah, it's pretty cool. I need the exercise.

JS: Rod, what happens if you get hit by a bus? Or trip on the cobblestones? Who is going to host tomorrow night?

RB: Well . . . er . . .

JS: Do it tonight. But don't do it again.

Rod didn't trip or get hit by a bus. But he didn't do it again.

On another occasion, Black's gregarious nature was a tremendous advantage for us. Sitting at an outside cafe near the IBC, Rod and I noticed boxer Evander Holyfield lumbering towards the building. Almost simultaneously, we said we should get him for interview. Rod jumped up from his chair, ran across the park, and introduced himself to the heavyweight champion, as if they had been longtime associates. Holyfield was very polite. He was, in fact, on his way to the NBC compound to do an interview about the boxing competition at these games. Then he eyed what we were eating:

EH: Is that an ice cream bar?

RB: Yes.

EH: Where did you get it? It's hot out here.

JS: There's an ice cream shop around the corner.

EH: Let's go!

JS: I tell you what, Evander. If I buy you an ice cream, will you do an interview with Rod for Canadian TV?

EH: I love Canadians. When would we do it?

JS: Right now, if you want?

EH: Let's do it. But I need my ice cream first.

JS: No problem. What flavour?

EH: Surprise me.

The three of us walked to the ice cream vendor and onto our studios for the interview. Only one problem: Holyfield was scheduled to be on set across the hall at NBC with Bob Costas. As we returned to the IBC, there was a contingent of NBC suits and hangers-on waiting for Holyfield. They were not very happy when Evander, ice cream bar (messily) in hand, told them he would be a few minutes late because he "has to go talk to Canada." Rod and I smiled. Our friends from America were not used to being told to wait, let alone wait for Canadian TV.

Those Olympics reengaged my love of television. The hours were long, but satisfying, even if we did finish at five in the morning. The people were friends, and I spent my time comforted that I would have a new opportunity in the business afterward at TSN in Toronto. All that needed to be done was sign the contract when I returned from Spain.

The man who hired me for TSN, Jim Thompson, actually spent some time in Barcelona during the Games, and we had a chance to reacquaint ourselves over a lunch. It was a rather strange afternoon—enlightening, but strange. It was in our Barcelona meeting that he gave a revealing, but not totally glowing, report about life at TSN. He suggested that the people at the network had some odd work habits and that an outside voice, like mine, would be invaluable to the future of the group. He was very complimentary and enthusiastic about my future there. He also said that there were some structural changes being made in the company. I would not report directly to him, as we first discussed. Part of our original discussion was that I needed to get my foot in the door in order to get a much larger role that Thompson had hinted would include their NHL package. I understood that philosophy, but never forgot that he had dangled the NHL carrot in front of me to get me to come. I would have done the same thing.

I would now report to Rick Brace, someone I had known for many years as well, but did not have a very good relationship with, at the best of times. Brace had worked his way up through the CBC, starting in master control, and left for TSN before eventually returning to become a network sports executive. He had recently been lured back to TSN by Thompson and network founder Gordon Craig as the cable network started to be a real difference maker on the Canadian broadcast landscape. This structural change troubled me. Not that I had any options; there were no jobs coming my way at that point from anyone. It was TSN or nothing. That was, until the day before the Barcelona Olympics ended.

On that Saturday in August 1992, my life took another turn. I believe, to this day, that it was for the better. The man in charge of those Olympic Games on a day-to-day basis for CTV was Scott Moore. Scott was and is a gregarious, creative producer. His style was a little different than mine, but he was very good at creating a team atmosphere, building alliances inside and outside the walls of the network, all the while building his own brand. Scott was ambitious. You could see it, hear it. Scott was very good, and he knew it. I'm not sure whether he didn't want to stay to run the next Olympic Games or the network brass didn't want him for some reason, but his role for the Winter Games in Lillehammer, Norway, was open.

On the Saturday before the Games were to end, I was invited to a small meeting room at the IBC in Barcelona. There were three other people in the room: Peter Sisam, who was the head of the Sports Group; Gary Maavara, the network's legal counsel; and Doug Beeforth, who was the head of sports production for CTV and my old college roommate and friend for twenty years. While Beeforth didn't need much convincing on my resume, I had had little or nothing to do with the other gentlemen until I was on the ground in Spain. But they had seen me work for the past month with the group of staffers and freelancers at the IBC.

For the Barcelona Olympics, Moore had made a decision to produce, actually sitting in the chair in the control room for a lot of key events during the Games. In many ways, it was a smart move, cutting down the level of bureaucracy that would occur if he had entrusted someone to make those split-second decisions jumping from venue to venue. However, it left a void outside the control room. There was no one available to make decisions on assignments and consult with various venue producers as the day went on, and to help the staff, most of whom had never been to an Olympics before, navigate through the daily grind of eighteen-hour days. It was a void that I gladly filled. Preparing and distilling content for our live prime time in Canada show was straightforward. Steering people through decision-making and production execution was a bonus. Apparently both Maavara and Sisam had noticed my expanded role, and how the results were mostly positive.

The conversation with Peter, Gary, and Doug was simple. Had I committed to TSN yet? Would I move to Toronto? Would I like to be coordinating producer for CTV's coverage of the Olympic Winter Games in Lillehammer, Norway, in February 1994, just eighteen months away?

The money was better than TSN was offering, but the long-term job security was not. There were no guarantees past 1994. I couldn't help but think back a few years to 1987. As was the case when CTV got out of football and hockey, Canada's second network was again giving me options. Options I dearly needed.

Discussions continued for the next day or two and became even more intense on the long charter flight back to Toronto. The money improved even more. Upon arrival in Toronto, I told Sisam, Maavara, and Beeforth they would have my decision in the next forty-eight hours, but I had to return to Minneapolis and discuss it with my wife. No matter what, we were returning to Toronto, whether it be for TSN or CTV. In the meantime, I had four hours to wait for my connecting flight to Minnesota. I felt it was important to communicate with Jim Thompson at TSN. I wasn't looking for more money, but I wanted him to know what had happened, and I would make a decision after talking with Mickee. Thompson wasn't shocked that CTV had approached me, but told me I should be calling Rick Brace to discuss the issues, because after all, I'd be reporting to him at the network. So I called:

> JS: Rick, it's John Shannon. I'm here at Toronto airport, on my way back to Minnesota, and I just wanted you to know that I've received another offer from someone. It's for more money, but doesn't have the job security that you're offering.

RB: What do you mean? We have a deal. You have a contract.

JS: Well, actually, I don't have a contract. The lawyers haven't sent it yet, but I'm just trying to be as transparent with you as possible. What I want to do is go home, talk to my wife, and make the best decision for me. And I promise, it will be quick. I don't want to leave you hanging.

RB: Well, I don't understand.

JS: Rick, I wanted to call you as a courtesy, as I was flying through Toronto. I really need to talk to my wife about this. It affects her, too.

RB: No . . . No. You need to make a decision right now.

JS: You can't wait a day?

RB: No.

JS: Well, I guess you've made the decision for me. I won't be coming to TSN.

The phone went dead. For the second time in my career, I was turning my back on TSN. My natural instinct had been, if TSN expected me to be loyal to them, and they couldn't give me twenty-four hours to make that decision, then it really wasn't the place for me. Loyalty was and is such a big part of my DNA, and a key reason for some of my successes. It wasn't going to change now. Decision made. Life goes on. Needless to say, I have pissed a few people off in my time. But I sleep well at night.

It was a huge decision, one that took just eight seconds. It changed my life, and for the better. The Lillehammer experience in February 1994 was one that couldn't have been duplicated. It actually gave me a higher profile in the industry than the TSN job would have, certainly much higher than I imagined. The Games themselves were successful. Canada performed brilliantly, winning thirteen medals. As the Games began, the spotlight was on the now-infamous Nancy Kerrigan–Tonya Harding episode. The drama began at the U.S. Championships in Detroit on January 6, when Kerrigan was attacked in a hallway at Joe Louis Arena by an unknown assailant (later identified as Harding's estranged husband, and which attack Harding ultimately agreed she helped cover up). It created such a buzz that everyone wanted to watch what was going to happen. Prior to the Olympics, there had been real doubt whether or not CTV could make a profit with the Games, but when the opening ceremonies drew more than 6 million viewers, every available commercial was sold for the remainder of the Olympics. Lillehammer was a perfect host city, not very big. It was like having the Games in Huntsville, Ontario, or Vernon, British Columbia. Small, quaint, fun.

Like any Games, they felt like they would never end, and when they were over, it felt like it happened in a flash.

What I remember most about these Games will surprise no one: the hockey tournament. This was four years before the pros were going to show up, and Canada was not certain of anything. This was a team coached by Tom Renney, with players including Paul Kariya, Petr Nedved, Corey Hirsch, Brian Savage, and Todd Hlushko. They were the last vestige of the Canadian National Program. Some would go on to the NHL; others would ply their trade in leagues around the world. But they were all in Norway, for Canada and a medal.

There was only one issue: these were the days before multiple channels. CTV had a single channel, covering every sport. Also, Canada does not have near the clout of our American friends. The people at CBS were salivating over figure skating. And it wasn't just the Harding-Kerrigan story that drew ratings. Figure skating has been the best way to attract female viewers to watch the Olympics. CBS wanted women's skating in prime time every night the first week. The International Olympic Committee (IOC) and the organization committee concurred. It was tough to argue. The problem was, skating was to take place at the exact same time as Canada's Olympic hockey team was to play, and it was the same story two nights later and four nights later. Skating was to prevail. The CTV network president, John Cassaday, wanted it that way, and so did the head of sales and Gary Maavara, the network's legal counsel, who was running the sports department now. Beeforth and I were not in agreement.

A hockey game is a continuous event. Figure skating is done in flights, with only a certain number of skaters up at a time. With just a few competitors really in contention to win, it is much easier to dip in and out of skating without totally disrupting what the viewer needs to see. If you leave a hockey game for a long period of time, you will have a viewer rebellion on your hands. It is pretty obvious.

The discussion of tape-delaying the hockey game made little sense to me. It was the same with the idea of leaving the game for skating while the game was still being played. Plus I feared that if we did tape delay a game here, then upper management might want to do it all the time.

There were no assurances on how good a team was, and how long it would be in medal contention. It was important, early in these games, to put hockey on live. In fact, we promised to the rest of the group that if Canada lost at any time during the rest of the games, we would not complain and would tape-delay all hockey from that point. We also promised to fill the intermissions of these games with skating and get to any additional figure skating events as soon as the Canada game ended. It was a good compromise: live hockey until they lost. Most believed our peace accord would last just a few days. Canada would lose at some point, and skating fans would win in the end. Well, as it turned out, it was a stroke of genius.

Our best female skater was Josée Chouinard. She was not really in medal contention. Our men were led by Kurt Browning, near the end of a brilliant career, and Elvis Stojko. Stojko would prove to be a star, but the men skated in the second week of the games, so we would have to wait for his performance.

The soap opera that was figure skating was best told in increments anyway. The practices were shown live, well before the hockey began. Harding did not skate well and Kerrigan didn't win, while Canada's men's hockey team won its first game and kept on winning. In fact, the hockey team didn't lose a game until the last day of the Olympics, in the gold medal game in a shoot-out, now commemorated by the Peter Forsberg postage stamp in Sweden. Our decision to use hockey as our anchor sport, and work around it, proved to be the right one. It also fueled my drive to return to the game.

As mentioned earlier, I spent the entire 1994 Stanley Cup playoffs studying every moment that was on *Hockey Night in Canada*. Making mental notes. First round, second round, the conference finals, and the Stanley Cup Final. Night after night. It must have driven my wife nuts. We had a three-year-old and a newborn and I was "buried in some stupid hockey game."

These were heady times at *Hockey Night*. Toronto and Vancouver were on a collision course in one conference final, and in the east the Rangers were facing the New Jersey Devils. While in previous years I was distracted by my own work, it gave me huge anxiety that my friends and all the people I worked with—heck, even hired—were now on the front line, and I wasn't: people like John Davidson, who was doing games for the Rangers; Chris Cuthbert, who had been with us in the West in 1984; Ed Milliken, who was a runner with me in the late 1970s; Mark Askin, who worked for me at Global; and of course Ron MacLean, Don Cherry, Bob Cole, and Harry Neale, who had become such huge stars on the show. I felt completely isolated from this institution I believed in so much. It was torture to watch, but watch I did. I felt I needed to be prepared for anything. It was no different than twenty years earlier, when I used the calling card of being a student to talk to people. To be ready, just in case.

But watching games wasn't enough—I had to create some presence. I needed some face time in front of the hockey world and network brass. The annual NHL Awards in Toronto, in late June 1994, was the perfect opportunity. I got a ticket from old friend and NHL vice president of broadcasting Glenn Adamo. Glenn had been with NBC when we produced the 1991 All-Star Game, and we maintained a strong relationship.

His passion for hockey was as deep as, if not deeper than, mine. Mind you, when he was at NBC working his way through the company on football, tennis, and Olympics, I was already doing hockey. We had a mutual admiration. I had done what he wanted to do, which was produce hockey. The relationship worked well for both of us back then and still does to this day, as we've continued to be friends.

The night at the NHL Awards was like a "fix" for me. I was around the game I loved and rubbing shoulders with league, team, and network execs. I felt proud of our success at the Lillehammer Olympics and through conversation about that (and the game, generally) hinted that I wanted back into hockey . . . badly.

It was early July when word broke that CBC would be creating a new position, executive producer of *Hockey Night in Canada*. However, the position is usually reserved for someone hired by Molstar Communications (the renamed Canadian Sports Network). There had always been a clause in the *Hockey Night in Canada* agreement that said the CBC had a right to its own executive producer, but the network never invoked the clause. Apparently there were some programming decisions made during the finals that the network viewed as purely "Molsonization," which they objected to and pushed them over the edge. Head of Sports Alan Clark made the decision to take over production control of the show.

My phone started to ring. Had I heard? Was I interested? Yes and yes.

Only one problem. Well, two, actually. Clark had pegged my co-hort at CTV Doug Beeforth for the job. He knew that Beeforth had a history with the show and was impressed with his organizational skills and his leadership. Beeforth's star was rising at CTV. Network president John Cassaday had grown to like his low-key manner, his preparation, his complex thinking. Beeforth had a key role in the CTV license application for an all-sports channel, one that while national, would also be regional in focus. I had helped a bit with the application, but Beeforth and Gary Maavara did all the heavy lifting. The application was done under the name "S3," and while it didn't come to fruition then, it was the precursor to Sportsnet. It might have been the potential of the new network that kept Beeforth at CTV, which meant, the *HNIC* job was still open. Then came the second problem: Alan Clark would not see me.

I had met Clark previously, outside a couple of television mobiles, in Pittsburgh and New York. I was working for SportsChannel America and he was with the CBC. Apparently, he felt I was not cut out to work for CBC. No reason was given; he just had no interest in me.

Crestfallen, I had no choice but to convince him otherwise. I created a simple, straightforward resume and letter and made two phone calls. One was to Ron MacLean, the other to Don Wittman. I explained the scenario to both, that I didn't necessarily think I was owed the job, but I at least deserved to be heard. Then I made a third call, to Doug Sellars. Sellars and I had maintained friendship from our time at Canadian Sports Network. Doug had migrated to the CBC and become the most important production person for Clark. Football, Olympics, and all the big events were on Doug's plate. Now he had hockey, in the interim, until they found someone. I just wanted ten minutes with Clark to convince him I was not the devil incarnate, and that I knew the show and its history better than anyone. If there was one person who could take the show up a notch with credibility and creativity, I believed I was the man. It was about leadership, decision-making, creativity, loyalty, and understanding.

For two weeks, I heard nothing. I assumed that any overtures from any of the guys I talked to had been deflected. I had given it my all but life must go on. I prepared to produce the Canadian Open for CTV and work with Director Ron Harrison. This is the same Ron Harrison who is the current executive producer of *Hockey Night in Canada*. In his time, Ron was one of the best sports directors on the continent. He had a great feel for sports and an even better feel for television. He had been executive producer at *Hockey Night* for about five years, in addition to directing some special events like golf.

The week of the tournament we spent a ton of time together plotting story lines and sharing production philosophy. Golf is a tremendously challenging sport to work on. Imagine 144 balls in the air, as opposed to a single ball or puck. The producer has to prepare for stories continually, based on a changing leaderboard. A director has the tougher challenge of ensuring he or she has enough cameras in the proper places to cover those stories, with players hitting simultaneously all over a golf course. It's a true partnership. Of all the sports, that coordination between producer and director might be the most important. In all the others, a broadcast can survive with a strong person in one of those two positions. In golf, you are joined at the hip, one person deciding where to go, the other delivering the pictures. It is an orchestral partnership. Ron and I had that in a television truck for golf. We enjoyed each other's company, and we thrived on the energy in the truck. It was fun.

We had been working together for fifteen years by now, mostly on hockey, occasionally on other sports, now on golf. In fact, Harrison was the director of my first Stanley Cup Final in 1980. He was the best hockey producer in the world. He had done the Summit Series in 1972 and the Lake Placid Olympics in February 1980. He carried an aura with him. He was larger than life, especially impressive for a man five foot seven. He smoked large cigars when he wasn't smoking cigarettes, and his personality made him the life of the party. He was very easy to like.

That 1980 Cup Final was difficult for him. Here I was, twenty-three years old, put in position as the producer of the games on Long Island of that Flyers–Islanders series. I was expected to lead a crew of men and women with much more experience than me, through half of the series. One of the men who trained me, Bob Gordon, produced the other half in Philadelphia, where I was around to assist him, learn, and soak up the pressure of a Final series.

My first challenge came early in Game 3, with the teams at a frenetic pace. Harrison was in his glory, barking out orders, calling replays, talking to the announcers. Only, that's not the way I like to produce. As I saw it, it was in my job description to decide on the editorial flow of the game, call the replays, and communicate with the announcers, particularly the two colourmen, Mickey Redmond and Gary Dornhoefer. I had spent the year working heavily with Dornhoefer in Edmonton, and Redmond and I had worked extensively in both Canada and the United States. Early in the first period, I was a nonfactor. Intentionally or not, Harrison was running everything. I could not tolerate it. When he decided to contradict an order of replays that I had set up, I knew I had to say something. On the next whistle of play we went to commercial, at which point I had thirty seconds to make my position clear.

"Ronny, listen. I know you don't like it, but I am producing. I call the replays and I talk to the announcers. You already have enough on your goddamn plate. We can do this together."

There was stunned silence in the truck. No one had talked to Harrison like that in years. Not an announcer, not even our boss, Ralph Mellanby. At this point, it could have gone one of two ways: World War III or peace in our time. Ron chose the latter. He understood the pressure we were all under to be great, and he took the high road. We became friends that day, and worked together many, many times after. Including golf. We both loved the sport, and both played it badly. Nevertheless, we worked well together because I didn't want him producing, and I couldn't direct. It was a great partnership.

Because of that, I felt a real need to tell him that I had applied for the CBC job. Harrison, who must have been justifiably disappointed by the CBC's move, was still going to be Molstar's executive producer of *Hockey Night*. He wasn't being removed, but rather aided in the job. He still had responsibilities with non-network games and involvement with the league. After all, Molstar was the conduit to the NHL on many issues, because they held the contract with the league. But Alan Clark's plan was to have the new executive producer in charge on the day-to-day editorial, production, and coordination of the show. The "tip of the iceberg," if you will.

On a quick trip to the clubhouse, the day before the tournament was to start, I told Ron that I had applied for the job, and I didn't want him to hear it from anyone else. He was appreciative, and it was a huge relief.

I wasn't sure I would get an interview at that point, let alone get the job. But I needed Harrison to know I wasn't going behind his back to be part of the *Hockey Night* family.

The golf went off without a hitch and I spent the remainder of the summer attempting to get some face time with Alan Clark. Unbeknownst to me, Wittman and Sellars became huge advocates for me. Both had strong voices in the CBC, and both had implored Clark to give me a chance to talk about the job.

I never did get a one-on-one talk with him. What I got was a formal interview, what the CBC describes as a "board" to interview for the job.

In early August, I met with Clark and Phyllis Platt, who was the executive director of the English-language CBC, and a human resources person. The room was rather dark, with four place settings for the three CBC execs and me. I sat at the end of the board table, Clark to my left, Platt and the HR person to my right.

I did not have a briefcase or a resume, or any papers at all with me. All we did was talk. We spent much of the time discussing how hockey is produced on television. I emphasized that we needed to be respectful of the history of *Hockey Night in Canada*, which I knew very well, and how change must come in subtle spurts, so as not to upset the conservative nature of the hockey viewers. I joked with them that we as a country have lived this notion every day for many years—after all, in what other country could one have a "Progressive Conservative" party in politics—an oxymoron, certainly. That seemed to hit a positive note.

We talked philosophy on every aspect of the show: replays, close-ups, features, editorial. I believed it would be my job not to tell everyone every word to say, but rather to give them parameters within which to work. Let people feel they are fulfilling their creative drives, all within a structure that allows the show to grow and thrive. That, too, hit a positive chord. We went through every announcer, producer, and director on the show. I knew their styles, their tendencies, their weaknesses, and their strengths. I truly believed I could make people better. I still believe that.

A planned one-hour interview lasted three and a half hours. As time passed, my enthusiasm for the position grew, as it appeared their enthusiasm did for me. They asked about my style of management. Was I too loud? Was I mean? Did I embarrass people?

I said yes, I have. "But I am passionate about doing things right. And I am a good teacher, and I am fair. Above all, I am fair."

I left not knowing if I had the job or not, but I knew I had left every ounce of energy and passion on the table. I was drained but satisfied that even if I didn't get the job, I had given it my best. If they had chosen to go in a different direction, it would be their loss, not mine. After all, I still had a job at CTV, and had been asked by the network president if I would consider moving to the news division.

The phone rang the next day. It was Alan Clark. The man who wouldn't take my call was now calling me. Could we have lunch? Today?

At that lunch, Clark was excited about what he had heard the day before. And while, yes, he had offered Beeforth the job before even considering me, he knew now that I was the man for the position. We hammered out the terms of a deal, then and there. I was soon to be named the executive producer of *Hockey Night in Canada*. This was one contract discussion I didn't have to ask my wife about before accepting.

TEN
REINVENTING THE BRAND

REBUILDING *HOCKEY NIGHT IN CANADA* DID NOT COME WITHOUT CHALLENGES. FOR one, there were, on paper, two executive producers: Ron Harrison and me. Ron still represented Molson's interests for the show and I was there as a contracted employee of CBC. The people who hired me, particularly the head of sports, Alan Clark, wanted the show to change. There were issues with portions of the programming—the biggest being the second intermission, which was inconsistent and flat, especially compared to the massively popular first intermission show, "Coach's Corner" with Don Cherry and Ron MacLean.

We also had the new challenge of the Saturday night doubleheader. Instead of just producing a single national game at 7:30 Eastern (with up to two regional broadcasts, as well), we also had a national second game at 10:30 Eastern, 7:30 Pacific time. The new format was giving Western Canada its own prime-time game. As a producer who cut his teeth in the West, this was music to my ears. The West had always been shortchanged on Saturday night games, so shepherding the new format was exciting. But it significantly changed the workload for all of us involved. The challenges of doing a network broadcast from one arena, while servicing multiple games, were daunting. But all that was still to come.

In the days following the announcement of my hiring, I did perfunctory interviews for some radio stations and local and national newspapers, including with Bill Houston at the *Globe and Mail*, Ken McKee at the *Toronto Star*, and Rob Longley at the *Toronto Sun*. The stories were pretty cookie-cutter: "Excited to Be Back," "Working with Friends," "Best Sports Brand in the Country." All true, but nothing controversial. After all, it's not as if this was a new show, with new people and new ideas. Any changes would come slowly.

I was joining the show because the network felt the interests of the program were not best served by the biggest sponsor being in charge of production and editorial content. My job was to make *Hockey Night in Canada* part of the CBC Sports family, not an island unto itself.

With this in mind, I met with Ron Harrison in his office in mid-September. The normally affable Harrison wasn't that affable on this day. He had in his hand a clipping from the *Toronto Sun*, with Rob Longley's article on my hiring. He wasn't happy with the tone of it, that things at *Hockey Night* could be better. But to me, it was obvious that the second intermission could improve, and now with a doubleheader to produce, we were going to need content for two more intermissions, plus whatever time there was between the games. We had to be ready for anything.

At the least, we agreed that we had to work together, to be a united front in the company. We shook hands and said no more. But I understood from that point on that keeping Ron in the loop was important. Ron, I believe, had the realization that he was no longer in charge of *Hockey Night in Canada*.

It may be surprising, but what happened next solidified my role: the NHL lockout that began on October 1, 1994, just after I showed up at the CBC building. The fight between the league, led by Commissioner

Gary Bettman, and the NHPLA, led by Bob Goodenow, would drag out until mid-January 1995, forcing a reduced forty-eight-game regular season schedule for the teams. All through the fall, both sides were entrenched, and both sides believed they had the best interest of their constituents, and the game, at heart. Bettman was looking for cost certainty for the owners, while Goodenow believed in a more open market. It took 103 days before the labour dispute—a lockout, really—ended. There is no doubt that it created animus between players and owners, union and league, Bettman and Goodenow.

All this was going on as I got familiarized with my new environment at the CBC's broadcasting centre in Toronto, and with the many people in the network and the sports department in particular. It was relatively easy to navigate. Many of the same names were still in place, even promoted, from the time of my first departure in 1986. Doug Sellars, who had advocated for me with management, was the obvious number two guy in the department. Olympics, CFL football, baseball, curling—Doug was in charge of all production, other than hockey. He and I had been friends for years, and that relationship made my transition smooth and easy. He also dispelled the myths about my style—that I had a temper. Doug had experienced firsthand my passion and directness. He knew that I was blunt but also knew, as I had said in the original job interview, that I was fair. And, most important, Sellars knew that the show needed me, and he told Alan Clark that. He truly had Clark's ear. The two of them had done a marvellous job reinventing the sports department. It was an exciting, upbeat place to work, with a ton of talented people, some of whom had never been given the chance to work on hockey. We were going to change that.

By mid-November, as the regular season was being cancelled in three-week increments, the powers that be at CBC were getting nervous. The lack of revenue driven by *Hockey Night in Canada*, which allegedly was responsible for 50 percent of *all* the network's revenue, was making many anxious, not just for the sports department, but the news and information department as well. Clark was trying to be pragmatic about our "hurry up and wait" world. His bosses were feeling the pressure, but he understood the issues between the players and the league, and as much as Canadian TV was the league's biggest partner, there was little we could do to prompt either side. Nor did we want to appear to support one side or the other. Regardless, Clark was constantly trying to figure out what we could do to drive revenue for the CBC Sports group.

One day in November, I received a phone call from Michael Barnett, who was Wayne Gretzky's agent. Barnett and I had been acquaintances for about fifteen years. Before he was with Wayne, he was the manager of a popular watering hole in Edmonton, the Sports Page, where we (not so surprisingly) ended up a few times that first year the Oilers were in the NHL. By 1994, Mike had become a huge factor in the hockey agent world. He represented far more players than No. 99. Brett Hull, Jaromir Jagr, Sergei Fedorov, Paul Coffey, Mats Sundin, Lanny McDonald, and Grant Fuhr were all part of Barnett's stable. Mike was a big deal now. He was associated with IMG, International Management Group, one of the world's great sports representation companies. Mike called to say they were investigating creating a team, led by Gretzky, to tour Europe in December, while the lockout continued. The idea was to play exhibition games overseas, to keep active and grow CBC's hockey brand. But before they would announce the tour, they wanted to secure some television coverage. We were the obvious choice. But if we did support the tour, it could create some controversy for us.

Televising any of those games might make it seem like a national NHL partner was publicly supporting a players' venture. But for some of us, this was about supporting Wayne Gretzky. By this time in his career, Wayne's influence was massive. Let's face it, it was his move six years earlier from Edmonton to Los Angeles that created Sun Belt hockey, with expansion teams in Florida and Anaheim, and the North Stars relocating to Dallas. The latter move, by the way, was a constant thorn in my side. Every time it snowed in Toronto, my wife reminded me about

Minnesota, and how if I hadn't screwed that up, we would be living in balmy Texas.

Nevertheless, it would not be in our best interest to turn away from "The Great One." One Friday afternoon, Alan and I walked over to Gretzky's restaurant, which used to be right by the CBC building, to meet with Barnett. He laid out a plan for a series of games in the Nordic countries of Norway, Sweden, and Finland. It was a pure barnstorming tour, much like the NHL teams did in Western Canada in the 1940s and 1950s. As a historian of the game, Gretzky would understand what those games so long ago meant to small-town Canada. In addition to creating some attention for the players' side of the labour dispute, Barnett laid out the plan to explain how the group of players would play six or seven games throughout northern Europe, with clinics for young hockey players, and practices open to the public.

Alan Clark was impressed. While I had been an acquaintance of Barnett for fifteen years, Clark was meeting him for the first time. That's not to say there wasn't some skepticism on Clark's part—he was being asked for a lot of money, some $400,000 to bankroll the whole trip, even though we were going to broadcast just two of the games, on consecutive Saturdays. Barnett explained that they would be using all the expertise of IMG to facilitate the logistics of the tour, including our travelling group. IMG had tentacles in every sport and almost every country. Their involvement put Clark's mind at ease about the tour's potential to deliver a quality product. He knew that the NHL would not be pleased that we were helping to finance the Gretzky tour, but this was our way of saying to both sides, the league and the union, that we needed hockey back on the air. More than anything, we wanted them to get a deal done. We couldn't control that, but at least we could make our own deal for hockey!

That's what we did. We walked out of the restaurant with a deal in principle to cover the series. Clark turned to me with a smile and said, "Well, you finally have some hockey to produce."

We now had a place to experiment with some programming ideas.

Those Saturdays in December allowed our group, driven by CBC personnel and help from the Molson production company, to make a new signature of hockey at the CBC. We didn't think we were in the business of planning and producing the show for the hockey world—we needed to put the viewer first. We needed to talk to the viewer in a manner that *they* understood. Being overly technical about the game was not the way to go. Telling people about what makes Wayne Gretzky so special, and what he's like as a person away from the game, *was*.

Our goal was always to entrench *Hockey Night* as the voice of the game, not just the NHL, in Canada. We needed to give coverage beyond the NHL, to the world of junior hockey, for example. With that in mind, we created a show called *Future Look*, which would give exposure to young stars of the three major junior leagues in Canada, as well as the odd Canadian playing in the U.S. college system. The rationale was simple: create a bond with the viewer, and the young player, all while building a library of footage that could be used for years, even decades to come.

Our first sojourn into this style of programming was sending Don Cherry to Belleville, Ontario, to talk with players from the Belleville Bulls. I remember it vividly because it featured a sixteen-year-boy from Newfoundland, Danny Cleary, who went on to be a first-round pick of the Chicago Blackhawks and then won multiple Stanley Cups with the Detroit Red Wings. The other part of the story was that Cherry got a speeding ticket on the highway to Belleville, and every once in a while in the ensuing years, when Cleary played, Don Cherry always brought up the ticket. No, I didn't pay it for him.

The reason we chose Don to be involved was twofold. First was his love of junior players, which had always been evident every year in the Stanley Cup Final when he interviewed the top five prospects from that year's draft. Second, if we could create a bond with Don and the feature, it would make it easier to place the feature in the first intermission of the show, albeit taking a few precious seconds away from "Coach's Corner." It was simple: if Don liked it, we wouldn't hear as much grief about not having enough time to do his regular Saturday shtick. How often did we hear "Folks, I don't have enough time around here . . ."

The other new programming was as close to journalism as *Hockey Night* could ever get. While it didn't get its actual programming name until January 21, 1995, the "Satellite Hot Stove" became the vehicle within our hockey programming to cover the latest news and gossip around the hockey world, and particularly at that time, the feud between the NHL and the NHLPA. *Hockey Night* had forever changed the viewing habits of Canadians in 1952 with the advent of television. Now we were doing our part to grow, change, and extend the viewing habits for Canadians from coast to coast to coast.

Before the lockout, *Hockey Night* had become a vehicle for selling beer and promoting Don Cherry—not problems, but the rest of the show suffered for it. We needed to create more and better programming that dealt with the game and the news around it. The challenge became one of time. With the new doubleheader format that we'd be dealing with once the NHL eventually resumed, we'd have to program five intermissions: two for each broadcast and a gap of time between the games (we dubbed that time "The Window" because it opened and closed at different times each week, depending on how quick the early games were). We needed to reflect the level of expectation of the viewers in what they believed *Hockey Night in Canada* should be. More features. More news. More Canadiana. As much as I'd like to tell you it was difficult, I had been preparing for this moment all my adult life. I had dreamt of being with *Hockey Night* for a long time, and I had yearned to return to it since that faithful day in late May 1986 when I was let go. I was ready. The lockout allowed us to test the new intermission show that would become "Hot Stove."

With the season delayed through fall and winter 1994, Alan Clark wanted our group to take back Saturday night with a selection of classic games that the fans could watch and vote on as the best. We needed a vehicle within the broadcast to discuss the issues facing the NHL, the NHLPA, and the lockout (for the record, if you supported the players, it was a lockout; if you supported the owners, it was a work stoppage). So I called my old friend John Davidson. He was firmly entrenched in New York as an announcer with MSG Network. By now there was little doubt he was the best analyst in the game, and he was making big money. Money that we couldn't afford at that point at *Hockey Night*, but we needed John. He was a credible voice, from outside the Toronto bubble.

Having John involved, albeit remotely, in one of our intermissions would be a huge plus for the new-look show. He had tremendous contacts through the league, had access to information from all the teams. In fact, the teams often phoned him to bounce ideas. He was perfect.

During those classic games, and the games of the Gretzky European tour we produced, John, Jim Hughson, and Scott Morrison of the *Toronto Sun* did a bit of a roundtable discussion on the labour war. That was one of the geneses of the "Satellite Hot Stove." For the longest time while I was away from *HNIC*, I had become a huge fan of cable news. CNN had reinvented the way we watch news. Tons of panels, boxes on the screen from New York, Los Angeles, Paris, and London. They used technology to tell stories. In my mind, in our business, it was magic. Putting people in different NHL cities and talking hockey would be new to our broadcast. Also, for years, during the Stanley Cup playoffs in Boston, I always read with joy Kevin Paul Dupont's Sunday hockey column in the *Boston Globe*. It was a full page of hockey nuggets in one of America's finest broadsheets. It combined statistics with gossip, and added some news. Kevin, who has become a friend, must have pored over the page for the six previous days to have it ready for the Sunday edition. It always bothered me that newspapers could do this, but TV couldn't. I was determined to change that with something that viewers would latch on to, like they did "Coach's Corner."

That's how "Satellite Hot Stove" was invented. After the trial runs in December 1994, it debuted in January 1995 with Ron MacLean as host and John Davidson (repping the United States) and Jim Hughson (repping Western Canada) as regulars. They had good chemistry, and when we added a fourth body, usually from the city we were hosting in, it became must-see television, as much as Cherry had become. The "Hot Stove," in my opinion, gave *HNIC* that great one-two national punch it really needed, to cover all of hockey: Cherry in the first intermission and "Hot Stove" in the second.

Those months of the lockout allowed me to acclimate myself to the world of CBC. We had a vision to reinvent *Hockey Night* in the last decade of the century. We needed to be more nimble, more newsy. We needed to be relevant and entertaining. To be clear, there was no manual on how to make the show better. It was just simple common sense, but having that time was a huge bonus.

The role of the producer is to be a conduit between the event and the viewer. It's important to understand the sport you are covering, but it is vital to understand who you are telling the stories to.

It's like being a translator from one language to another. Imagine how futile it would be to translate from Russian to English, but your audience needed to hear French. In sports television, we can know as much as we want about the sport (sometimes too much), but if we can't put it in the form of simple, effective stories, in a language the viewer understands, we have failed.

It's called *broad*casting for a reason. We work in *mass* media for a reason. Broad strokes for the masses.

Remaking *Hockey Night in Canada* for a broader, bigger audience was a challenge I relished. It was, at the time, the biggest job on sports television in Canada. The game was changing. The league was changing. *Hockey Night* had to evolve.

ELEVEN
MAKING CHANGES

THE TIMING OF MY RETURN TO *HOCKEY NIGHT* COULD NOT HAVE BEEN BETTER FOR ME, even though the NHL was going through difficulties with the lockout.

In 1994, the New York Rangers won their first Stanley Cup in fifty-four years. The sports world, outside of hockey, was paying more attention to the NHL. *Sports Illustrated* had its now-famous cover story that had everyone in our game salivating: "Why the NHL's Hot, and the NBA's Not." It was a great time to think about growing the game and the appeal of *Hockey Night in Canada.*

We took a long, hard look at what worked and what didn't work for *Hockey Night,* as well as what needed to change, improve, or be adapted to the new Saturday night doubleheader format. The challenge for all of us was to ensure that the tradition of *HNIC,* what it stood for, wouldn't be compromised as we moved from three hours to six. Eventually it became seven hours of content with the addition of a national pregame show, and the after-hours program that Scott Oake adopted as his own.

While every network was morphing into panel shows for the NFL, CFL, NBA, and MLB, the strength of *Hockey Night* was in individuals and in-depth stories told through features or interviews. We had the best broadcasters. We had the most compelling sport. We had the tradition of the *Hockey Night* brand. What we needed to do was build off that foundation, not destroy it or reinvent it. Change for change's sake was not our intention. We had customer loyalty that any retailer or business would view with envy, bordering on jealousy. Those four simple words—*Hockey Night in Canada*—opened doors anytime, any place around the world. In many ways, it's like renovating a building of tremendous historical relevance without changing the facade. We needed to be modern. We needed to be current. We needed to remain a Saturday night institution. It looked great from the outside, but it needed new plumbing.

I couldn't get to work fast enough, stay late enough, talk to enough people. It wasn't that I couldn't sleep—I didn't *want* to sleep. From the time I was hired in August 1994 to early January 1995, we spent hours thinking about what could work and how we could do the job properly, and how to bring in the cutting-edge technology that CBC had but was never used on *Hockey Night.*

There were people at CBC who had tremendous vision and built a state-of-the-art, world-class facility. The broadcast world was shifting, from analog to digital, and the CBC was changing with it. *Hockey Night* needed to change as well. For most games in Canada, we were always able to use CBC equipment and people. They had a tremendously high level of professionalism and an understanding of what made great TV. There was no need to teach the camera operators how to follow the puck, or what made a great close-up picture—they knew. Their skills truly defined what a "home" game was for *Hockey Night*, no matter what Canadian city we were in.

What we changed in 1995 was the amount of CBC equipment and personnel we used in the United States, which rarely happened prior to that season because it cost money. But we needed to ensure a higher level of quality control for the show, no matter what city we were broadcasting in, Canadian or American. Being more entwined with CBC also helped us create a more positive team philosophy within the organization than had existed before. No longer were people at the corporation just working in Canada and becoming viewers for games in the United States; they were now working in any NHL city, putting a true *HNIC* stamp on every game we produced. It built a pride of ownership and camaraderie at all levels of the production.

For the longest time, many within the walls of CBC had thumbed their noses at our show. Even though we generated about half of the network's operating profit, people did not like that we hijacked the prime-time lineup for sixty days in April, May, and June. Admittedly, it didn't help that we walked around with a chip on our shoulder and the confidence that we always had the best ratings on the network. Call it envy or whatever you will, but there was no air of cooperation with other departments at the CBC. Our move to involve more people in more games helped the show's reputation internally.

The other part of our mission, and this was personal, was to make this show about all of Canada. For far too long, the demands and the passions of the two largest fan bases dictated the tone of the show. The Toronto Maple Leafs and the Montreal Canadiens had followings not only in their own cities and regions, but across the country. It is the tradition and age-old quirk of cheering for the team one's parents did. We were still less than twenty-five years since Vancouver got a team, and less than fifteen years since Edmonton, Calgary, Winnipeg, and Quebec became members of the exclusive club. For decades, the only teams across Canada had been the Maple Leafs and Canadiens, and fandom has deep roots.

By this time we had eight teams in our small country. The Ottawa Senators had been the latest to join the league, dividing up television revenue in the country yet again. It was hard to imagine how eight teams in a country of 30 million could coexist. It would be like putting eight NHL teams in the state of California. It speaks to the passion of hockey fans in our country. However, it meant servicing all those fan bases, without taking sides, and trying on a daily basis to be fair to everyone.

That might have been our biggest challenge. After all, each member club had a stake in the success of the national show. In addition to receiving a rights fee from the network, each team attempted to commoditize all aspects of their marketing plans, when they were seen in a national television window. For example, the rink-board advertising that was controlled 100 percent by the clubs was primarily sold on the basis of local market exposure (both in arena and on television). However, those rink boards would increase in value every time the national game emanated from the home arena. Increasing national exposures from five or six games to perhaps eighteen games would significantly raise the value of those rink boards. The teams all had expectations that they would be treated fairly, regardless of market size. Of course, much of that had to do with how many games the network would televise. Obviously, there were expectations that Toronto and Montreal would be on every Saturday night, as had been the tradition for decades. But now there was pressure to do a game or two in Quebec City or Ottawa. When I say a game or two, I mean a game or two. Fan followings for both the Nordiques and the Senators may have been passionate, but they were minuscule markets compared to the Maple Leafs and Canadiens. It made little or no sense to broadcast the games from the then Corel Centre or Le Colisée if they were playing a non-Canadian team.

That didn't make us feel welcome in either city. Ownership in the newer markets thought that being a member of the NHL would give their teams the same status. That was just not the case, and it was truly frustrating that both the NHL and the teams would try to force our hand by scheduling home games on Saturday nights. By the letter of the contract between the CBC and the NHL, if we didn't broadcast the game, no one else could, even on a local level. The contract protected Saturdays as strictly for *Hockey Night in Canada*. We would get all the blame, all the time, for ignoring the teams. But it made no business sense to broadcast three games "early" on *Hockey Night in Canada*. We would have added very few viewers by doing so, and would have increased production expenses by 50 percent. Not that viewers cared about that, but it was a fact of business.

Make no mistake, it is business, which completely contradicts the perception in our country that watching NHL hockey on TV is a right. It goes hand in hand with the belief that the NHL is a public trust in Canada, as opposed to a coldhearted private business. Imagine the complaints we would get when a Saturday night matchup of the Sens and the Philadelphia Flyers was seen in Pennsylvania and Delaware, but not seen in the Ottawa Valley. Fans were not happy, but they didn't understand the business side of television.

About fans being unhappy: well, it is a reality of being a fan. I don't ever recall receiving or reading viewer comments that were positive. Never once did the phone ring or the daily call logs appear saying, "We really love what Ron did in the opening," or, "Harry Neale was so fair in talking about both the Senators and the Maple Leafs."

It just never happened. It didn't matter that commentators, during the game or in the intermissions, were fair, honest, and without bias. It only mattered if it seemed they were critical of one of the teams, invariably the losing team, and that gave those fans license to phone, write, and later email that we were unprofessional, unprepared, and, for example, in the back pockets of the Maple Leafs. Nothing could have been further from the truth, but it was a useless exercise to engage in debate. As a friend of mine reminded me recently, the great coach Marv Levy of Montreal Alouettes and Buffalo Bills fame used to say, "If you start listening to fans, you'll be sitting with them soon enough."

In my first tour of duty at *Hockey Night* I was lucky to produce most Edmonton vs. Calgary games, and at least three "Battle of Alberta" playoff series. It was some of the most ferocious, vicious, physical hockey of the 1980s. On the ice, the teams reflected the great rivalry between the two cities in the province. It's a rivalry that few truly understand until they live in Alberta. White-collar Calgary, business suits with cowboy boots. It had a more transient population of people working to get up the corporate ladder than in the East and the United States, and the most head offices west of Toronto. Blue-collar Edmonton, the provincial capital, gateway to the oil patch and the North, with a population more likely to be born and raised in the city. The sports teams, in football and hockey, became a true projection of that rivalry. Winning meant a lot. Losing meant more.

Playing it fair on television became almost impossible. Every word was analyzed, every picture critiqued. It made it even more important to get it right. In one playoff season, on an off day, our production team was walking down a street in Calgary after dinner. The announcers Don Wittman, Gary Dornhoefer, and John Wells were with us, the faces and voices of our production. We were enjoying a quick laugh on the walk back to the hotel when it was shattered by a passing car: "Hey, Dornhoefer, you suck! You love the Oilers."

Moments later, an approaching bunch on Fourth Avenue noticed Don in our group: "Hey, Wittman, you always cheer for the Oilers—you must just love the Whiner. *Oops*, we mean Wayne."

Wittman, who was a master of managing the public, just smiled and said, "Thanks for watching." Even today, when I get negative criticism, Don's words resonate in my brain, and I (usually) reply, "Appreciate the feedback—hey, thanks for watching."

Wittman, who died far too soon, never received his due as an announcer. He came out of the CBC's great training system and could do absolutely everything. News, any sport, hosting, play-by-play, lotteries. For two generations he was the voice of sports in our country. He was by far the most talented, underappreciated announcer I ever worked with. Never once did he have a bad performance. Maybe more important, if he felt he did, you'd never know. He always did it with a smile on his face, a glint in his eye, and a quarter in his pocket. "Hey, you want to play the coin game for the bill?" Invariably, Don would win. Don would always win.

During that same Battle of Alberta series, on an off night in Edmonton, the same group of *Hockey Night in Canada* people walked down Jasper Avenue, to the same kinds of jeers. It was only then that we truly believed we were doing our jobs: even, fair, and hated by all.

Nothing has changed. In 2022, the development and maturation (I use the term lightly) of social media has only amplified these levels of unhappiness. More instantaneous, more raw, more powerful. It's not fair, but it is a reality.

Being fair wasn't easy. There were far more fans of the Maple Leafs and Canadiens than there were of any other team. Sure, Vancouver owned everything west of the Rockies, Edmonton was a dominant force through the prairies, and Calgary and Winnipeg had small but loyal fan bases. And then there was Ottawa. Through the first few years of the franchise, we could not win in the nation's capital. Fans in the Ottawa Valley were divided in three, and I truly believe it was in this order: the Maple Leafs, Canadiens, and then the Senators. Along with our friends at the NHL, we had the decision-making power of what game appeared in what market across the country. It wasn't up to the team, or the local station—it was up to the network, and those of us at *Hockey Night in Canada*. If you produced and broadcast a Toronto game into Ottawa, Canadiens and Sens fans were angry. If you put a Montreal game into Ottawa, fans of both the Leafs and Senators flooded the switchboard (people under thirty are no doubt now googling "switchboard"), and if you put a Senators game on, the long-faithful fans of both Montreal and Toronto were apoplectic. We could not win. Plus it was so expensive to produce a game for just Ottawa, we actually let the game be played without any Canadian production. With two Canadian teams we could justify it, but if it was Ottawa playing a U.S. team, the TV market was dark and we would invariably have the Maple Leafs on in English, and Canadiens on in French. The Senators and their fans were a small group, but vocal.

I remember one summer when I was driving down the coast of California with my young family and received a call from Bruce Garrioch of the *Ottawa Sun*. I liked Bruce but did not know him very well. The NHL schedule had just been released and the television schedule was still being hashed out. Bruce was doing a preemptive story on the broadcast schedule and was wondering how many games the Senators would get on the schedule. This was a team that had yet to have a quality season. They were still haunted by drafting Alexandre Daigle and choosing a dead man in the expansion draft a few years before. The new building in Kanata was certainly an improvement from the Ottawa Civic Centre, but the team hadn't improved as much as the venue. Bruce's question was fair, but my answer was hardly diplomatic.

> JS: Oh, I would say two or three.
> BG: Two or three in a twenty-five-week schedule? The Leafs will probably have twenty-five, and Montreal not far behind.
> JS: But Bruce, perhaps the team should win a bit more. Then we could justify it.

Well, Bruce did his job, and reported my comments verbatim. I was not very popular in Ottawa for a few days before the comments died down. Also, the CBC head office was in Ottawa. The civil servants at headquarters were not happy with a sports guy making light of anything in their city that could cause a ruckus at a cocktail party. Luckily for me, Alan Clark was a lifelong Canadiens fan and loved to stick it to Ottawa anytime he could.

In the end, though, the Senators did improve, and we did put them on the air more, even at the expense of the English version of the show in Montreal. The English market in the province of Quebec had been dwindling for years, probably since the 1976 election of the Parti Québécois, to the point that it was the same size as that in the city of Regina, Saskatchewan. With relatively little or no pushback, we would produce a Senators game in English, all the while pushing fans of Canadiens to our French-language show, *La Soirée du Hockey*. It was logical and simple. It didn't hurt us that the Senators were actually a better team than the Habs for a few seasons.

Beyond moving to the doubleheader format, the biggest programming change was the "Satellite Hot Stove" in the second intermission of the early game. The concept was simple: marry the old with the new. Pay tribute to the traditions of *Hockey Night*, all the while taking advantage of technology to talk about hockey, linking people on-screen from different locations, in real time. A great deal of "Hot Stove's" technical success was built on the capabilities the CBC was building in Toronto. Their cable news network, CBC Newsworld (now CBC News Network), was doing this type of thing every day, connecting CBC hubs across the country. Our goal was to do the same using the NHL arenas where we had games, plus small production houses across America where one of our original panelists, John Davidson, could easily access us on Saturday afternoon.

The original concept was basic. Ron MacLean would host the show from whatever game was deemed national. Because we produced the national segment on-site, in addition to hosting Ron and Don, it was called "the circus." Three other guests would participate in the discussion. Davidson was there to represent the "American" stories of the NHL; Jim Hughson, who lived in Vancouver, was part of the show to represent Western Canada; and a third rotating guest was used based on the location of the circus, or the biggest story of the week. Those initial years we had up to a dozen contributing panelists on the show. Some were better than others, but once the format became accepted and well known, we had reporters and TV personalities lobbying to appear on the show.

Davidson and Hughson were perfect. They understood their roles, could combine opinion and information in an entertaining way, and had excellent chemistry together. We began those initial shows with Scott Morrison, who was the sports editor of the *Toronto Sun* at the time. Scott was plugged in, low-key, and always full of information. He would prove to be a good foil for John and Jim, and Ron of course. But we needed to expand the contributors. I was always cognizant of the famous "Toronto bias" that has haunted every sports television show in this country. Too much Toronto is not a good thing. It was always difficult when the Maple Leafs drove the ratings, and Don Cherry made no bones about being a Leaf fan on every Saturday night. Still, it was vital to reflect the whole country. After all, the name of the show is *Hockey Night in Canada*, not *Hockey Night in Toronto*.

It was also important to ensure that when we travelled to any NHL city, we showed a level of respect to the media in that town. When we travelled throughout the league in the late 1970s, there was a combination of awe and envy from local media. Many thought it was great that this band of television people were in their town; others were jealous that the "Canadians had invaded." While there was an admitted swagger in all of us, we realized we would get much more cooperation and press coverage if we were inclusive. Any chance we had to put other people from other cities on was important to the lasting acceptability and credibility of our show.

For that reason, for "Hot Stove" we tried to use people like Red Fisher and Yvon Pedneault in Montreal, Terry Jones in Edmonton, Eric Duhatschek in Calgary, and John McKeachie in Vancouver. That is in addition to others from the United States, like Larry Brooks of the *New York Post*, Kevin Paul Dupont of the *Boston Globe*, and Jim Kelley of the *Buffalo News*.

Then there was Al Strachan. In my life before running *Hockey Night*, Al had become the best "inside" hockey writer in the country. While I was aware of him writing in Montreal, my first real introduction to him was when he moved to Alberta, to write for the *Globe and Mail* as their Western Canadian columnist. I wouldn't say we were friends then, but I enjoyed his writing and his ability to dig up inside information from the NHL Board of Governors and the general managers. He seemed to have a couple of regular pipelines, which made his stories so important to read, if you were compelled to follow the NHL on a daily basis. Over the years, and over a few beers, Al and I became very comfortable with each other. In many ways, he was all about supporting the players, and I could respect that. Early in the first season of "Hot Stove," it became apparent to me that this format was perfect for Al's knowledge and sense of humour. He was unafraid to challenge authority. My saying to everyone was that "there's nothing wrong with a little sandpaper." Al was to be our sandpaper.

However, it created a huge dilemma for the show. By then Strachan was actually working for Scott Morrison at the *Toronto Sun*. In our desire to be fair, and spread much of the "glory" of being on the show, I felt we couldn't have two writers contribute from the same newspaper. As much as I liked and respected both guys, after that first year Scott would not be on the show. It was a difficult conversation to have. After all, he and I were friends. We had seen each other around Maple Leaf Gardens for more than fifteen years. I know he wasn't happy with me when I gave him the news, but I hoped that his "corporate conscience" would kick in. After all, someone from the *Sun* would still be on the show, which would help sell papers. It just wouldn't be Scott.

One writer who wasn't as forgiving was the great Red Fisher. I had been around Red from my early years at *Hockey Night*, when I was sent to Montreal during the Bowman era. Dick Irvin had always treated me with such kindness in that time, which seemed to give Red the green light to be polite to me, too. Throughout the 1980s, when our regional shows travelled to Montreal, our best intermission programming was always Dick and Red, chirping at each other, telling stories about hockey's most storied franchise. It was great, simple television. Adding the game's best writer to our list of contributors just made sense.

Like Strachan, Fisher was plugged in, opinionated, and full of sandpaper. Over the years, though, as Red aged, his commentary got more acerbic. Many on the show, and many off it, didn't enjoy him as much as I did. After all, he was old hockey. He was a true throwback to a time of the six-team league, and the great names in Montreal of Richard, Blake, Harvey, Plante, and Béliveau. Over the decades, he had been a part of the

Hockey Night family with his "Fisher Report"—he always had an association with the show. The least this new edition of the show could do was put Red in a rotation of presenters for the "Hot Stove." It was a perfect match of old with new. For the first few years it indeed worked that way.

As was customary, at the end of the summer, as our preparations for the new season began, the senior members of the production staff would sit down and talk about what worked, what didn't, and where we had to go to improve the show, to keep it fresh. By this time, we had distilled the group down to five or six rotating people: Strachan, Duhatschek, Pedneault, Greg Millen (when he wasn't doing colour), and Davidson and Hughson. All at the table agreed we were on the right track, that is, until we got to Red. I went around the table, asking everyone if we wanted him back. By my count, there were eight nos on the table. And zero yeses.

To me, it was settled. I announced to the group, "All right, then—Red's back!"

The room looked at me like I had two heads. Some people groaned. So I explained that Red Fisher was part of our family. He brought tradition, continuity, knowledge, and grit to the table, every time we used him. We owed him loyalty for all his years of great storytelling. Beyond that, I liked him.

As was my tradition, while these men were not under contract, they would receive a formal letter from me, outlining the dates they would be required and the fee they would receive for the appearance. On the first Saturday when the circus was in Montreal and Red was to be used, he stormed up to me waving his letter of agreement. He proceeded to tell me that the twelve dates on his letter just wouldn't be enough. He wanted to be on every Saturday, and that was all there was to it. I explained to him that we had made commitments to other people already, and the schedule was set in concrete, but if he didn't want to do the dates suggested, and so wanted to forfeit the money, I would totally understand. Red folded the paper up, walked into the studio, and sat beside Ron, ready to go.

A few years later, during the Stanley Cup Final in Dallas, we were taping the "Hot Stove" with MacLean, Strachan, Davidson, and someone else (I honestly can't remember) when someone came up to say Red was looking for me. Unbeknownst to me, Fisher's newspaper had sent him to Dallas for the Stanley Cup Final, and he had seen the "Hot Stove" being produced, on a monitor inside Reunion Arena. Eventually we spoke and he was livid. How could we put someone else on the show while he was there? It was unprofessional, he thought. Why would I embarrass him like that? I tried to explain that I was unaware he was travelling to Dallas, and had I known he was there, we could have planned for that event. I tried to reassure him: perhaps next time. "There won't be a next time," he said. There never was. Loyalty was important to me and Red, and it's a shame we didn't see eye to eye on this.

Eric Duhatschek was another longtime professional, and he made a lasting impression on me. We had had a long relationship. Duhatschek, Dave Shoalts (who worked for decades at the *Globe and Mail*), and Steve Simmons were the beat writers for the Calgary Flames in 1980, when the team arrived from Atlanta. We were all about the same age and have maintained an acquaintance for all these decades. Eric is the only one who never moved from Calgary, and with that became a strong western voice in hockey, first with the *Calgary Herald*, then the *Globe and Mail*, and then the *Athletic*. Initially. When the circus came to Calgary, Eric was the obvious choice to appear alongside Ron.

Only one problem: Eric is a writer, a long-form writer. With eight full minutes of content, and four voices talking, that means everyone should contribute for about two minutes, in conversation, not a soliloquy. Eric, who was excited to be on *Hockey Night* anyway, had a difficult time with . . . well, time. His first statement wasn't twenty or thirty seconds, as the show required. It was a dissertation. Well over two minutes after starting the show, we stopped recording (thankfully we weren't live).

JS: Eric . . . *Eric* . . .
ED: Too long?

JS: *Too long?* Eric, I asked you for the time, not how to build the
fucking watch!

At that point, MacLean, Davidson, and Hughson all broke out in laughter. To be clear, Eric's content was outstanding. He always delivered pertinent information. We just had to teach him how to distill his verbosity for television. Over the next three or four years, invariably, we would stop the show just so Eric wouldn't dominate the first segment, and never be heard from again. To this day, we laugh about those moments, even the part about building "the fucking watch."

Eric's professionalism came into play years later, during his tenure at the *Calgary Herald*. In 1999, the *Herald*, which was being run by then publisher Ken King for media magnate Conrad Black (through his company Hollinger International), was in a terrible, drawn-out labour dispute with the unions over editorial control, working conditions, and wages. It was a strike that lasted more than eight months and changed the landscape of newspapers in our country.

From a distance, I was aware of the strike. I suppose I took a little more interest in the event because I had lived in Calgary for thirteen years, time that had moulded me as a producer, a person, a husband, and a father. I had met my wife in Calgary, and our son, Jake, was born there. But I also took interest because the strike meant that one of our guys was on the picket line, and receiving only strike pay. It was not a positive situation for Eric and his family.

I am the son of man who believed in helping others. My dad was a socialist. While not a card-carrying member of the NDP or CCF, he believed certain aspects of life were a right, not a privilege: health care, higher education, welfare. He also believed in a constant healthy debate in anything political. He claimed he was in Regina during the riots in the 1930s. He didn't expect us to always agree, just have an opinion. He was a true believer in the labour movement, and the role of unions.

With that in mind, and the hockey season well on its way, some thought we had a real challenge in Calgary when it came to the "Hot Stove" contributor. As a group, we didn't see it that way. Eric Duhatschek, after all, had helped build the brand of the program. We were not going to turn our backs on him while his regular job was in flux. In fact, we did the opposite.

Over the next few months, Eric appeared regularly. When I say regularly, I mean every week. After all, we were probably his only source of income at that point. He had always shown *Hockey Night* a great deal of loyalty, so it was just common sense that we would show that same loyalty in return. He would be identified as "a hockey writer based in Calgary" as opposed to "from the *Calgary Herald*." That titling seemed to irk a few management types at the newspaper.

One week I received a call from a senior manager at the paper. They were concerned that we were using a striking newspaper writer on the show, as opposed to an authorized "*Herald* person." I assured the person that we were very aware of the labour situation at the paper and therefore didn't give Eric any affiliation for his on-air credit. But that *was* the problem. They liked the recognition on the nights that "Eric Duhatschek of the *Calgary Herald*" appeared on the show. So far, during the season and on the air, they were receiving no acknowledgement. After all, it was free advertising. The new way we introduced him was a constant reminder to those within the paper's hierarchy, and supposedly their readers, that "Eric from Calgary" was on strike.

It was at that point the management person offered someone else to appear on the show. A person still writing with the paper. A scab. Somewhere in the back of my mind, I could only think of R. J. Shannon, my father. By now he was years into dementia, but alive. His words were with me when I declined the offer: a scab is a scab. Always was, always will be.

Eric appeared on the show a great deal that year, including eight straight Saturdays. I hope it made the difficult decision to picket just a little easier to stomach.

Over the seven years I was back at *Hockey Night*, the "Hot Stove" became a staple. So many times it was the highlight of the game coverage. It also allowed us to balance our coverage with what Don Cherry said in the first intermission. Most of the time, they were complementary segments. Every once in a while, when Don felt "Hot Stove" was getting a little too much TLC, I would remind him that it took three commentators to match his show. He seemed to like that. The other aspect many didn't seem to realize was that once Strachan became a regular contributor, and was around the studio much more, it seemed to calm Don down a great deal. They had many of the same political philosophies and a love of history. As outspoken as Don always was about his role on the show, he remained very loyal to his friends. Al was a friend and ally of Don's and *Hockey Night in Canada*.

The power of the "Satellite Hot Stove" was never more visible than in April 1999. On a Saturday night, John Davidson announced to the country and the hockey world that the Gretzky "retirement meter" had moved a great deal in the past few weeks. Davidson, who was also the lead analyst for MSG Network in New York City, where Wayne was playing, indicated literally with his hands that the meter had moved from 50 percent (his arm straight up in the air) to 99 percent (his arm moved completely to one side). Davidson hinted that Sunday, April 18, 1999, would be Gretzky's last game. With the Rangers not qualifying for the playoffs, that game versus Pittsburgh would be massive. Within hours it became national news. We were questioned by newspeople on the authenticity of the story. Davidson, multiple times, was challenged to reveal his source. It became one of the biggest hockey stories of the decade, perhaps only matched by the story in August 1988 that announced Gretzky had been traded from Edmonton to Los Angeles.

On Sunday morning, I phoned John at his home in Westchester County, New York, to ask him for the details. It had been, in fact, Wayne who told him of the decision. Moreover, it wasn't 99 percent—it was a 100 percent done deal. It spoke to me of Wayne's loyalty to John that he gave him the story. It also spoke to me of No. 99's loyalty to the show—after all, it was our group that helped finance the Gretzky tour in 1994 to Europe. There was only one problem: it was a Sunday afternoon game. Not a Saturday. We didn't have rights to broadcast the game. We had seven days to rectify that.

Within minutes of talking to John, I called Alan Clark to ask him to please talk to the network and the league about making the game available to *HNIC*. Remembering that we were on the verge of a two-month journey through the Stanley Cup playoffs, and a ton of network prime-time hours, it was not that easy to sell CBC on giving us yet another three-hour window for hockey. But it had to be done. We were the show of record for the game in our country and we had to cover the Great One's last game.

In my mind, from the moment Alan and I talked, it was a done deal. The planning began the moment he agreed, my brain whirring at 3,000 RPMs. Features, talent, staffing, openings, closings, musicals. We needed to work on all of these things and be ready for the playoffs that would start three days after Gretzky's last game. It was a week of work that everyone in our business dreams about. Not enough hours in the day. Ideas constantly erupting out of conversations both in our group and beyond. The electricity in the office was palpable. A dream come true.

But by Tuesday morning the network had still not signed off on carrying the game. As an add-on game, there would be an additional cost to the network of about $350,000 ($250,000 in rights fees, plus production), advertisers would have to be approached quickly to gauge interest, and, finally, the network had to determine if it was worthwhile to bump the planned programming.

At about 10 a.m. on Tuesday, Alan and I met with Slawko Klymkiw, who was the head of the English CBC network. Klymkiw was a Winnipeg boy who had worked his way up the corporation's ladder and viewed himself as a great programmer. Within the CBC hierarchy, he was a powerful person. We needed to convince him of the importance of this event. I was shocked it wasn't already decided. Moments like these reinforced the stories that *Hockey Night* was never appreciated, or even liked, within the walls of the CBC. Jealousy I could understand; lack of appreciation was a completely different story. There was another revelation that morning: not every Canadian is a hockey fan.

Crazy, I know! But it's true.

I couldn't believe we had to explain why Gretzky's last game was important, not just to hockey fans but to all Canadians, across the country. Why it was important to the show, to the network. Finally, I had to convince Klymkiw that Wayne wouldn't be changing his mind; this was, for sure, his last game. "Okay," he said. "But if he changes his mind"—he said this pointing at me—"this is all on you!"

Clark and I left the meeting relieved, but it shook me how short-sighted some people could be, and how close we came to not covering that game. It's my belief, and I've never confirmed this, that our biggest ally was someone who wouldn't have liked that we hijacked his airtime for two months during the Stanley Cup playoffs every year. Peter Mansbridge, the network's number one anchor, was a huge hockey fan. Of the people within the corporation, he knew the importance of that last game, not only as a sporting event, but as a news story. I'm sure that Peter, who wielded a ton of power at the CBC, endorsed our decision. While the game was secondary (Pittsburgh won 4–1), the broadcast was the highest-rated non-Saturday regular season game in the history of *Hockey Night in Canada*. It proved to be a great business move and a great news story.

My memories of the actual event are vivid. Our best producer, Paul Graham, and director Sherali Najak (who would go on to be executive producer of the show well after me) created great drama and moments all afternoon. It was right out of the *Hockey Night* handbook. Read and react to the environment, tell simple but effective stories, and most of all, let Wayne's actions dictate the story lines. What Graham did with those stories, and how Najak cut the cameras, puts that game at the level of our best work ever at the CBC. While I'd like to take credit for all of it, I can't. In fact, both Sherali and Paul will acknowledge that the best thing to happen to the show was that midway through the first period, I left the television mobile, which allowed them the artistic license to do what they did so well.

Admittedly, I was wired for this show. In many ways, my career had paralleled Gretzky's, from a time-and-place perspective. We are about the same age, cut our teeth in Edmonton and Western Canada, and had some success. Obviously, Wayne's successes dwarfed mine, but I did feel a kinship and a responsibility to guide this final game to its conclusion. Except, I wasn't doing a very good job of it. For the first portion of the game, I was a complete backseat driver. I was loud. I was uncompromising. It was not helping the show.

Between Paul and me, we decided that my best utilization was not in the truck, but rather at ice level, between the benches in the arena. With that, much to the joy of everyone working in the mobile control room, I departed. From the position between the benches, with a headset on, I was able to guide Paul and the crew through the events that were going on in the arena bowl. Because Paul, Sherali, and I had worked together so much, our communication was quick, concise, and to the point. When it became apparent that this was going to work well for the show, Paul joked that I was "the world's most expensive spotter." While we all got a chuckle, it reminded me of where it all started, in the late 1970s, running, spotting, doing stats. All the frontline rolls that help make quality television.

Sometimes being the executive in charge can be frustrating. This day, Wayne's last day, put me back on the front line, and it felt oh so good. The broadcast made all of us proud, but what happened after the game is the stuff of legend.

Let me first say, I love chartering airplanes. I have always loved flying privately, leaving when we want and travelling only with people we like. All the way back to the days of CFL broadcasts, if we could financially justify the cost, I loved to charter a flight. At one point, the joke became that *Hockey Night in Canada* always flew "Air Shannada" for the big events.

We did fly a charter into New York for our technical and production crew for Gretzky's last game. Combining the regular Saturday night show with the urgency of the upcoming playoffs, the special Sunday game demanded we be as efficient in travelling people as possible. It just made sense. However, in extenuating circumstances, being able to fly a large group (around forty) home right after the game was going to be difficult, especially if some people had been given a special invite. That invite was one of the great celebrations of hockey and its greatest player. Wayne Gretzky had a party on the 106th floor of the World Trade Center, the same World Trade Center that would no longer exist twenty-eight months later.

Walking through the back hallways of Madison Square Garden, I ran into Mike Barnett, Wayne's agent. He quickly invited me to come to the WTC party, "and bring whoever you want." I thanked Mike and went on walking down the long ramp to where the television compound was located. I had about two minutes to figure out how to get off the charter that I had arranged and in a cab down to the party. As usual, I was the last to arrive on the scene, outside the arena. In fact, my lengthy departures from arenas had become somewhat of a regular occurrence. There's always someone else to thank, or say good-bye to, or shake hands with. As much as it became a ritual, I always enjoyed life at the arena. They were and still are special places. By the time I arrived at the compound, most people had boarded the buses we'd arranged to get to the Teterboro, New Jersey, airport, where our charter was located. Outside the bus were Bob Cole, Harry Neale, and Paul Graham. At that moment, it occurred to me that if any group of people deserved to be at the party, it was those three gentlemen. Cole and Neale had been involved with many big games in Wayne's career, and Paul, who was from Edmonton, had been working on shows with the Oilers since 1979 and had been a partner in crime with a few of us in television for three decades. Discreetly, I walked over to them and said, "Don't move." All three looked at me with curiosity. Cole was the most surprised, but Graham could see the glint in my eye and knew something was up. "Bob," he said, "if John says don't move, just don't move."

I walked to the buses and said they could go ahead and leave without us. We would take a cab to the airport. I also told them that if we weren't there by the time the plane was about to leave, they should depart.

As the buses pulled out, I turned to Paul, Harry, and Bob and told them where we were going. Bob pointed out that we now had no way home and had checked out of the hotel already.

So I phoned the charter company in Toronto and requested a second plane, for four people, for 2 a.m.—and put it on my American Express card. As the three guys heard me book the plane, they exploded with laughter. The party, after all, was the perfect way to end a great day of television.

My time as executive producer wasn't always perfect and fun. I was loud. I was direct. I was hard on people at times. I demanded almost as much from others as I did from myself. Preparation was paramount. Execution was the ultimate. In the 1997 playoffs, one of our directors and I had a disagreement on his camera-cutting pattern during a playoff game in New York. The run-in carried on outside during an intermission break, and I was suspended for yelling at him. I was summoned home to meet with by boss, who gave me other instances of my actions that were creating issues for the network and him. It was not a criticism of the product, but rather of my style. Once it was decided I would be suspended, the news broke like wildfire, throughout the hockey world and in the newspapers. It was an uncomfortable time. The most difficult aspect was having to look my wife and children in the eyes. This was not their doing. This was not their fault. Yet they were being tarnished by my actions. That was the hardest part.

At the same time as my suspension, Don Cherry's first wife, Rose, was losing her battle with cancer. It was especially hard on Don because Rose insisted he continue to work and travel to games in Dallas and Denver. It hit even closer to home for me because my wife, Mickee, had just been diagnosed with cancer and would have major surgery in November of that year. It was a difficult challenge to balance my professional life with my personal life. Ten days after my suspension, and just three days after Rose's death, I saw Alan Clark in the parking lot of the funeral home. Clark was polite but coy. Something had happened in that time. The small group of people who were still working at *Hockey Night*, and responsible for my time away, were unable to match the passion, creativity, vision, and quality that we brought to the show. That small group had been isolated from the many people who worked on the show who supported my philosophy on the program. In just ten days, the person who brought me in to change the course of *Hockey Night* realized that I was doing most things right.

Did I have to mellow? Yes. But Clark knew that with all the differing personalities there had to be a decisive, creative leadership style 24/7/365. Otherwise the ship would list and the show would lose focus. He had also polled enough people on the show to know that while I was loud, I was also loyal and fair, and most if not all on the show knew my intentions were pure. While I did not return to the show for the remainder of that Stanley Cup Final, within a week I was on a plane to Nagano, Japan, preparing for the upcoming 1998 Olympic Winter Games, featuring NHL players for the first time.

The public embarrassment actually turned into a bit of a positive. In a show of support of my job as executive producer, Clark allowed us to replace certain people behind the scenes. Also, I was able to hire a couple of people in tune with what we thought the show should be. Those who had supported my return became that much more loyal to the change and creativity the show required. In short, the changes that the show needed were embraced wholeheartedly.

In the end, those who questioned my style and leadership were the catalysts for my role at *Hockey Night in Canada* to become even more cemented.

TWELVE
GRAPES

I AM A FRIEND OF DON CHERRY.

Our political beliefs are different, but that doesn't mean we can't or don't get along. The one thing we shared was the passion and belief that *Hockey Night in Canada* had an important place in the game, and in the hearts of all Canadians.

I have already discussed how we first met, while Don was the coach of the Bruins. It was that relationship that allowed me to push the envelope with him over the years. Even in his time coaching in Boston, Cherry had become a go-to guy for Ralph Mellanby and us at *Hockey Night in Canada*. When the Bruins were eliminated, Don would get a call to join us as a guest commentator. In his short time in Denver as coach of the Colorado Rockies, I actually saw Don a great deal, as I was producing games in Western Canada. Don was his bombastic self, but always happy to see me.

Our bond grew to the point that one night I convinced him to sit inside an adult-size Christmas box and jump out on cue, as part of an opening we did. Don burst out (despite his knees hurting, crouched inside and waiting for his cue) and kissed Santa Claus on the cheek! As only Cherry could. It was television gold.

He also joined us as a colour commentator for games in the late 1970s, after the Bruins had been eliminated. His best line from these games occurred during an intermission conversation one night in Philadelphia, with play-by-play man Dan Kelly, who asked Don for some analysis. Don's answer was pure Cherry: "I'd love to answer you, Dan, as soon as this guy stops talking in my ear."

Dan and Don were positioned in the lower press box, along with all the other writers and reporters, but closest to the exit. Every once in a while, a media member would walk by the announcers and Don would be his friendly self. "Hi, how you doing?" and "Good to see you." Only one problem: Don's mic was always on, and our TV audience heard every greeting Don said. It was like he was a greeter at Walmart. Everyone wanted to say hello to Don. He was always polite to say hello back. That hasn't changed, after all these years.

Once he was dismissed by the Rockies and moved to southern Ontario, Don did a ton of work on both regional and national media. He actually did more games as a colour man early on, before "Coach's Corner" became his domain. He was in the booth for a Calgary Flames game in Boston when the Flames employed a Finnish defenceman named Pekka Rautakallio. That was the Saturday afternoon when he said, "Pekka? Pekka? I don't think I can say that name in B-ahhston." Needless to say, that was the last Flames regional game Don worked.

Not long after, Don was the colour man on December 30, 1981, when Wayne Gretzky scored five goals against Philadelphia to accomplish the amazing feat of 50 goals in 39 games. What Don displayed then, and I maintain he still does, was an innate ability to distill the events of the game, any game, better than most. He saw things that most didn't, and he explained them in a very simple, straightforward way.

Don't think for one moment that I agreed with every word he uttered on *Hockey Night*. I didn't. I viewed Don as if he were an important columnist of the largest newspaper in the country. It was up to the viewer to decide if they agreed or disagreed with him. He made people think. He made them laugh. He made them angry. He entertained. He did his job, and he did a damn good one.

All the stories about Don being the common man, saying what everyone was thinking, I'm not sure I buy that. There is no doubt that Don's "brand" projected that. But Don knew what worked. He was very observant about the broadcast world, what worked and what didn't, and he perfected what best worked for him. For example, by the time I returned to the show, the set and production for "Coach's Corner" was a simple single camera on a two-shot of Ron and Don, and Don refused to wear an earpiece, by which the producer could talk to him. Don was always concerned about lighting—simple flat lighting with a small bit of light from the back (or backlight, in television vernacular). That's all Don wanted. Simple production, simple lighting, in order for his content to be the focus. In order for Don to be the focus.

It was in mid-December 1994, during the lockout, that I witnessed Don's temper. We were running two games from Gretzky's all-star tour of Europe, and some classic games, and I was still learning how to be the executive producer. How the moment was handled perhaps helped us cement a solid, loyal relationship.

We were running the famous 1979 Boston vs. Montreal playoff, Game 7 to be exact. Montreal won after tying the game late in the third period on a power play goal. Cherry's Bruins had been called for too many men on the ice.

The show was hosted by Ron MacLean and Dick Irvin. Don was sure to be part of it, as well. But we were also in the middle of a labour dispute between the league and the players. That was more the story this Saturday night than a game that was almost sixteen years old. Running these old games was not so important—we had no studio from which to broadcast.

All of the assignable space was being used for shows like *Royal Canadian Air Farce* and other CBC programming. Instead we were forced to be flexible, and all the on-cameras would take place right in the control room. It was the only way for us to mount these shows through December.

Needless to say, everyone was excited to be working on something that resembled hockey as we limped through the lockout. Some, like Don, were hyped to talk about his May 10, 1979, game at the Forum. Still, it was rather uneventful to start. Ron and Dick opened the show, and Don did a mini version of "Coach's Corner" in the first intermission. The second intermission was planned for news. John Davidson would be at the CBC studios in New York City, Jim Hughson was at CBC Vancouver, and Scott Morrison of the *Toronto Sun* would be with Ron in studio (the control room) to discuss the latest labour-related ramblings between Bettman, Goodenow, et al. This format became a bit of the blueprint for the "Satellite Hot Stove," which would make its official debut when the shortened season started in the new year. We planned on giving Don some time between periods to explain what was happening in the game, too. Everything was going great until the panel discussion got involved in the intricacies of the labour war and went longer than planned. That would leave Don just ninety seconds to explain his position, and what to watch for in the third period and overtime.

Once the satellite panel was finished, Don came in and sat down with Ron to tell some stories. At that point, he was told he had only one and a half minutes to set up the period. He was not amused. Now he wasn't sure what story to tell. Like most people, when he got flustered he tended to talk faster, and not finish his sentences. Once Ron threw it back to the game, Don blew up. He stood up yelling that what he was saying was more important than "those other guys." He walked right over to the front desk of the control room, where switcher Tim Rohal, script assistant Karen Sebesta, director Sherali Najak, and producer Ed Milliken were sitting, working away. He started asking them if they agreed with him, and why did it happen?!

I had no choice but to speak up. After all, this group of great people were just following my orders.

JS: I'm in charge here, Don. I made that decision.

DC: Oh, you did, did you? Why? I had great stuff about the game!

JS: I know you did, but it was more important to talk about the lockout.

DC: You think so? You really think so? That's stupid.

JS: I tell you what, Don, these people in here need to keep working. Let's go outside and settle this.

DC: You want to go outside? You want to settle this? Okay, let's go outside.

With that, Don put on his overcoat and left a rather tense control room. Here I was, the new guy on the job. It was important to get Don out of there and stop the distraction. I picked up some papers, told people I would be back, and proceeded to the hallway, where Don was . . . nowhere to be found. Don had, in fact, left the building and was, presumably, on his way home.

This was far from a triumphant battle won by the new leader. It was an unsettling argument between the biggest star in Canadian sports broadcasting and a brand-new executive producer. It stayed with me for the rest of the night, and the following two days. On Monday, I sat in my office, adamant that I would not make the first move. I would not phone Don at home, to discuss the issues. Then the phone rang.

DC: Hey, John-boy. Don Cherry here!

JS: Hello, Don. How are you today?

DC: Great, just great. Just want to tell you how much fun I had on Saturday.

JS: That's good, Don. I thought the show was solid.

DC: It was. I would have liked more time, but I understand.

177

JS: Yup. We just got tight for time.

DC: I know . . . Anyway, just wanted to say thanks. Talk to you
soon. Toodle-loo!

And so our disagreement evaporated into the ether. It was over. My
relationship with Don became much stronger after that. There was trust
between us. He wouldn't belabour the rest of the show, and I would support Don in making his segment as strong and successful as possible.
That didn't stop the complaints, mind you. There were times when he
would talk about the show openings ("Nobody watches those things")
or "Satellite Hot Stove" ("What did the pretty boys say tonight"), but
he did it in the good-natured way that teammates trade jabs and barbs.
There was a touch of competitiveness to it that kept everyone at the top
of their game. There is little doubt, in my mind, that Don became better
as the show's content became deeper and more complex. There is never
anything wrong with a little sandpaper.

The event also showed the entire staff, prior to the season actually
starting, that I just might be up to doing this job. I'm not sure I believed
it yet, but that Saturday night, standing up to Don, told me I had a
chance.

Two other events stand out in my time with Don: one where we cen-
sored him, one where we didn't. Both, in the end, got little or no notice
in the media, but I suspect the viewing public understood fully what was
going on.

In the first case, we were taping Don's "Coach's Corner" segment at our
Maple Leaf Gardens studio. Don and Ron got into a rather heated discussion about some innocuous event that occurred during the week, then Don
turned to Ron and said, "That sucks." Well, for some reason, that really
bothered me. It was not something that I viewed as proper, for *Hockey Night
in Canada* and for people of any age to hear from one of our announcers.
I never minded a good argument or a little friction on the air, but I always
believed we should present the stories with class and dignity. When we

finished recording, I left the television mobile and walked through the bowels of MLG to the studio. The whole way, I was constructing my argument that we would have to retape the show, which Don hated to do.

I explained to Don and Ron that everything in the seven minutes was fine except when Don said, "That sucks." In my opinion, while it wasn't a swear word, it wasn't a word that should be heard on national television (my, how things have changed). Particularly from Don Cherry, who talks to hockey fans from ages eight to eighty. Don understood, but he didn't want to retape the segment. I suggested we bleep it out. It was either that or redo the whole segment. Don elected for the two seconds of censorship, which went off without a hitch, or any notice, as far as I can remember. I guess viewers had to imagine what he had said.

On the other occasion, Don was justified in swearing on the air, and did. It probably reflected what the entire country was feeling. In November 1996, Sheldon Kennedy bravely came forward with the horrendous stories of abuse at the hands of his junior hockey coach, Graham James, a decade earlier. It shook the hockey world and the country as a whole. It was a topic that *Hockey Night* and "Coach's Corner" could not ignore. We believed that there were many Canadians waiting to see what the show would say about these events. While much of the story was being handled adeptly by the journalists of the CBC News division, and it wasn't directly part of the day-to-day NHL, there was no doubt that we had to say something. Don wanted to say something. And he did.

We were hosting the national show from Vancouver, with a single early game in the East, which meant Ron would open the show live in Vancouver at 4:00 p.m. Pacific time, and "Coach's Corner" would follow about ninety minutes later, live. The topic of discussion for the segment would indeed be Graham James and Sheldon Kennedy. While we often discussed the topics for the show before they went to air, usually when Don was getting makeup, we were also aware that sometimes those topics, and the approach to those topics, changed as Ron and Don digested them for the duration of the first period. The preparation they went through could be described as a sparring match, both trying to argue their own points, both believing they were "psyching" the other up for the show, both trying to bring the best out of each other. Don usually had a page of notes, and Ron wrote his and the order of points from Don's. A couple of coffees later, they were ready to go.

None of us had anticipated Ron being the devil's advocate and trying to give James the benefit of the doubt. I'm not sure he believed the position he was taking on national television, but MacLean indeed did. It was not a good look. The on-air argument was real. At one point, Cherry said James should be "drawn and quartered" for what he did to Kennedy and others. Ron tried to state that any person charged with such crimes is innocent until proven guilty. To that Don uttered, "BULLSHIT!"

It reflected, I'm sure, what most people felt at the time. Except Don had said it, live. I was standing in the production mobile, inside the Vancouver arena. Directly in front of me were a half dozen people sitting at the console with their hands on buttons or keyboards or intercom panels or stopwatches. Almost in sync, a millisecond after Don uttered "BULLSHIT," they all turned and looked at me. It was a moment of sheer panic. Except, we couldn't panic. We were on the air. Ron and Don, sitting side by side, were yelling at each other, Ron pleading for sympathy, Don getting louder with hopes that Ron could actually hear him. Maybe he could yell some sense into his partner. I said the only thing I could: "Keep going, folks, it's already on the air."

Mercifully, the seven minutes ended without any more profanity. It was probably a blessing that the production crew involved had a few hours to gather themselves before actually producing a game in Vancouver that night. But Don and Ron had made the case in a manner that many in our country had been having. Don's outburst did later receive some notice. But it was hardly a controversial moment in the show's history. Only one media writer, Ken McKee of the *Toronto Star*, phoned to ask me about it. For me, then and now, all Don did was reflect the state of mind of most Canadians on the topic. It truly was bullshit. Don had never been more powerful about a subject so abhorrent. In this case, he was every Canadian.

In my time as executive producer we had healthy working relationships. We all had jobs to do, and there was a mutual respect, even when we didn't get our way. Mostly I did not want to be an obstacle between Ron and Don. They had built a strong working relationship for the seven years before I arrived and I didn't feel I should inject myself between them, even though there were times when I'm sure it was needed. Instead, I chose to manage both of them separately.

With Ron it was usually a daily call leading up to Saturday night, maybe a breakfast meeting in the neighbourhood (we lived about ten minutes from each other). There was constant communication. After all, Ron MacLean wasn't the weatherman in Red Deer anymore; he was the face of *Hockey Night*. I valued his opinion and the depth of his knowledge, even though I didn't always agree with him and often would not go down one of his "rabbit holes."

As far as Don went, we had built a system of support for him as he prepared for those first intermissions every Saturday. The assignment fell to the desk of Kathy Broderick. Really, she became Don's personal producer. She was available to Don all week as he found the need for video highlights, pictures, and background information. In 1994 she was an employee of Molstar, but that didn't concern me. What we needed was what was best for the show. Don needed someone to work with on a constant basis, and as the show grew from three hours to six hours and then to seven, it was difficult for me to be there for Don's every whim. Kathy fit the bill perfectly. She knew hockey, she was opinionated, she had a very high standard, and she was tough. She might have been tougher than any of us. I liked her ability to tell the unvarnished truth—to me, to Don, to Ron, to anyone. What made her so valuable is she loved *Hockey Night in Canada* and what it stood for. She understood the history of the show, and believed in it. She became such an integral part of our success. Not just "Coach's Corner," but "Satellite Hot Stove" and the first attempt at a studio show for the Stanley Cup playoffs. So much of Don's success, and his ability to make his seven minutes on Saturday nights the best it could be, was due to his total, undying trust in Kathy's work. Whether it was a video clip from an NHL game, the World Junior anthem, or pictures of fallen soldiers and front-liners, Kathy delivered for Don each and every week.

Cherry was a pure showman. Like Jackie Gleason, who I'm sure he loved. As simple as Don wanted the production to be of "Coach's Corner," he was demanding of himself, of Ron, and of anyone directly involved. Like Gleason, he understood what made for good, entertaining television. He knew that perceived conflict made people sit up and watch. He also had tremendous comedic timing. Combine that with spending a whole week planning such a short segment, and things could get combustible. Fun, but combustible.

Often I was asked how I could let Don do what he wants on his segment. As I noted earlier, I viewed our Saturday show like a newspaper. Don, in that instance, was our number one columnist. As editor or publisher, I didn't want to tell Don what to say or how to say it. In many ways, what we did for Don (as we did for the boys on "Satellite Hot Stove") was create parameters within which to work. It was a liberating feeling for all and spurred a diversity of opinions and information for the viewers. We held them accountable for their actions, but we didn't want voices and views to be homogenized.

I truly believed I understood Don and his playbook. It was easy to sense what his topics would be on any given Saturday. If there was something controversial in the NHL that week, we were fully aware that the country would wait until Saturday to hear from Don, and the guys on "Satellite Hot Stove" for that matter.

Maybe the best example of managing Don and to a lesser extent, the message, was the last week of February 2000. On Monday, in the last minute of play between the Boston Bruins and the Vancouver Canucks, Bruins defenceman Marty McSorley slashed Canucks forward Donald

Brashear in the head. Brashear collapsed, bouncing his head on the ice, unconscious. Vancouver goalie Garth Snow charged at McSorley, and the few seconds remaining in the game became nothing more than a quagmire of pushing, shoving, heckling, and booing. The moment I saw the events occur, my first thought was that we had five days to work with Don to temper the message of the next "Coach's Corner."

You see, McSorley was one of Don's favourite players, while Brashear was not very high on that list. Also aggravating the situation was the fact that Brashear had been taunting the Bruins players, in particular their goaltender Byron Dafoe, all night long. Despite the fact that Boston had fired Cherry so many years ago, he had always had a soft spot for the club and the city of Boston. Combine the love of the team and the affection for Marty McSorley—and the following Saturday had the ingredients of an incendiary bomb. Over the week, it became more than a hockey event. Vancouver prosecutors and police were now investigating a potential crime. Our job was not to make McSorley a martyr and become part of the story.

Tuesday was a typical preparation day for us, reviewing our long-term plans, made over the previous months. First, discussions of what our big feature of the week would be, as well as confirming who would be our regulars on "Hot Stove." For the late game, our first intermission was always some sort of packaged event, like the "Labatt Blue Shoot-Out," our Canada-wide venture to have a regular person score on a breakaway. Plus we had Kelly Hrudey and his segment "Behind the Mask"—our attempt to create programming specifically for the Western Canadian market. Kelly had made the move from player to broadcaster flawlessly. He combined a keen eye with a folksy, no-nonsense approach and quickly understood what it meant to be on *Hockey Night*.

Second intermission was "Scoreboard Saturday," which gave us one more chance to review all the key events and highlights of the day. This was an item that the national show always built, and 99 percent of the time it was on tape well before the intermission began. If there was late-breaking news it created an issue and more work for Ron MacLean, but it was the best, most effective way to build the perception of Ron anchoring the whole night, without having our host and a whole crew having to stay until one in the morning. We also had the luxury of talented people like Sherali Najak (when he wasn't directing games) and Kathy Broderick (the same Kathy who managed Don Cherry's demands) to make sure we didn't miss anything all night long. Simultaneously, we always knew that our western host, either Scott Russell or Scott Oake, could manage any last-minute curveballs, like a trade or other news, if need be.

We also felt comfortable that whatever our main feature ("The Head-liner") didn't cover, Don or the panelists of the "Hot Stove" would. We had built-in safety nets to ensure that no major item in the NHL or the game of hockey, for that matter, would be missed. This was before the instantaneous world of social media. The two cable channels were doing a great job of covering the game, but we had built enough brand equity in our show and our personalities that viewers would wait to see what *HNIC* would address, and how.

There was no question the McSorley-Brashear event would be dis-cussed on our Saturday broadcast. By Wednesday, we were aware that Don wanted to protect McSorley and probably criticize Brashear for the events of Monday night. Don was smart about building the drama. He would always refuse to comment publicly about what he was going to say. "You'll have to tune in on Saturday to hear what I think."

We had three days to polish the message, without compromising how Don did his job on Saturday night. I never wanted to tell Don what to say, or how to say it, so long as nothing compromised what *Hockey Night* stood for. I was passionate that our show had a role to play in making the game a welcoming, enjoyable, entertaining escape from everyday life. We wanted it to be a destination for people to feel Canadian. We felt that we could promote and protect Canadian-style hockey and buffer it from big busi-ness (particularly American big business) and keep it real and keep it ours. Most who worked on the show understood that vision, including Don.

The 1985 Stanley Cup Final. Ralph Mellanby's final year, and my fifth Final in five years.

The first broadcaster of the Calgary Flames, October 1980. Don Wallace and I flank our announcers, host Jim Van Horne, colour man Gary Dornhoefer, play-by-play man Ed Whelan.

I make a pregame cameo appearance during rehearsal with our host Chris Cuthbert, May 1986. This was just prior to my final game as producer of *Hockey Night* (the first time).

The Canadian Football Network was part of my life for four seasons. We had a great production crew that included Dave Moir, Jim Eady, Larry Isaac, and Larry Brown (July 1987). Longtime friend and broadcaster Dave Hodge and Grey Cup champion Neil Lumsden were part of our announce team.

Spending some quality time with two greats, Herb Brooks and John Davidson, 1989.

In Barcelona, Spain, at the Olympic Games, July 1992, with Doug Beeforth and Rod Black.

For the first time at *Hockey Night in Canada*, we created the Stanley Cup Playoff Studio, April 1996. That's Ron MacLean talking with Doug Gilmour, Kelly Hrudey, and me.

In October 1998, *Hockey Night in Canada* changed sponsorship from Molson to Labatt. We had to rebuild our broadcast team. *Back:* Pat Flatley, Mark Lee, Steve Armitage, John Davidson, Scott Oake, Al Strachan, Alan Clark, Ron MacLean. *Front:* Me, Dick Irvin, Scott Russell, Don Wittman, Labatt President David Don Kitchen, Harry Neale, Bob Cole, Kelly Hrudey, Chris Cuthbert.

Left: A quiet moment on the Ice at Maple Leaf Gardens, February 1999. It was just hours before MLG hosted its last NHL game. The Maple Leafs hosted the Chicago Blackhawks.

Right: Not many producers get their own hockey card. For the 1997–98 season, Pinnacle made a set for all the *Hockey Night in Canada* announcers. They surprised me with my own. Certainly a collector's item.

Summer of 1998. Dick Irvin announces he doesn't want to work in the broadcast booth anymore. I wouldn't let him retire, telling him, "He was the last link to the history of the show." While he didn't do games anymore, he still made regular appearances on the show telling pertinent historical stories.

MLSE President Richard Peddie and I launch Leafs TV and Raptors NBA TV, September 2001.

An emotional moment for me, as I speak at the funeral for Frank Selke Jr., March 2013. Frank was a huge influence on me for many years. Just days before he passed away, he phoned the house to say, "I love you . . . don't change." I was a puddle of tears for hours.

The closing of Rexall Place in Edmonton, April 2016. It was one of the highlights of my on-camera career. Particularly when I could spend time, on ice, with Bob Cole and Wayne Gretzky.

As part of the salute to the 1984–85 Edmonton Oilers, voted the greatest team in NHL history, Dave Hodge and I interview some of the players on that team at the Hockey Hall of Fame, January 2018. *Left to Right:* Dave Hodge, Kevin Lowe, Wayne Gretzky, Paul Coffey, Mark Napier, Pat Hughes, Mike Krushelnyski, me.

Being inducted to the BC Hockey Hall of Fame, in July 2017, was a special night for me. It was made that much better being inducted by friend Bob Nicholson.

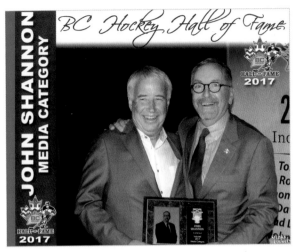

I have spent plenty of time around the Commissioner of the NHL, Gary Bettman. We have not always agreed on issues, but we have much more in common than we do differences. My respect for the man is immense.

Our Sportsnet free agent crew, July 2019. Say what you want, we always had fun. *Left to Right:* Doug MacLean, Kevin Bieksa, Marc Savard, Sam Cosentino, Colby Armstrong, Caroline Cameron, Jeff Marek, Nick Kypreos, David Amber, Brian Burke, Kelly Hrudey, Elliotte Friedman, Chris Johnston, me.

The McSorley story, however, required some special massaging. That meant a quick visit to Don, at his house. Coffee in hand (we both drank it black), I appeared Thursday morning. Don, dressed down in a sweatshirt, came to the door with Blue on his tail. This was Blue No. 4, I believe, a beautiful American bull terrier, always at Don's side or asleep at his feet. Petting Blue was like touching a seventy-pound piece of pure muscle. Don and I settled in at the kitchen table to discuss, in a roundabout way, what Saturday's content about his friend Marty would be. Over the two hours, our conversation wandered in and out of the McSorley situation to what was right and wrong with the Maple Leafs or Canadiens or Bruins. It was also interrupted by the phone ringing, with people trying to lobby Don to talk about certain things, or promote their charity game, on the next show. He was always polite, welcoming, and compassionate on the phone, without making any promises. He was a master at making all those around him, or on the phone, feel special—truly a kind and gentle man. Our conversation on McSorley was conciliatory. I knew exactly what he wanted to say, but believed that it would not be an opinion many outside of the McSorley family would support. What we at *Hockey Night*, I explained to Don, must not do is inject ourselves into any legal discussion that the Crown attorney or the Vancouver police were having. Our job was to entertain.

Telling Don what he could or couldn't say would never work. In fact, it might exacerbate the situation. But it was important to discuss all of the aspects of the incident, and discuss what role *we* wanted to play. Don needed to appreciate that much of our audience were in Vancouver. They wanted blood! We couldn't prey on Marty and we couldn't protect him at all costs, either. We needed to be fair. We needed to explain what happened. While I never once heard from Commissioner Gary Bettman on the topic, you knew that the people in the New York office would also be interested in Don's take. While McSorley had already been suspended indefinitely, Bettman hadn't ruled on the incident. We did not want to make any statement on the event and be wrong. That would hurt not only Don's credibility, but *Hockey Night's*, too. That, in a nutshell, was the difference between his job and mine.

On Saturday, while Don was getting his TV makeup on, I made one last visit, coffee in hand. Again, we talked it through. By this time Don had formulated a story line and an opinion that worked for both of us. If memory serves me, I suggested one more turn of phrase and we left the makeup table both satisfied that what we were doing was fair and balanced. I'm sure Don thought I had overstepped my position a bit, but he also knew that I always had his best interest in mind. He trusted me, and I always believed in and protected him.

The fact that the memory of the actual show has faded tells me one thing: Don did a solid job, without fanning the flames. I'm sure he felt he protected McSorley, but we also got the message across that Marty had to pay the price for the slash.

The real and genuine Don Cherry showed up for me after my contract wasn't renewed by the CBC in August 2000. We had finished the Stanley Cup Final that year in Dallas. The New Jersey Devils won Game 6 at Reunion Arena and our season was over. The playoffs that year had been like any other: passionate, physical, exhilarating, long, and exhausting.

Management at CBC had gone through a major overhaul. The friendly faces of Jim Byrd and Alan Clark and others had been replaced by those who didn't appreciate the value of sports and *Hockey Night in Canada*. It had gotten so bad, one of our country's finest producers, Doug Sellars, sought greener pastures at Fox Sports Networks (with another Canadian, Arthur Smith). Sellars was the man who back in 1994 had convinced the CBC that I wasn't the devil incarnate. We became key components of what Alan Clark had built at CBC in sports. I ran hockey; Doug ran the rest of production. It was a great partnership. In fact, it would flourish once more in our careers, before Doug's tragic death in Los Angeles in 2013.

So there we were, Don, Ron, and me leaving Dallas. We usually flew together, simply because it was so entertaining for me to be around them. It was good for them, too—someone had to carry the Sharpie pen they both needed to sign for fans, and someone had to take the pictures with fans, too. But mostly, on the plane we had a bit of privacy to enjoy each other's company and discuss some ideas for the upcoming production.

Invariably, Don and I would end up discussing history and the greatness of Sir Francis Drake, Admiral Horatio Nelson, or Winston Churchill. Like many who ended up coaching, Cherry studied these men for their tactics and their ability to create and reinforce loyalty of those around them. But this was a different flight home. No production ideas needed to be discussed. We were all tired of the grind. Sixty straight days of work, travel, airports, arenas, hotels, and, by June, Texas heat. It was a quiet flight, until Ron tapped me on the shoulder and shoved a piece of paper in front of me. It was out of the American Airlines in-flight magazine. The page he tore out was a story about Tim Russert of NBC. Russert was by then established as a strong political commentator with his election "whiteboard" and job as the host of NBC's *Meet the Press*. Ron was adamant I should read it—an article about how Russert had started as a producer but became an announcer.

Not only did I read it, I kept it. It's somewhere in the scrap albums in my office. I had a sense of two things that day. I knew my days at CBC were numbered—whether Ron knew was another story—and I knew I had a future goal in mind. Ron didn't specifically suggest I should become an announcer, but the implication was there. It wouldn't happen right away, but it would happen.

There were changes coming to the CBC. New senior management didn't understand what we had done to reinvent *Hockey Night*. They didn't appreciate how the hockey group interacted with other departments and viewed our group, fairly or unfairly, as arrogant. I believed the show needed to be nimble and proactive, and quite honestly, I didn't want to wait for input from people who didn't understand what the show stood for, and what our group had done to make it the gold standard of sports television. Management had grown intolerant of hockey's position at the network, that the rules didn't apply to the "one and only" *Hockey Night in Canada*. Also, my contract was to expire at the end of August, with nary a word of a new one.

I made a few tactical errors with the new management. I was a big name and I was not happy that the people who made my life so enjoyable at the corporation, Clark and Sellars, were gone.

In June 2000, I overstepped my bounds publicly. Bill Houston had long been the media writer for the *Globe and Mail*. His "Truth and Rumours" column was the premier media read in Canadian newspapers. Bill had always been very supportive of both Ralph Mellanby and me, probably because we loved to read our names in print and, for the most part, always spoke on the record. We spoke with authority, from a big pedestal.

After that final season, Bill asked me to grade the announcer teams at *Hockey Night*. A report card, as it were. Whether it was exhaustion from the playoffs or frustration with management, I did it. It reflected my frustration with some announcers, exasperation with others, and very little admiration for a few. It was a stupid, stupid move. I knew it, the moment all those words were on the broadsheet. I intended it to be a silly display of my own ego and power, but it became a reminder that I was just a cog in the wheel.

Within hours of publication, my words came back to me in the form of an internal memo reminding me that the CBC doesn't air its dirty laundry in public. They were right. I was wrong.

My dismissal from the executive producer's job came by phone in early August. It was over in four minutes. Numbness set in. It had been the one job I had always wanted. I had fought my way back to the show. Back into the country. It had been seven years with the best job in television in our country. We had moved the show from a 1970s rerun to a proactive voice of the people in the game that our country loves beyond reproach.

Oh my God, it hurt. I was embarrassed. I had been told I wasn't good enough. It would be in the paper. Again.

Though I felt sorry for myself, I felt terrible for my family: my wife, Mickee, and my kids, Jake and Maja. They had been proud of what we had accomplished. They had sacrificed so much family time with me, as I focused every hour of every day on making *Hockey Night in Canada* the show of record in the game.

It had been just three years since Mickee's cancer surgeries, when I made a bad decision to return to work rather than be with her. Now I had to ask, was any of it worth it?

After the announcement of my departure, the lines of support were tremendous. Many calls, thousands of kind, consolatory words. I was surprised by many who called, disappointed by those who didn't. But that's to be expected. Learning how to manage one's dismissal should be a life lesson at university. It's a very practical, real skill. Mickee always calls it "the bloodletting." Like she had said eighteen years earlier in Minnesota, there's always a group of people who are truly concerned for your welfare, and then there are those who want to see how miserable and angry you are about the events that took place.

The first group, those who care, will phone again and again because they are true friends. The "bloodletters" will call once, commiserate for ten minutes, tell you how miserable they are in their job, hang up the phone, and never be heard from again. As a person who has lived this saga more than once, there are bloodletters on every corner. It has also motivated me to call people when they lose their jobs and make a mental note to call again in two weeks, just as a checkup.

MacLean and Cherry were avatars of that first group. They have been long and loyal friends, through thick and thin and the three different variations of *Hockey Night in Canada* that involved us.

In December of that year, Don, Ron, and I had a celebratory holiday lunch at one of Don's restaurants in suburban Toronto. It was the first time we had been together since that flight home from Dallas. Both of them were in the throes of the *HNIC* season. I, on the other hand, was trying to project an air of confidence in a time of uncertainty. No jobs were to be found and, at that point, there was very little promise. Publicly I tried to convince everyone that something would be coming down the pike soon. Trying to tell them. Trying to convince myself.

As the lunch ended and we were leaving the restaurant, both men extended their hands in friendship. In the palms of their hands were cheques. Not small amounts. I told them I couldn't take them, but of course, they insisted. "And it's not really for you, anyway," Don said. "It's for Mickee and the kids. Christmas is coming." It was a display of loyalty and friendship I have never forgotten.

Three weeks later, on Christmas Eve, I had to make a late run for milk and bread, only to return to the house to find Mickee visibly shaken. In my short absence, Donald S. Cherry had appeared at our front door. Under his arms were gifts, Christmas presents labelled for Jake and Maja. "I wanted to make sure Jake and Maja had a merry Christmas," he had said. That's why Don Cherry is my friend. And Ron MacLean, too. Loyalty, above all.

I felt bad for Don when he was removed from the show a few years back for his comment about "you people." For as long as I can remember, Don had taken time in his segment to promote the sale of poppies for the veterans in the first two weeks of November. He had become part of the dying breed of Canadians who understood the pain and suffering of the world wars, and had wanted to honour those who served. But even in that period of time, when Don started his advocacy to the end of his tenure at *Hockey Night*, the makeup of our country had changed. Throughout the 1980s, the 1990s, and into the new century, Canada became a welcoming, diverse country. It made our nation better, stronger, more worldly. To believe in Canada, we needed to understand how our many cultures were changing the country. As in tune as Don was with his audience, he didn't necessarily change at the same speed as the country. It really is a shame. He loves our country. He loves our game. He has done far more good things for people, privately and publicly, than his departure would suggest.

THIRTEEN
THE MIRACULOUS
MR. BROOKS

IT SEEMS I HAVE AN AFFINITY WITH COACHES. GOALTENDERS AND COACHES, ACTU-
ally. I always believed that goalies, more than other players, would make
better analysts because they have to play every minute of the game, or
watch every minute of the game. Similar to catchers in baseball, goalies
never relax and are always thinking about what happens next. That is
perfect for a broadcaster.

Davidson, Millen, Hrudey, Healy, Garrett—should I go on? It's the
same story for coaches like Bowman, Neale, MacLean.

Then there was Herb Brooks. If any friendship could be considered a
wild ride, it would be the one I had with Herb. American vs. Canadian.
Both alpha dogs, both passionate hockey experts, and two men who always wanted the last word.

I first met Herb during the 1980 Stanley Cup Final. Mellanby had
hired Herb to do a guest appearance for *HNIC* during the Islanders vs.
Flyers final that year. It was a brief handshake and a five-minute interview

with Dave Hodge for the hero coach of the recent U.S. men's hockey Olympic gold medal in Lake Placid, New York. My second meeting was not as cordial, in the Stampede Corral in Calgary while Brooks was coaching the New York Rangers. His team was playing the Flames, coached by Bob Johnson. I wanted to expand on the personal relationship between Brooks and Johnson—Brooks had been the coach of the University of Minnesota Golden Gophers, while Johnson was at the University of Wisconsin, coaching the hockey Badgers. This was perfect. Now all I had to do was get the two coaches to talk about each other. Easy, right?

Johnson loved to talk and loved being the centre of attention. He could speak for five minutes and say very little. I had learned to tell him what I was looking for in a statement, and while he would tweak a few words, I would always get what I needed. He loved looking smart and being the voice of the team, to the point that when we were at practices, before we interviewed any players, we always talked to him first. If we didn't, our player sessions were often short, or eliminated totally. So Johnson (whose son Mark played for Brooks on the Lake Placid team) played along with my story line about Brooks vs. Johnson, Minnesota vs. Wisconsin, Gophers vs. Badgers.

Herb—not so much. I reminded him that we had met a few years earlier at Nassau Coliseum, then home of the Islanders, but that didn't seem to impress the Rangers coach. His mind was somewhere else. He didn't really understand the world of media and television, but as an NHL coach, he knew it was a necessary evil. Herb loved being in charge, controlling the message, and I suppose doing media interviews meant he wasn't in charge. With initial introductions out of the way, I made a simple ask of Brooks: just tell us what you think of Bob Johnson.

HB: I don't want to answer that.

JS: We are just trying to put context to the two of you coaching against each other again.

HB: I don't like that question.

JS: We aren't looking for *War and Peace* here, Herb. I just want to hear about two old rivals.

HB: Listen, I'm happy to talk about my team, about our road trip, about lots of stuff about the Rangers. But I'm not talking about him.

JS: Well then, you can go.

HB: Wait, what?

JS: You can go. I don't want to waste your time. And I'm not making you do something you don't want to do.

HB: Hold on, what do you want me to say?

With that, Herb gave us some inane comment about college hockey and how heated it gets, without mentioning Bob Johnson's name, and he was gone.

To Herb, hockey was only for winning, not for entertainment.

Only later did I understand how much these two hated each other. Johnson, the consummate showman, was happy to wax poetic in the name of entertainment. Brooks, the consummate coach, couldn't bullshit his way through to have fun. It went beyond the two men. Legend has it that one night in Madison, Wisconsin, Bob's wife, Martha, was ringing her cowbell constantly, directly behind Brooks's visiting bench. At one point Herb turned around and told Martha, in no uncertain terms, that he was prepared to take the cowbell and put it somewhere unpleasant. And so the rivalry grew.

My third meeting with Herb was the beginning of a four-year relationship on American cable television, and it could have easily been one of that network's reality shows. We were both hired by the Cablevision people in the summer of 1988 to work on the national package for SportsChannel America. SportsChannel was controlled by the Dolan family and existed primarily in five or six eastern states. Buying the hockey rights was their first foray into trying to get national coverage from all the cable and satellite providers. Quite frankly, it was twenty years ahead of its time.

However, it quickly became apparent, from both a financial perspective and a distribution perspective, that buying those rights was a major mistake. The fledgling network had spent more money than any previous U.S. network on the rights to the NHL and had not been able to grow its subscriber base or footprint. It was a financial disaster. There were a few who did flourish with the new deal, though. I was certainly one of them. Still living in Calgary, I was able to produce a game or two per week, all over the league, particularly in Los Angeles, where the SportsChannel deal would be able to highlight the arrival of Wayne Gretzky to play for the Kings. I think in the first two seasons, I made forty trips to California, which was *not* hard to deal with. It was in L.A., and Marina del Rey specifically, that my next meeting with Herb Brooks occurred.

Prior to the 1988–89 season, I went to dinner with Brooks and play-by-play announcer Jiggs McDonald at a seafood place called the Black Whale, a frequent haunt of many hockey people in Southern California. Our reintroduction was cordial enough; the most nervous person at the table was Jiggs. He was concerned that "Fiery John" and "Opinionated Herb" would not get along. After all, our paths to our positions were completely different, and as Jiggs knew, we both expected to be captains of the ship. In many ways, it was a science experiment. You would either get the combustibility of nitroglycerin or the satisfying taste of a dry martini.

We got through dinner without argument, although I do recall Herb moving the salt and pepper shakers, the vinegar, the napkin holder, and the cutlery all over the table to explain how his flow system of hockey would work in the NHL. I got the sense he would have rather been plotting a game plan with his coaching staff before opening night of the season than sitting with two TV guys.

The ritual then on game days was to have a quick breakfast meeting, attend the morning skate, and then head to the team dressing rooms to talk to the players and coaches. While Jiggs and I did that, Herb wanted nothing to do with talking to players, and he certainly wouldn't sit with coaches and listen to them. That was not in his DNA. My disappointment with Herb for not participating was obvious. On the way back to the hotel at noon, I told him that if he was to make a go of working in broadcasting, getting some time with the coaches and players was vital to creating story lines for the show. He was not interested. It was apparent, even before our first broadcast, that Herb was using the exposure as a placeholder—until his next coaching job.

It was even more apparent after that first game. That night was Gretzky's debut with the silver and black of the Los Angeles Kings. The show—the event, because that's what it was—went relatively well. We made sure to focus 99 percent of the show on No. 99. It was opening night for a new national rights holder in the United States, and the feedback as the night went on was very positive. Even Herb seemed to embrace the magnitude of Wayne's first game for a new team, in a new country. But after the game, he was anything but ebullient. He sat in the backseat of the car with a scowl. The rest of us were rather pleased with ourselves. Good game, great show, first night on a new network. But Herb wouldn't even crack a smile.

JS: Herb, come on, I thought we did a good job.

HB: Did you see what he did?

JS: Who?

HB: Ftorek [Robbie, the Kings' coach].

JS: What did he do?

HB: The fucking power play. It was awful.

That, in a nutshell, was Herb Brooks as a broadcaster. He really had no interest in being on the air. He just wanted to be behind a bench. He had such a competitive drive to win, that was the only thing that mattered.

On another occasion in St. Louis, we were still trying to convince Herb to play the broadcast game. The powers that be at SportsChannel believed that Herb's marquee value would drive viewers. Joe Micheletti, who had played for Herb at Minnesota, was an assistant coach for the Blues under coach Brian Sutter. After some prodding, Sutter agreed to have an announcers' meeting with our group, including Herb, who reluctantly agreed to attend, I suspect because one of his players (Micheletti) was on the staff. What occurred during the meeting was right out of a western movie: a classic standoff.

Sutter—a tough, rugged Albertan—sat at his desk giving little or no information. Brooks—a stubborn, college-taught Minnesotan—sat stoically in the corner. The meeting was going nowhere. Trying to prompt a conversation, I noted that Brian's wall calendar showed ten games in the next twenty days, with no back-to-back games. That's a lot of travel. I asked him what he planned for a practice schedule. Before Sutter could answer the question, Brooks interrupted by telling the Blues coach how to run his off-day schedule. The conversation was one-way, for about five minutes. Our private announcers' session, with a fuming Brian Sutter, was over before you could say, "Do you believe in miracles?"

Brooks was a legend, particularly in the United States. No one was more passionate about the game of hockey—the pure game on the ice—than Herb. For that alone, I had tremendous reverence for him. No one quietly enjoyed his celebrity more than Herb. On one trip to Los Angeles, it became truly evident just how famous he was.

It was a rare Saturday afternoon game between Mario Lemieux's Penguins and Wayne Gretzky's Kings. Both put on a show that day, but nothing as memorable as what would occur a few hours later at a nearby hotel bar. Unlike most trips, the Penguins had elected to stay in L.A. for the night before travelling on to their next game. Sitting in the hotel lobby, Brooks and I were kibitzing about the show, the two stars, and how their two respective coaches weren't using them properly. Moments later, Penguins broadcaster Paul Steigerwald and Mario Lemieux walked by and said hello. Mario was very polite, and obviously respectful of Herb, and invited us to the hotel bar, where Mario said a friend was joining them for a drink. This was perfect. It was the type of conversation we had been imploring Herb to have with many players, and here was one of the game's greats.

So there we were, at the Sky Bar at the Marriott by Los Angeles International Airport—Brooks, Steigerwald, Lemieux, and me—talking about the afternoon game, when Mario's friend arrived. It was Michael Keaton, who had just finished shooting the first Batman movie and was on the previous week's cover of *Time* magazine. Keaton was a Pittsburgher, and obviously had become friends with the Penguins' best player. It truly was a great table to be at. That night, many fans came by the table to say hello to the trio and get an autograph. If we had fifty autograph seekers at the table, forty-nine of them were for the coach of the 1980 U.S. Olympic team. The Miracle on Ice team. A team that transcended the game. Herb loved every minute of it.

We also had some rocky experiences as two competitive guys who wanted to be in charge. One night in Pittsburgh, Herb was in the broadcast booth working alongside Gary Thorne. Herb was not at his best this night, and I was not shy in trying to help him get through the game, talking in his earpiece, as the night went on. I was also forcing Herb to analyze replays that I viewed important, but he probably did not. According to Thorne, he had to restrain Herb from coming down from the booth to the TV mobile to fight with me after the second intermission. Then, after the game, Herb was nowhere to be found.

On another occasion, late in one regular season, for a game in Edmonton, Herb elected to travel the day of the game rather than the day before, which was against network policy. He neglected to tell anyone of his plan. By midnight, I finally tracked down Brooks, at his home in White Bear Lake, Minnesota. I told him in no uncertain terms that I found it hard to believe the game's greatest coach refused to be part of a team. I told him he was selfish. With that I hung up. As the producer, I began to worry when we were short an announcer at the morning skate. By five o'clock, I was apoplectic. When Brooks finally arrived at the arena, he made a beeline for me:

HB: Hey—no one has ever talked to me like that ever before.

JS: Well, there's a first time for everything.

HB: Listen, I thought—

JS: There's your problem, Herb: you were thinking again. Just do
your fucking job.

It was hardly a great motivational speech, like the one Brooks gave his
team in 1980. But it was the most effective thing I could think of. The
rest of our stint together at SportChannel was stilted, but professional.
We only ever had brief, cold conversations over those two years. Even
when I moved to the Twin Cities to produce North Stars hockey, and
Herb was living just miles away, we never spoke.

In October 1994, after I had returned to *Hockey Night in Canada*,
I received a letter from Regina, Saskatchewan, on stationery from the
Regina Inn. Inside the envelope was a newspaper clipping from the Regina *Leader-Post*, with the announcement of my return to *HNIC*. In the
margin, scribbled in that left-handed scrawl that Herb always used, was a
note of congratulations and the line: "I always knew you were the best."

By then Herb had already been behind the bench for Lou Lamori-
ello's New Jersey Devils, and was then scouting for the Pittsburgh Penguins, who were managed by Craig Patrick, his old assistant coach from
the Lake Placid team. He was comfortable being in the game, around
the rink, trying to help the Penguins stay at or near the top of the stand-
ings. With his reputation, he was still viewed as an international hockey
legend. That's why he was hired by the French Ice Hockey Federation to
coach their team at the 1998 Olympic Winter Games in Nagano, Japan.
We were responsible for the coverage of the men's and women's hockey
tournament, and not long after our arrival at the rink one day, before the
Games began, I heard yelling across the arena. It was Herb—slim, trim,
and decked out in a blue French Olympic hockey sweat suit.

"Hey, Hockey Night in Shanada!"

John Davidson, who was standing beside me, doubled over in laughter.

At that moment, the animosity, the edge, disappeared. It was replaced by a deep, sincere friendship. We both had succeeded in accomplishing our lifelong goals: Herb returning behind the bench and me back at *Hockey Night in Canada*. We laughed, told stories, and shared our love of the game. It carried through his time as coach of the Penguins and then to his last great hurrah at the 2002 Olympic Winter Games in Salt Lake City. Every time we spoke, whether privately or in a group, it always started with "Hockey Night in Shanada."

Just seventeen months after the Salt Lake City Olympics, where Pat Quinn's Canadian team defeated Brooks's American team, Herb returned to the Twin Cities, where he was always viewed as a hero, and died in a single-car traffic accident. Apparently he was travelling back from the set of *Miracle*, a film about the Lake Placid hockey story, starring Kurt Russell as Herb. He was acting as the technical director on the movie. He fell asleep at the wheel, rolled his car, and died.

Our friendship of almost twenty years had its ups and downs, but it was one of mutual respect and love of the game of hockey. It took almost a decade for us to realize that we had much more in common than we had differences. The laughs we were able to share at the Olympics in Nagano and Salt Lake City cemented our bond. Herb's death put into perspective the importance of being more open and honest, and respectful of others.

FOURTEEN
THE TURNS AT THE TURN OF THE CENTURY

MY POSITION AS EXECUTIVE PRODUCER AT CBC ENDED, AS I SAID, WITH A PHONE
call. It came at a time when the television universe was exploding. We had entered the digital age.

In Canada, the governing body of radio and television, Canadian Radio-television and Telecommunications (CRTC), had just granted more than forty new licenses for new specialty television signals. Some of those were for sports. Included on that list were TSN, a hockey channel co-owned by the NHL, and a Toronto-based company called Insight Sports. TSN also had plans for a women's sports channel, WTSN, and Maple Leaf Sports & Entertainment (the parent company of the Maple Leafs and the NBA's Toronto Raptors) had plans for not one, but two channels. One was dedicated to the Maple Leafs hockey team; the other was to be a basketball channel with a focus on the Raptors and the Vancouver Grizzlies (who at the time were rumoured to be relocating to St. Louis or Memphis). While I already had an agreement with NBC to work in Salt Lake City two years hence, I felt in my bones that one of these ventures could be a good landing spot for me.

For obvious reasons, I ruled out any chance of working at TSN. I had turned down two quality job offers from them in the past, and my relationship with Rick Brace was far from rosy. But I did phone the commissioner of the NHL, Gary Bettman, to suggest I would be a great candidate for his new NHL Network. The league was partnering with TSN to create an all-hockey network in this new digital sphere in Canada. As always, Gary was supportive and polite. But an opportunity to join the new network never came.

As August turned to September and the last few months of 2000, my opportunities for employment grew slimmer and dimmer. And as *Hockey Night in Canada* came back on the air, it became clear that the show actually could go on without me. That hurt—a lot. I don't think I let my guard down in public, but I know that Mickee could see it every time she looked at me. At one point, in late October, I joked that perhaps I should get my real estate license. She just laughed.

The low point came in November, when my severance package ran out and we were running short of money. Humbly and embarrassingly, I had to ask a friend for a loan just to make sure we could get through the winter. In an act of friendship and charity, that friend couriered the money to the house the next day. I assured him that he would be paid back when I got back on my feet, and he was repaid, with interest. I will never forget what he did for my family and me. We remain friends to this day.

As fortune would have it, everything began to happen at the same time in December 2000. I received three phone calls: one was from Vancouver, one from New York City, and the last from Toronto.

The Vancouver call and subsequent meeting was with Paul Carson, a local media legend who was launching an all-sports radio station in Vancouver that would eventually be called TEAM 1040. Carson and I had known each other for almost twenty years, from my many visits to the West Coast to produce games, and a brief working relationship in the

North American Soccer League. It seems that Carson had heard of my interest to go on the air, after all these years. He wanted to gauge my interest in moving to Vancouver and doing just that. He had heard my appearances on radio in Toronto, predominantly *Prime Time Sports* with Bob McCown, and thought I might fit into their plans. Though the money wasn't great, it was a psychological boost at a time when I truly needed it. We met for a long conversation over breakfast in Toronto with Paul Reinhart, the retired NHL player whom I knew well from my time in the West. Paul was to be an original investor in the station. As interesting as the opportunity sounded, there were no guarantees for success, and it meant a move of some sort for our young family. But I wasn't saying no—after all, I didn't have a job and needed to be flexible.

Not forty-five hours went by when the phone rang again. This time it was Glen Sather, who was now running the New York Rangers. He had heard of my frustrations through mutual friends in Edmonton and wanted me to consider coming to New York to run the in-arena presentation for the hockey club. As much as I had been part of running in-arena productions before, it wasn't ideal. But again, it was a relief that something positive was happening.

Then, on the eighteenth, a call came from the Toronto Maple Leafs. It was, to my surprise, the team's president, Ken Dryden, whom I had known from his playing days in Montreal. In fact, I had had some interesting conversations with Dryden in my time at *Hockey Night*. Those conversations had put a strain on our relationship.

The first involved an idea Ken wanted to do for the show. He proposed a twenty-minute mini-documentary on the history of the goalie mask. The concept actually intrigued me. Dryden had already produced his award-winning book *The Game* into an eight-part documentary series for the CBC. A new Ken-produced series was something I could get into.

There were pitfalls, though. We had no time for a twenty-minute feature. *Perhaps* we could go for two ten-minute features on adjacent nights, but twenty just wasn't possible. The other concern was cost. Ken thought he needed north of $50,000 for the feature. A regular season game—two and a half hours of airtime—costs about that. Features for *HNIC* in those days were budgeted at $5,000 each. Two features for the cost of ten was not even worth considering. While Dryden was not happy with my answer, I felt he understood my position and our conversation ended cordially.

The other conversation was not so cordial. It surrounded a presentation of an award to Curtis Joseph, the starting goaltender of the Toronto Maple Leafs. Joseph's agent, Don Meehan, called one day early in the week to discuss whether or not *Hockey Night in Canada* would be interested in covering the presentation before a game in the coming weeks. At the time (and in many ways still), Meehan and his company, Newport Sports Management, was the most dynamic hockey player agency on the planet. Saying no to a Newport client might have ramifications, perhaps with the more than one hundred other clients they have, or perhaps in getting quality "insider" information for our show, particularly "Satellite Hot Stove." But I didn't need convincing of this. Joseph was, by far, the most popular player on the team, and maybe, at that time, in the country. Working with Newport on this was a win-win.

I immediately agreed to cover the ceremony, with one caveat: while we covered the presentation, the lights in the arena had to be on.

Every time the Maple Leafs had one of these events, the first thing they did was turn out the lights. It's a nice effect for the fans in attendance, but it makes for bad television.

Meehan agreed and went back to the Maple Leafs. Whether he neglected to say anything about the lighting, or the team ignored the request, something got lost in translation. The first iteration of the pregame scripting from the hockey club came back with plans for a darkened arena. At that point, we informed both Newport and the Maple Leafs that this was not satisfactory for us, and had to be changed.

Follow-up phone calls with Meehan were straightforward and polite. Don understood our position and respected it. He again went back to the club to coordinate the procedure. Minutes later, the phone rang in my office. Ken Dryden explained that it's far more dramatic for the fans if the lights are out for these types of things. I understood that, but we had a policy of not covering ceremonies in any arena where the lights are off.

That policy was an agreement between our senior producers, Paul Graham, Sherali Najak, Tim Davis, and me. It wasn't written anywhere; there was no decree from on high. It was just our group saying we refused to cover bad-for-TV ceremonies for teams and their fans. Most teams understood or complied. It made for simpler television. In fact, our rules for pregame were often more complex. It went beyond ceremonies to include the singing of the national anthems. We didn't mandate coverage of the anthems in any arena, except if it was a Canadian team against a Canadian team and so we only had to cover one anthem. Obviously, we made exceptions for special match-ups or special events and the playoffs. The reason for not covering anthems was to allow our producers up to three more minutes to set the game up. These were the nights before pre-game shows and multiple channels; the three minutes before the opening puck drop were like gold. Every team, the league, charities, sponsors were always trying to find ways to leverage *Hockey Night in Canada* for those three minutes. But this is airtime that we controlled and we weren't going to give it away and compromise what the show stood for and looked like. We were damned if we would be covering a ceremony in the dark!

Dryden was not happy with our stance and tried to convince me to make an exception. But allowing the Maple Leafs to do it would open the door to other teams. We did not want to give any team that option.

Dryden's final word on this was that the ceremony would occur with the lights out and a spotlight on Curtis Joseph. I said that was fine with me, but it would not be on television. Then I asked, who would call Don Meehan to tell him of our decisions?

If memory serves me, the ceremony did occur, on television, with full arena lighting. I always felt after that that Ken was a bit more aloof, and a little less cooperative with the show.

The call in mid-December 2000 was to gauge my interest in assisting MLSE in building not one television channel, but two: the Toronto Maple Leafs channel and the Toronto Raptors channel. The CRTC had already approved the licenses; now MLSE was plotting whether or not to execute the plan. To do so, they needed people with expertise in sports television, in start-ups, and in creating content. Whether Ken put personal grudges aside or they were never there to begin with, he was very polite and forthright in telling me that they had done their due diligence and multiple people had pointed them in my direction.

It was so gratifying to hear something this positive, I would have accepted the job, on the spot, for twenty cents on the dollar. I still needed to sit with a few of the company's top management people and let them gauge if I could work in the environment of MLSE. Those conversations wouldn't occur until the new year. Ken cautioned me that if I did get the job, the challenge of launching the two new channels in just eight months would be daunting.

Just after the calendar turned to 2001, I spent time with senior managers at MLSE: Chief Financial Officer Ian Clarke, Chief Operating Officer Tom Anselmi, and Senior Vice President Bob Hunter. All the conversations were polite, pleasant, and brief. None of the meetings were longer than twenty minutes. My next conversation was with Dryden himself. I expected that one to be longer—much longer. Ken is polite, but direct, and there was little doubt he had an agenda in discussing how the project was going to work.

I felt he was trying to challenge me, which was a good thing, to think differently about the content on the hockey channel. I also felt he was trying to admonish me for our previous conversations. He didn't want to live by regular television rules. He was not interested in conventional television. He wanted creativity, and depth. Like the books he had authored, he wanted storytelling. He wanted to be different.

Dryden's desire to remove the shackles of conventional television made me that much more excited about the project. The only thing that dumbfounded me was that the conversation ended in less than an hour. I had expected a classic Dryden oratory about hockey and television. I had expected him to tell me why his approach to the hockey club, and by extension the network, was going to revolutionize the NHL. But I didn't get that. I was quickly ushered into the chief executive officer's office, where Richard Peddie was on the phone. I had met Peddie just a couple of times, after he assumed his position within the company and they had moved from Maple Leaf Gardens to the Air Canada Centre, now Scotiabank Arena. In fact, I knew Richard's brother Tom Peddie from my days at CTV and the 1994 Lillehammer Olympics, when Tom was CTV's chief financial officer. Richard had come from the Raptors side of the business and assumed the top job when the Maple Leafs, under the ownership of Steve Stavro, Larry Tanenbaum, the Ontario Teachers' Pension Plan, and TD Bank, bought the basketball team from Allan Slaight. Peddie had been part of Tanenbaum's failed bid to get the NBA in Toronto in the early 1990s. He was a perfect person to run the new company, MLSE, as it began its ascent as a sports conglomerate. He had been part of the packaged goods world. He was formerly CEO of SkyDome stadium and previously had a role within NetStar Communications, TSN's parent company.

Peddie was persuasive. He also had vision. His vision was always big. Bigger than Toronto. Bigger than Canada. He wanted MLSE to be in the same conversation as the Yankees, the Lakers, and Manchester United.

Once he was off the phone, Richard shook my hand and began to espouse his vision for his two TV channels. He approached the project with the eagerness of an evangelist. He believed that the company needed to grow beyond the "engines" that were the two teams. He sat for just a few minutes, before jumping up and opening a wall-size whiteboard that he had been working on. When he opened it, there had to be fifty different thoughts, 150 more arrows that linked all the ideas, and tons of questions marks. There was no doubt that Peddie was the driving force behind this company joining the media world. What occurred for the next few hours was truly memorable. His enthusiasm was infectious. And as much as he spoke, he listened. He also did an amazing job of making me feel integral to the project, even before my name was on any contract. I learned very quickly that Peddie made everyone feel special in the Air Canada Centre. From interns to power forwards, custodians to superstar winners, Peddie made sure they knew they contributed to the success of the company.

Despite the respect that Peddie had from all the employees at MLSE, it did not translate on the street or in the media. That amazed me. Inside he was viewed as a collaborative visionary, outside as merely the voice of corporate sports. The loyalty he built with his staff was remarkable and admirable. Of all the people I worked for, Richard Peddie and CBC's Alan Clark top the list in that regard. Neither had an air of superiority and both created the perception of listening more than speaking. It was a recipe for success for those two gentlemen.

Despite being owned by a company that had buckets of money, our venture into the digital television world was far from rich. It wasn't the case of being forced to cut corners; they were already well rounded off. Budgets were small, staff were underpaid, equipment was broadcast quality, but barely. This required ingenuity, creativity, and flexibility.

In year one, on both the hockey and basketball side, we had few or no live games because they had been sold to the two cable networks, TSN and Sportsnet. Let's face it, live game broadcasts are the only real pillar of sports television. Without games, a fledgling cable sports network is filler. That didn't stop us from trying to be creative. But something else almost did.

We launched the two channels on the first Friday in September that year, September 7, 2001, just four days before the hijacked jets hit the World Trade Center in New York City. As part of our launch month, we were preparing to televise a game from St. John's, Newfoundland, the next Wednesday. It was going to be a glorious start for the new venture. A live game for our new, little channel. It would have set us apart, even it was just for a night. But the events of 9/11 changed everything—for everyone.

The arena where our game was to be played in St. John's was turned into a hostel for stranded airplane passengers whose flights were forced to the ground as air traffic was halted. The game was cancelled. The advertising world's investment in sports television plummeted. No one was spending money on commercials and sponsorships. Our networks were on hold. The world was on hold.

The strange thing is, if not for the attacks, it's possible our channels might have been shuttered within a year. Advertising was already scarce and so had been the appetite from cable subscribers for another regional hockey network and a national basketball channel, neither of which carried live games. We were trying to sell the sizzle, with absolutely *no* steak. The attacks put a pause on almost everything, and gave us more time to get organized. Also, in between our content and the fans were the distributors, the Big Five: Bell, Rogers, Shaw, Cogeco, and Eastlink. In 2001, cable and satellite operators viewed themselves as programmers, not the conduit between the programmers and the public. They were going to decide whether or not to give us a "slot" on the new digital tier, but only after looking at our content and deciding whether it was compelling enough.

The basketball channel, Raptors NBA TV, was a much easier sell to the distributors than our Maple Leafs product. That may be surprising, but the NBA brand was strong, and the channel would be the number one (and only) complete basketball product in the country. What killed Leafs TV was the fact that it had to be regionalized. That meant, even though it took up the same amount of satellite transponder space, it had to be restricted to just the region the NHL dictated was the team's market. Because we used the Maple Leafs trademarks and name, we couldn't go into Vancouver, or Montreal, or Winnipeg. I understood the rules, but it created a ton of distribution and sales issues for all of us. After all, we were dealing with the most iconic hockey brand in English Canada. There were (and still are) a multitude of Maple Leaf fans in all ten provinces and three territories, but we were subject to the rules of all the other

NHL teams and the league itself. The NHL was in this game, too—they were partnering with TSN to launch the NHL Network at the same time.

Even operating under these restrictions, in many ways, these five or so years working at MLSE and running the channels were the most fun I ever had in television. We were a group of fifty people, most with less than two years of experience in television and pro sports, and a few with a ton of experience and a great deal of patience with people learning on the job. Truthfully, some had more patience than others (he said sheepishly).

The first thing I did was surround myself with friends and veteran broadcast people. Frank Hayward and I had worked together producing hockey and Olympics. His personality is the complete opposite of mine. But he was a thinker, a schemer. A longtime television production person, he had seen firsthand how the business was changing from a methodical, long-term planned business to a spur-of-the-moment, reactive industry. He knew what to do, and just as vital, he could predict what I would do.

Duncan Blair was a veteran television technician from the CBC. I first met Duncan when I returned to *Hockey Night* in 1994. As a Maritimer, he had a "no bullshit" mentality. His commonsense approach was combined with a vast knowledge of sports television production. In addition to being a key technical guy at *HNIC*, Duncan was also our senior audio person at the hockey venue at the Olympics in Japan in 1998. He was a salt-of-the earth guy. Totally trustworthy.

Finally, I brought along Karyn Savoia, my executive assistant from the CBC. Karyn was my shadow. She protected me, at all costs. She confronted me when I needed it and she promoted me when others were questioning me.

These three made our two channels work. I trusted them implicitly and they believed in what we were creating. They were always—*always*—two steps ahead of me. I gave them headaches. They saved my bacon.

We tried to act like we were in the big leagues. We wanted to compete with TSN and Sportsnet, who had many more people and resources, and a lot more money. As the early years wore on, and our viewership remained limited, our budgets were cut. It wasn't fun, but we just couldn't justify spending money on content that wasn't being viewed by many people. For example, in year two we were able to carry a few Maple Leafs pre-season games. Our viewership probably peaked at 65,000 viewers. That was a far cry from *Hockey Night's* 2 or 3 million viewers on a Saturday night, but it was still television—quality television that might have lacked resources, but made up for that in passion, enthusiasm, and knowledge.

Our two-hour Sunday morning panel show *The Reporters with Paul Romanuk* was a great way to start a Sunday. That special group of media people truly enjoyed contributing to a show that allowed them to tell their stories, have an opinion, and never feel rushed. The payment for our guests? A fresh Subway sandwich after the show. They did it because it was fun. Paul Romanuk, who had left TSN to be involved in an ill-fated all-sports radio network, was a perfect host. He was known to hockey fans across the country for his NHL and Hockey Canada work, and had a deep knowledge of the game. The format of the show was a thin frame-work of topics that allowed for solid discussion, debate, and disagree-ment. In so many ways, it was the "Hot Stove" on steroids—not eight minutes of content, but two hours of free-for-all discussion on everything hockey and Maple Leafs. It quickly gained a small, but loyal, following.

My favourite concept, one that really encapsulates what Leafs TV stood for, was a show called *In Conversation*—a thirty-minute interview show with our host Brian Duff. It was hardly an original idea, but it was something that we could do quickly and inexpensively.

The guest list was basically my phone directory. If I had a friend in the hockey community coming to Toronto, I would try to conscript him to show up at the studio. Brian, who has gone on to great things in Buf-falo for the Sabres' broadcasts, invariably got less than ten minutes notice of who the guest would be. Part of our promise to the guest was that the whole thing, from hotel pickup to hotel drop-off, would be less than an hour—guaranteed! With those parameters, how could anyone who's stuck in a hotel room on the road refuse?

So, on any weekday when we could make it work, our little shop sprang into action from the moment I got off the phone and told Frank Hayward, our coordinating producer, that, for instance, Coach Marc Crawford was coming over.

With that, I'd walk to my car while Hayward informed Duff of the guest, the producer Chris Clarke found two pictures of the guest, and the technical crew got in place. As soon as I came back it was a quick dust of makeup, then Crawford's in the chair and answering twenty-four minutes of questions. Then right back to his hotel, all within an hour. Before exiting the studio, Crawford would have been given a DVD copy of his show. Lean, nimble, creative, passionate—and fun for us. That was Leafs TV.

We may have been lacking resources, but the project had the power of the brands. Richard Peddie always talked in terms of the two engines, the Maple Leafs and the Raptors. It allowed our group to be front and centre with these two teams every day of the NHL and the NBA seasons because we had access that other networks never could. It gave us great license to create content and eventually produce more than 120 live games a year, for other networks. On most nights, we had pre- and postgame shows that lasted more than the length of the actual games.

We were producing the games with some of the best production people in the industry. By year three, we were able to negotiate production control—for the Leafs and Raptors—from both TSN and Sportsnet. Our logic, which both networks bought into, was to make a quality production, and there was great efficiency in having one production unit do those games. The simplicity of our group fostered artistic and financial success. But the real benefit to them was keeping MLSE happy. Both networks privately admitted that keeping the NHL and NBA teams satisfied with rights renewals always around the corner was a smart business move. At that point, our group was producing more live sports content than *Hockey Night in Canada*. In addition to some of those young lions we developed internally, we were able to secure Paul Graham and Gord Cutler to work on our NBA games. Graham has become the most important live

TV sports executive in the country, guiding all of TSN's game coverage: NHL, NBA, CFL, IIHF. His career has been remarkable, and in 2002, after a fallout at CBC, he became a linchpin for us. Similarly, Cutler was a quality producer for years at both TSN and Sportsnet. I began to work with him when he was a green production person way back in 1986 and 1987. His resume, like Paul's, is exquisite, including Olympics and the NHL. Having two of my friends, two comrades in arms, to navigate the world of the Toronto Raptors was essential to our higher production quality, and thus our success.

On the hockey side, the Maple Leafs' regional broadcasts were still being produced by Molstar Communications. Molstar was going through some changes. It no longer produced the national packages, and in a short period of time, they were getting out of the hockey production business, too, as their number one client, Sportsnet, was in the process of switching to using their own staff to produce the regional broadcast packages across the country. It wasn't lost on a few of us that thirty years earlier a small group of people had produced almost every hockey game, including national and regional broadcasts, in Canada. Two of us, Doug Beeforth and myself, produced many of those games. Now, three decades later, it was Beeforth as president of Sportsnet and me at MLSE who were pushing the Molson-backed production company out of the hockey production business.

Given all the power of Maple Leaf Sports and Entertainment, and trying to ensure that our little television venture was successful, we thought we should produce the hockey games for other people, namely Sportsnet and TSN, who split the regional games. By year four, we were producing the Maple Leafs with Mark Askin, the longtime Maple Leafs producer, and Jacques Primeau, who had become the best hockey director in the world while working games at the Montreal Forum.

We knew that Askin and Primeau, both big personalities, could work well together. In 1996, they were paired for the first World Cup of Hockey; in 1998, they worked well together as our lead production team at the Olympic Winter Games in Nagano, Japan.

Askin's passion for Maple Leafs hockey was deep. No producer alive could analyze a play quicker than Mark. His editorial strengths, on the fly in the truck, were unmatched. He was built for Leafs TV. Primeau had been a mainstay at *La Soirée du Hockey* for many years. His feel for the game was unmatched. Perhaps it was his days as a junior player that made him so good. He had a great eye.

The shot that made Primeau the best was the December night in 1995 at the Forum, which all Canadiens fans know as Patrick Roy's last game as a member of the team. Primeau's understanding of the emotion of the goaltender, the stubbornness of the coach, and the concern of fans was measured in every shot. He was able to show the passion of Roy as he was left in the net for yet another goal. He had the patience to stay on the shot of Roy as he left the ice, walked past coach Mario Tremblay, dropped his mask, and walked back past Tremblay again to team president Ronald Corey to tell him he was done as a member of the team. It was magical television. It was also a classic case of knowing when *not* to cut away—watching the monitor and knowing this was hockey history in the making.

Then, to cap it off, at the beginning of the next period there was the long zoom from the end zone camera all the way beyond the Canadiens' bench to the empty seat of the team president. It was simple, dramatic, and so effective. Panic was setting in for the Bleu, Blanc, et Rouge. Jacques made the position of director into an art.

By the time Leafs TV was in a groove, and a factor in the market, we had quality people running the shop in Hayward and Blair, and I also knew Karyn Savoia always had my back. We had the best live sports production group in the country working on the teams' games: Graham, Cutler, Askin, and Primeau. We had come a long way, in a very short period of time. It was amazing to think that just a few short years earlier, I couldn't get a job.

Still, the leadership learning curve was steep. I arrived with one type of style, but became a much more complete manager, which has put me in good stead over the years since. Much of that had to do with the people around me. I had to listen more to those in better positions to judge the work ethic and creativity of our young staff. Some of that had to do with Richard Peddie's approach to business. Internally, he believed in "Visions and Values." He treated everyone with respect and transparency. There was no better example of his skill than how he ran the company during the 2004–05 NHL lockout.

Much like a decade earlier, the league and the players were in a dispute about, primarily, revenue sharing and the implementation of a salary cap. Negotiations failed over the summer and this time the entire season ended up cancelled.

In that window of no NHL games, and so much lost revenue, Peddie was under extreme pressure to ensure MLSE would stay solvent. There were still Raptors games to be played, but at that time the revenues of the basketball team were dwarfed by those of the Maple Leafs. Peddie talked about the "two engines," but financially it was really one big engine doing the work. As the NHL games began to get cancelled in two-week increments, many employees began to worry about the future and their job security. At no time over the lost season did Peddie or ownership ever panic and begin to furlough employees or put them on shorter workweeks with less pay. There were more than five hundred full-time employees continuing to work, without worry of a lost paycheque. Richard's ability to manage the company's board of directors was tremendous and created a true sense of loyalty and team at a time when other teams were laying people off and cutting back wherever they could. He really did exhibit the "Vision and Values" he preached to everyone, every day.

One of the driving forces of the development of Leafs TV was ensuring that television rights revenue continued to increase. It was something that teams like the Boston Bruins (who are minority owners in NESN) and the New York Rangers (MSG Network) have always been able to leverage. Heck, beyond hockey, what NESN did for the Boston Red Sox and YES Network did for the New York Yankees were back of mind for the Leafs' ownership group and Peddie.

In the year before our venture started, Maple Leafs regional TV rights were around $100,000 per game. By the time I left MLSE, they were over $400,000 per game, split between the two networks (Sportsnet and TSN), with an allotment on Leafs TV. There was little doubt the business model had an influence on the market. I also believe it was a key contributor to why Rogers and Bell decided to partner to purchase 75 percent of the company, in order to control content distribution and manage rights costs.

FIFTEEN
CHANGING THE GAME FROM WITHIN

FROM THE TIME I STARTED IN THE LATE 1970S, I ALWAYS THOUGHT I WAS HELPING people watch and enjoy the game of hockey on television. I also believed that through my various jobs, I was trying to help the NHL. Whether it was *Hockey Night in Canada*, Global Television, SportsChannel America, or the two teams I worked for (the North Stars and the Maple Leafs), my relationship with the league office was open and transparent. If we did our jobs well, they looked good. If they did their job well, we looked good. It was a quality, reciprocal relationship.

I always had access to senior management, at any time, whether through John Ziegler Jr.'s tenure as president or Gary Bettman's as commissioner. Over the years, there had been informal discussions about creating a role for me at the NHL, but I was always reluctant. I very much liked my independence from the league. There were some philosophical differences between us (mostly on what was good in the United States for the game versus what was good in Canada), and I felt I was better off outside the walls of the NHL. That all changed in 2006.

The 2005–06 season was the first following the year-long labour dispute between the NHL and its players. It also marked two new broadcast contracts in the United States, with NBC and Comcast. Midway through the season, I was approached by a friend at the NHL about whether I'd be interested in talking to Bettman about a role in broadcasting at the NHL office in New York. At this point, with Leafs TV and Raptors NBA TV up and running, I was intrigued by the suggestion. In mid-January, I met Bettman in Toronto to discuss. He admitted he was thrilled with the new broadcast partners in the United States, but felt the league wasn't doing enough to support NBC and Comcast. He knew of my passion about broadcast styles, of storytelling rather than numbers, and was well aware of the programming successes both at *HNIC* and MLSE.

Over the next few weeks, we continued our dialogue. In fact, during the Winter Olympics in Turino, Italy, Gary and I were having a prolonged email discussion about philosophy, money, and logistics. I was in my office in Toronto and he was in the seats at the hockey venue in Turino. During one of the Canada games, the broadcast cut to a shot of Bettman, buried in his BlackBerry, at the same time I was receiving a reply from him. At one point I mentioned to him that our conversation was taking place on television, which elicited an emoji from the commissioner. What I didn't know then is that Gary has an amazing talent of being able to conduct about a dozen conversations simultaneously via text. But at the time, I felt special, thinking the world was watching him text me in Toronto.

After the Olympic Games ended, so did my time with the Maple Leafs and Raptors. I accepted the job at the NHL and I was on to my next adventure. I spent five days a week in New York City, commuting in and out of LaGuardia Airport, as my family (with two kids still in school) elected to live in suburban Toronto.

That first year with the NHL was amazing. Bettman allowed me to be an agent of change. We took elements from decades of broadcasting and finally put them into practice across the member clubs and broadcast partners. We became more aggressive with all the broadcasters when it came to monitoring content and production philosophy. Some of the networks welcomed our input with open arms. Most of the teams welcomed our new style with questions of their own, wondering if we could assist with improving the quality of their regional broadcasts.

It was all about building features, game philosophy, and feedback. And it worked. With the acceptance of people like Doug Sellars, who had left CBC and was now in charge of production for all the Fox Sports regional networks out of California, Mark Milliere at TSN, and my old college roommates Doug Beeforth and Rick Briggs-Jude at Sportsnet in Canada, we built a broadcast department at the NHL that actually became a resource for the broadcasters and the teams.

Both NBC and CBC were a little less enthusiastic about our daily or weekly roles in their worlds. Both believed they knew more about producing hockey on television than the NHL. That may have been true in previous years, but it wasn't true in 2006. Sam Flood was running NBC's hockey. Sherali Najak was the executive producer at *HNIC.*

Flood and I were rarely on the same page, simply because we were both strong-willed, with differing philosophies of how to produce games. We differed on play-by-play styles; we differed on the style of camera cutting during the game. What we didn't differ on was our love of the game. In the best interest of the relationship between NBC and the NHL, it made sense to have one person manage NBC, while the rest of our group managed all the other broadcasters. Adam Acone, who was a vice president of broadcasting for us, did a great job of nurturing NBC and keeping Sam and me relatively happy.

Najak, on the other hand, knew my style well. I had actually hired him for *Hockey Night,* twelve years earlier. Our relationship with him and the rest of the CBC became one of facilitation. After all, what the NHL was now trying to build was fundamentally what *HNIC* had been pushing for decades.

The NHL broadcasting department had always been a facilitator, co-ordinating the league's events, like All-Star Games and the NHL Draft. The department had never before proactively suggested how to produce content and tell stories. We were changing that.

We created content that told stories about the players away from the game, with their families (with one rule: no hockey footage). We built a system of broadcast accountability through quarterly reports that provided teams with solid information and feedback on whether their broadcast partners were doing the job they were expected to do. While many people, even owners, think they know television, they aren't sure why they like or dislike something. My long-standing joke is that "everyone is a TV expert—they have one in their family rooms." Our report card program gave teams and broadcasters simple, fair, and direct feedback. Four times a year, we supplied the teams and the broadcasters with written evaluations of the quality of their production:

Were the announcers fair? Did they understand the rules of the game? Did they make the game enjoyable for the viewer?

Were the camera angles acceptable? How did the replays help the story lines of the game?

Were the features of a high quality?

Did the broadcast put the NHL in a positive light?

It made people accountable. We also created weekly communication for all broadcasters and rights holders to discuss best practices and monitor "hot spots" (like the quality of the broadcast and camera positions, or team cooperation and in-game timing) and complaints.

Our group, which started as four and grew to a dozen, became what a broadcast department at a league should be: proactive and receptive. Respecting our partners and challenging them to be better. Giving guidance, taking heed, and working through the problems as a team. Beyond re-building *Hockey Night* and starting two television channels from scratch at MLSE, this was one of the most satisfying times of my career. We were making a difference.

Part of my job at the league was to make sure the teams had a re-source at the league level, to help the regional broadcasts be their best—and regional broadcasts are very important. The NHL regular season was 1,231 games long, and fewer than 200 of those games were on national television, in both Canada and the United States. Most fans were di-gesting their hockey hunger through the regional broadcasters. Up until 2006, those broadcasters did not get more than cursory attention from the NHL, beyond worrying about camera locations and broadcast posi-tions. As a group, we were determined to make a difference on every broadcast, on every day of the week, not just Wednesdays, Saturdays, and Sundays, when TSN, CBC, and NBC aired games. The networks had much bigger budgets, larger staffs, and a high demand for quality. The league's job with them was more that of a facilitator: ensuring teams cooperated, monitoring live microphones, and protecting the league's in-terest with their largest corporate partners. Our position—that we should spend more money, more resources, and more time in managing the other one thousand games—was greeted well by the hockey operations group at the league, the rights holders, and the teams. It meant a far greater in-teraction with people and teams on a daily basis, whether that be Sellars at Fox, Briggs-Jude at Sportsnet, or any of the other broadcasters. These names from my past, after all these years, reinforce how small the hockey community was (and still is). We had constant communication with the teams, even if just touching base—a combination of "Big Brother" watch-ing and "Best Friend" saying hello. Becoming a resource for content, and a production consultant for broadcasts, became one of our primary objec-tives over five seasons.

It didn't hurt that most teams knew of my long tenure at *Hockey Night in Canada* (a broadcast partner) and my six years at MLSE (a member club, and production group). Calls were most often returned, and problems were solved rather than created.

We were actually able to orchestrate a couple of "acquisitions" for teams and their broadcast partners. The Florida Panthers, in an effort to be credible in the market, signed former ESPN broadcaster Dave Strader to a deal to be the play-by-play broadcaster for the regional rights holder, Fox Sports Networks. Only one problem: the hiring of Strader did not move the needle. His abilities as a national broadcaster were never in question. Hockey fans in South Florida, the small group that did watch Panthers hockey, were thrilled to have such a quality broadcaster on their shows. But the fan base, along with ratings and advertising revenues, didn't grow by much. After just one year, Strader's contract was becoming a liability, and the team's president, Michael Yormark, knew that at some point Strader had to go. It was not going to be a good look for the team, the network, or Strader. Dave, who still had time on his contract and had been a team player throughout, didn't deserve any fallout, and it would be best if we could avoid any public embarrassment for him or his family. I considered it part of the reason I was brought to the NHL: we needed to help the clubs, and level the broadcast playing field, in order for NHL games in every market to look as professional as possible.

At the same time, in Phoenix, the Coyotes were looking to mount a "network" quality broadcast for a team struggling in its market. Team president Doug Moss had been a major player at MSG Network in New York and truly knew the value of a quality broadcast and quality broadcasters. Darren Pang was already in place, and Coach Wayne Gretzky, who had a tremendous amount of power in the organization, at every level, truly believed that the broadcast was one of the key ways to grow the game in Arizona.

Yormark explained his issue, that Strader, unfortunately, had to go as the Panthers continued to bleed money. Moss checked in (as he often did), asking if we could help improve the broadcast for the Coyotes. The two calls occurred within forty-eight hours. It was a eureka moment and exemplified what a league broadcast department should be doing. Don't create problems, solve them. It was as close as I ever came to being a general manager, engineering a trade. It felt satisfying.

It amazed me how often a problem could be solved with a phone call to the right people, at the right time. In spring 2008, John Collins, the league's chief marketing officer, was smack in the middle of orchestrating the first Winter Classic in the United States. We were in his office with Larry Quinn, CEO and president of the Buffalo Sabres, who were one of the participating teams. Quinn had always been a "league-first" guy and was a willing participant in making the Winter Classic a reality.

To make it work we needed a team that was prepared to sell a home game out of their season-seat packages to the league. In exchange, the team received a sum of money equal to the average gate receipts and concessions from the previous season. In addition, as part of relinquishing responsibility for the game, the team's season subscribers would get first crack at tickets for the event. It was a win-win for the league and the team. In this case, the Sabres received just less than $1 million for selling the game back to the league.

In one of the logistics meetings early on, Quinn, Collins, and I were talking about what needed to happen to keep the Sabres happy, when Larry took a phone call from someone at the team's office. When he hung up, you could tell he was upset. It seems his longtime TV analyst, Jim Lorentz, had decided to retire, leaving the team's broadcast without a colour man.

This was right up my alley. Quinn's people were quickly coming up with a list of potential replacements and I asked him, flatly, who he wanted: "If you had a single name, no matter where he worked or if he was available, who would you want?" The answer: "Harry Neale. I just think he's the best."

It was another eureka moment. In my previous life, with the Toronto Maple Leafs, Harry Neale had been a mainstay on our regional broadcasts, in addition to his work on *Hockey Night in Canada*. He was beloved in the market, and worked very well with both Joe Bowen (regionally) and Bob

Cole (nationally). But you could tell Harry was starting to slow down. While his wit still came through, his analysis of games and events was not at the level it once was. He had become rather predictable, citing stats rather than using key observations. In my opinion, he had become far too reliant on his producer, Mark Askin, to analyze the game and tell stories.

Before I left the Maple Leafs, we had hired Greg Millen to work on the Leafs TV side of the broadcasts. Millen, another guy I hired multiple times, had come to work for us with the long-term plan of replacing Harry, at the appropriate time. There was no timetable for the Millen promotion, but make no mistake, it was on the mind of many at MLSE, who were famous for always building succession plans (something that senior management, under Richard Peddie, met twice a year to discuss).

Following our meeting with Larry Quinn, I put a call into Tom Anselmi at Maple Leaf Sports. He was chief operating officer, under Peddie. With the knowledge that Neale's contract was expiring (a deal I helped construct), I put it to Tom that I might have a remedy for him to avoid offering Harry a new deal without being embarrassed about not wanting to bring back the seventy-year-old legend to the Leafs' broadcast booth. After that, I phoned Don Meehan at Newport Sports Management, who had represented Harry for many years and multiple contracts. I put it to Don that we had a chance to extend Harry Neale's career by three or four years, and allow him to actually work games in the city where he lives, Buffalo. Don was intrigued but didn't want to compromise his client's position in the Toronto market. A fair concern, but I explained there was no way, in my view, that Harry would get a lengthy contract in Toronto, and we could orchestrate one in Buffalo—*and* in American dollars! We weren't looking for a decision immediately, but it couldn't wait four months, either. Negotiations would have to start quickly, with the hope that Harry would do games before the hockey season ended.

This was all within two hours of the original discussion in John Collins's office. I tracked down Quinn in the New York office and told him about my phone discussions. I think he was shocked. Perhaps not that

Harry was in play, but rather by how swiftly we were able to lay the foundation of the Sabres and Harry Neale partnership. I don't believe Harry ever fully knew about my role in getting him to the Sabres—or if you want to put it another way, my role in avoiding an embarrassing end to his career in Toronto, which might have happened if not for Quinn and the Sabres voicing their need and opinion at the perfect time. I hoped this partnership would last three or four seasons; I was thrilled by the decade it became.

As year four at the NHL began, one of my key responsibilities was to run the NHL Network, which we had launched the previous year in the United States, piggybacking on the success of the network in Canada. We needed to produce some content for the American market (and in high definition, as our contracts with distributors dictated), but it was not as challenging as the previous three years had been trying to assist all the broadcasters, on a local and national level, to improve and give them better content.

By spring 2009, I could sense my influence and position within the NHL waning. Collins, who had been brought in after a time in the NFL world, was now the chief marketing officer. He had completely restructured or removed key people who had been in Gary Bettman's inner circle, and created, ostensibly, a more progressive, prolific group to build content for the web and big-time events. Events like the Winter Classic, which Collins had championed with our friends at NBC, became key "tent poles" for the NHL.

Even though I had a big title and an inflated salary, my authority had been narrowed. Meetings started to occur around me, without me. It was apparent that my skill set did not fit the vision of an evolving NHL broadcast/content philosophy. Collins, whom I reported to, had become less and less accessible to me. My desire to continue to support the regional broadcasters, at least as much as we supported the national broadcasters, was no longer the corporate outlook of the league. Monies that were earmarked for regional content were diverted to other projects. I'd say the writing was on the wall, but the reality was *there was no wall to write on anymore.* I was not happy, they were not happy—something had to happen. I would love to tell you that my departure was mutual, but it wasn't. Yes, I wanted out, but my love for the game and my loyalty to the people I worked with would have kept me there indefinitely.

I was fired—and allowed to stay on for an additional five weeks to manage the Red Wings/Penguins final and the draft. The official transfer of power would be during draft week, in Montreal, at our annual broadcast meetings. The story was framed, by both the league and me, that it was time for me to move on, the need for full-time people in New York (as opposed to me commuting from Toronto), and the development of the digital side of the business, which required a more hands-on approach than I could give. Most people bought it.

It was in my best interest not to burn the bridge with the commissioner and his cohorts. I still intended to work in or around the NHL. I had finally learned, after scorching my previous employers, that enjoying the short-term spotlight of martyrdom did not outweigh the long-term advantage of being professional and holding your head high (not to mention future employment). As much as you may want to publicly humiliate the other side, it does absolutely no good. Perhaps it's an unfortunate reality of business. Companies that have power and control purse strings also control the narrative. And companies can hold grudges. It's not fair, but it's real. I have learned that the hard way.

During these moments I've often asked myself, am I compromising my integrity? I don't think so. Taking the high road means maintaining some discretion at a time when every bone in your body is aching in despair. It would be easy to yell from the nearest rooftop that you were being discarded like an old pair of socks. But maybe the hard thing to do is the right thing. And, like much in life, it's simpler than it seems: leave on a positive. Make it look like a mutual decision. Create the illusion of choice. That was always in my own best interest.

I left Montreal at the end of the draft a free man. No more commutes to New York. No more delays sitting at LaGuardia Airport. No more late-night texts and emails from the commissioner about an issue on the air at NBC or anywhere else. I left proud of what our group did to make the NHL broadcast experience better—for the teams, for the networks, for the fans. Even today, the effects of what we as a group put forward are visible on the air across the continent. Not many would realize it, because they are subtleties of production, like more isolated replays, better camera positions, and more storytelling. But it makes me smile.

As part of my deal to leave, I was offered an on-air position at the league's satellite radio channel on SiriusXM. My relationship with Collins was candid enough that he knew of my desire to be on the air. The channel needed some new voices, and with offices located in Toronto, it made sense for the NHL to put me in a position to continue to promote the product. Still, it was a peculiar position I was put in, when you think about it.

"We don't want your broadcast expertise, but we want your voice of reason on the air." It's kind of like getting kicked in the groin while being presented with a small bouquet of flowers.

I truly believed, at age fifty-three, that my career was winding down. Networks weren't hiring men in their fifties to produce television, and I knew that my infamous direct approach when it came to business scared some people. I understood that; I accepted it. I had to evolve as a person if I was to continue in the business. On the other hand, I was confident that if I accepted the position on satellite radio, I could contribute to the growth of the game, particularly in the United States.

Within a few days of returning home, I received a phone call from David Akande, the head of production at Sportsnet in Toronto. He said, "I'd like to talk to you about announcers." I took that to mean they had been impressed by what our NHL broadcasting department had done in mentoring television announcers across the league, and he wanted me to consult with the network—an announcer coach, as it were.

Admittedly, spending so much time in the United States for years, I had not watched much of the network (other than game coverage). They controlled regional broadcasts across Canada, but not national rights. At this point, Sportsnet produced games in Vancouver, Calgary, Edmonton, Toronto, and Ottawa. They did not have the biggest budgets, and at times that was reflected in the quality of the shows. By now, however, they had started to build a level of talent in guys like Daren Millard, Nick Kypreos, Doug MacLean, Bill Watters, and Scott Morrison, who were giving the network some presence at the national level. Millard, Kypreos, and MacLean in particular had excellent chemistry and had become the cornerstone of Sportsnet's hockey group. In addition to television, their daily radio show (simulcast on the television side) had been seeing a ton of growth in popularity, more because of the bombastic styles of both Kypreos and MacLean, but also because of the quality of guests they were able to procure.

It seems that as the first decade of the 2000s moved on, more and more players found Daren, Nick, and Doug entertaining after coming off the ice from practice or a morning skate. In many ways, it was becoming the players' show of record. Millard, Kypreos, and MacLean treated their show like a locker room—full of laughs, quick wit, and the latest hockey gossip. It was a show that featured personal chemistry as much as it was about hockey, and many players seemed to love that. I assumed that with my connections in the television world and the hockey world, I would be asked to help sand some of the rough edges off the announce group at Sportsnet. In the short term, that would suit me just fine. The previous five years at the NHL had been relentless. A *good* relentless, but relentless nevertheless.

So it was much to my surprise that Akande did not suggest I work with their announce group, but rather join it! The offer was flattering, shocking, and inspiring all at the same time. I had always wanted to be on the air, but I was a production person. It was a career that offered a ton of influence and profile, and even a bit of notoriety. It wasn't so simple to leave that and go in front of the camera or behind the microphone. I always believed, and still do, that getting the next job, the next assignment, in production or television management is just a matter of patience and evolving with the times. I always believed that I would rebound. Moving to the other side seemed like giving up on that. Also, I felt it would expose me to new insecurities. What if people didn't like me? How would I look on television? What if I got fired from an announcing job—who would hire me then?

I wanted to do it but wasn't sure I would be good enough to succeed. That's why, initially, I turned Akande down. "David," I said, "I'm not sure I would hire me."

Akande chuckled and explained his thinking. I would fill a void on the network's hockey coverage, as a "hockey lifer" who could explain league stories. The group was losing the "scoop" battle with TSN, the league's official cable broadcast partner, and he thought I could help with that. He also said I would provide some balance to what Kypreos, MacLean, and the others had done, all the while expanding Sportsnet's hockey brand.

That still didn't sway me. I really didn't have much of a desire to do television—I had a tremendous desire to do radio. That was my first love. I felt radio played more to my strengths—my general sports and history knowledge. As those around me tend to remind me a great deal, I also do love a good argument. I love to be the "devil's advocate." Radio programming allows more time for that kind of back-and-forth.

Akande wanted me for TV and some radio, while I wanted radio with some TV. Two weeks later, Akande called me again to see if I had changed my mind, and if I had warmed to the idea of being more on television. I told him I would consider it if he could guarantee me a (mostly) regular position on *Prime Time Sports* with Bob McCown. From 1996 to 2002, I had been a regular member of the Friday roundtable with Bob and cohost Jim Hunt. I enjoyed it a great deal while I was at *Hockey Night in Canada*, and then in my early days at MLSE. It was those weekly appearances that had reignited my love of radio, and confirmed that if I truly put my mind to it, I could have a career on the air. Nelson Millman, the program director/station manager at The FAN radio in Toronto, had become a dear friend, and never discouraged me. If you know Millman at all, you also know that right now he'd be chirping me, saying, "But I never said you'd be good, either!"

We eventually settled on a deal that set the ratio at fifty-fifty TV and radio. It gave me the comfort of working with McCown, the boys at *Hockey Central*—Daren Millard, Nick Kypreos, and Doug MacLean—and other talented broadcasters like R. J. Broadhead, Mike Brophy, Scott Morrison, and Bill Watters. All the while, I'd be making a conservative, cautious venture into the TV world.

It was a nervous excitement. This was something that I had always wanted to do, but never had the nerve or the opportunity for. In many ways, it was uneventful, particularly in the first two years, where our role as the number two sports network was evident. We filled a void, behind TSN, in the hockey world, trying to compete nationally but without the national television rights (albeit with TV content in Montreal, Ottawa, Toronto, Calgary, Edmonton, and Vancouver). There were bumps in the road—I had to learn about being on television—but everyone pulled in the same direction. It was a fun and comfortable place to work.

One of the biggest differences for me was the recognition that came with being on television. Here I was, now in my fifties—with more than thirty years of being a policy maker or an influencer of how people watch sports on television. I had had much more important jobs behind the scenes, affecting how people consumed the NHL product. Now, after just a few months of being on camera and on the air, I was being recognized on the street. These new contributions on the air were minor compared to what I had done before. I always felt sheepish acknowledging any praise because this job was so much easier and less stressful than the management and executive jobs I had.

It was a thrilling time. Good people. Nelson Millman on the radio side. My college roommates Doug Beeforth and Rick Briggs-Jude on the television side, plus a group of announcers who became friends as we had fun on TV. But, within five short years, the TV landscape, at least when it came to hockey, would change forever.

SIXTEEN
EPISODES

WHEN I STARTED THIS PROJECT, I VOWED NOT TO HAVE A BOOK OF SIXTY CHAPTERS, two and a half pages each. To me, a chapter should expand on a theme, a major story. But a life in hockey provides many stories that are just anecdotes, worthy of a paragraph or two, and hopefully a good chuckle.

One of those involves the return to Maple Leaf Gardens of legendary Leaf Dave Keon, but as a member of another NHL team, the Hartford Whalers. Early in the 1979–80 season, and newly added to the NHL from the dissolved WHA, the Whalers made their inaugural visit to Toronto. The Whalers' biggest name was obviously Gordie Howe, the former longtime Detroit Red Wing now in his fifties and playing alongside his two sons, Mark and Marty. That was a huge story for our broadcast of October 30, 1979, one of the first times I produced a game at the Gardens.

I'm not sure why I was given the assignment. The regular Maple Leafs producer, Bob Gordon, was around, but perhaps Ralph Mellanby wanted me on a game that many viewed would be the weakest competition for the Leafs early that season. Regardless, it was a thrill. With the Howes and the return of Keon, there were juicy story lines for a young producer to gnaw on to create some good television. The Howe part was easy. The Keon angle was a little different.

The Maple Leafs, by now led by a reinvigorated Punch Imlach as general manager, were a soap opera. General Manager Jim Gregory and Head Coach Roger Neilson had been let go in the summer by owner Harold Ballard, who felt that the players, like Darryl Sittler, Lanny Mc-Donald, Ian Turnbull, and Mike Palmateer, were a little too influential. Imlach was brought in to bring back some of the authoritarian style he wielded in the 1960s that won the team four Stanley Cups. It became an unmitigated disaster. The return of Keon, while dramatic, was the least of Imlach's worries as he tried to change the culture on his team. Keon had jumped to the rival WHA in 1975 after Ballard had publicly soured on his captain. Originally playing for the Minnesota Fighting Saints, then the New England Whalers, the thirty-nine-year-old had played a few games at Maple Leaf Gardens in the interim, against the WHA Toros, but those nights were invariably in front of a half-filled arena, and little, if any, television audience. Keon's return, in an NHL sweater, was big. At twenty-three, I was still learning on the job. For two previous seasons, I had observed other producers' work and thought I could handle the pressure of the moment, and believed I could prepare as well as any of them.

But the Keon story deserved special attention. The day before the game, I set up a meeting with the Whalers' public relations man, John Hewig (who went on to great success in the LPGA and PGA communications world). We met at the team hotel, where I suggested how important it was for our show to cover Keon's return to Toronto, in order for Dave to get the acknowledgement he deserved. Hewig's response was predictable.

JH: We understand how important it is. That's why he will take the
opening face-off.

JS: I was actually thinking of something different. Because, if you think about it, he will take that face-off right after the anthem is finished. There will be no time for the fans to applaud Keon as they sit down again. It really isn't as dramatic as it could be.

JH: Well—what would you suggest?

JS: I think he should take the second face-off of the period. Think about it. On the first whistle after the game has started, your coach makes a line change, and Keon comes over the boards. Every Leaf fan will see it, and we will be prepared for it on television. We will follow him to the face-off circle, and the crowd will roar. It's perfect.

JH: I'm not sure Don [Blackburn, the coach] will do that. And I'm not sure Dave will like that.

JS: Well, why don't you ask?

I wasn't sure that Hewig had bought into the idea, but at least he hadn't said no. The following morning, Hewig, Blackburn, and I met in the empty seats at Maple Leaf Gardens, where I again explained the idea to the coach. Blackburn actually liked it and agreed. I don't know for sure, but I suspect Blackburn explained to Keon that this was about giving him a better special moment.

The night went off without a hitch. The first whistle, in the first minute of play, put the face-off in the Maple Leafs' defensive zone, to the left of goalie Mike Palmateer. Our camera was already on Keon when he hopped the boards and scooted, the way he always did with that jump in his stride, to the face-off circle. The Gardens erupted.

The story had been told. The player had been appreciated. My job was done. But Keon's night was far from over. He had one goal and one assist that night, as his new team defeated his old team 4–3. At that time in Keon's career he loved nothing more than to scupper Harold Ballard's Maple Leafs. It was a sore point that lasted long after Ballard's death and into the twenty-first century, when team president Brendan Shanahan was able to mend the very frayed relationship by receiving him for an event in which they finally retired Keon's No. 14.

I felt truly blessed to be around Scotty Bowman's Montreal team. When you consider that I got to cover the Islanders and the Oilers in the 1980s, I have witnessed perhaps the last three true NHL dynasties. Others, like Detroit or Pittsburgh or Chicago or Los Angeles, have been tremendous, but, for whatever reason, none of those teams sustained winning like the teams of Bowman, Arbour, and Sather.

What stays in my mind the most is not the great hockey these teams played, but the interactions I had with all of them. The Sather events speak for themselves, as I have discussed already. Al Arbour was bigger than life during his team's four Stanley Cups. When he spoke, you paid attention. I still remember in the 1982 Cup Final, at the Pacific Coliseum in Vancouver, one harmless interaction that left an indelible mark in my relationship with the great Isles coach.

It was about two hours before Game 4 (which was the final game) of the series, and Arbour was outside the visitors' dressing room at the Coliseum, smoking a cigarette. This was years before the laws that forbid indoor smoking. Here was a Stanley Cup champion, both as a player and a coach, taking one last quiet moment to relax before the game. I was eighty feet away, near the TV mobile, which was parked inside the arena, halfway between the two dressing rooms. I saw Arbour and respected his space, particularly this close to game time. After all, he probably had no clue what this kid in the blue blazer did anyway, except that it was a *Hockey Night* blazer. As I turned away to walk into the mobile, he bellowed, "John!" I turned and looked. That was Al Arbour, yelling at me. And he knew my name! "John! Come here!"

I knew of Arbour as a coach, obviously, but I also knew him as a hockey player, a guy who was on our black-and-white spartan television in the 1960s playing for Bowman's St. Louis Blues. He was the only player I knew who played wearing glasses. And he was talking to me! I walked over, in total fear that we, or worse, *I*, had done something wrong. After all, he was an NHL coach on the verge of winning his third consecutive Stanley Cup. He wasn't just saying hello for the hell of it.

JS: Hello, Coach. How are you?
AA: Doing fine, John. I just need a favour.

I was growing taller, every time he said my name.

JS: Anything you want.
AA: You see that TV light over there? That big one? Anyway, you can turn it off for the next few minutes. I feel like I'm getting a suntan here.
JS: Al [I'm confident now], I think I can do that.
AA: That's great. Thanks so much. How are you doing?

What followed was a brief, social conversation between a grizzled NHL coach and a young, green television producer. He made me feel important. He didn't have to, but he did. I never forgot, and I never will.

Over time I learned that most coaches, that close to game time, have little or nothing to do. They need someone to chat with or, in this day and age, text with. During the 1999 Stanley Cup Final in Dallas, Ken Hitchcock was so engaging and enthralled in our conversation about Civil War reenactments, we spoke right through the pregame warm-up, almost to game time. These days I would have little or no caution in speaking with a coach about a lineup issue or just to say hello and wish him luck. I suppose it's more about my forty years of understanding that these guys aren't that much different than the rest of us after all, or perhaps it's about the trust you build up with people who have become friends, or at least acquaintances.

Those small moments, like the one with Arbour, stand out. But then there are the nights of greatness, historic nights that make you proud, but still create a cringe or two. One of mine occurred on December 30, 1981.

Most hockey fans know that date: the game when Wayne Gretzky scored five goals, to reach the amazing total of 50 goals in 39 games. It had been an amazing night of hockey. The Philadelphia Flyers were making their annual end-of-calendar-year trip to Western Canada. The Flyers and Oilers had become pretty good rivals in just two seasons—the Flyers started their trek to the 1980 Stanley Cup Final with a three-game sweep of the Oilers in the previous year's playoffs. Philadelphia was still a star-laden team with Bill Barber, Bobby Clarke, Brian Propp, and Reggie Leach, with the great Pat Quinn behind the bench. In a seesaw battle, Gretzky ended the night with that famous empty net goal for his fiftieth. It is one of the great television moments in the last half century of the NHL. The call by the late Tim Dancy was short and sweet: "Here is an empty-net chance for Gretzky . . . Five seconds . . . He's moving in . . . Scores!"

What followed at Northlands Coliseum in Edmonton was bedlam—pure, unadulterated bedlam. And we showed it all. It was an ovation that felt like it never ended. The players mobbed Wayne. The crowd rose and stayed on its feet. It was a surreal moment. Perhaps one of the greatest moments I will ever be part of.

What we never did see on TV, however, was a replay of the empty-net goal—no end zone, tight follow, or low-angle look for the fans watching. I would like to tell you that it just didn't feel right, but the truth is that we—no, *I*—was so caught up in the moment that we just didn't think to.

Other replays were used in our postgame interview with the Great One. But with the technology of the time, some of those other angles just disappeared. That still makes me cringe a little.

By the way, despite what people think they remember, the game was not on *Hockey Night in Canada*. Nor was it a national broadcast. It was strictly produced for our audience in northern Alberta. Also for the record, our colour man that night was Don Cherry. He was pretty darn good.

My first Olympic experience was unforgettable, for many reasons. It was in Calgary, where I was living, in 1988. It's also the same time when I started dating my wife-to-be, who knew little of my TV background. Four decades later, she still calls us a "bunch of old gossips."

Access to coaches is different at the Olympics than in the NHL. While media have access to NHL players and coaches at key times, the same cannot be said for the Olympics. The world's greatest sporting event is full of protocols and politics, and there's a lack of direct, discreet contact. Calgary was no different. This frustrated Dan Kelly to no end. Here he was, the voice of Olympic hockey in Canada, and he had little or no time to talk to the team, and in particular head coach Dave King. It drove Dan crazy.

He had already had a run-in with King at a pre-Olympic event the previous December, when he told King he was "fucking stupid" for not putting Brett Hull on the Canadian roster. (As a result, Hull became an American player for the next fifteen years on the international stage.) On top of that, King was reluctant to make himself available for media. Dan needed help. He needed his daily update from the head coach on the roster and the game plan. He came to me to see if I could coerce the Canadian coach to give him fifteen minutes on game days.

Living in Calgary, I had spent a ton of time around the Olympic program and enjoyed a really good relationship with King. But these were tough times. The pressure on King to put a quality team on the ice, at home, was intense. He was not his affable, approachable self those days. My access to him was limited, as well. But I couldn't let Dan down. After all, in a few weeks we were to be back on the Stanley Cup trail again with Davidson and Hodge for the second straight year. For the next two days, I must have seen Dan a dozen times. Every time he saw me, there was no "hello" or "how are you doing?" There was just "What's going on with King?"

The games began on a Sunday with no resolution in the Kelly-King summit. My pal Dan was not very happy. He couldn't understand why he couldn't have the same access that Al Michaels and Ken Dryden, who were doing ABC's hockey, had with USA coach Dave Peterson. In fact,

Peterson would sit backward on a chair in the hall outside the USA locker room and talk to anyone who would go by. Canada played again on Tuesday. It needed to be solved or else Dan would have another meltdown. On the Monday following the first Canada game, the phone rang in the TV mobile. It was Dave King. He needed a favour.

It just so happened that he had planned to make coaching videos with all the different angles from our host broadcaster feed for Hockey Canada's coaching tapes, and he needed the high end-zone camera, a little wider in its coverage of the game. He needed it badly.

> DK: So, John, how do I talk to the cameraman to get him to do
> that?
> JS: Well, Dave, you can't talk to the cameraman. That would be like
> me talking to one of your players during the game. I think I can
> help you out. But in return, I need a favour.
> DK: Anything.
> JS: Okay, we will have our end zone camera shoot "board to board"
> for your videos, if you give Dan Kelly fifteen minutes on the
> afternoon of your games at the Saddledome.
> DK: How important is that?
> JS: How important is your end zone camera?
> DK: Tell him he can come up to my office at four o'clock on game
> day.
> JS: Every game day.
> DK: Yeah, every game day.

With one phone call, two problems were solved. And a happy Dan Kelly is a good Dan Kelly. We weren't even working together, but he was my friend. "You, Shannon," he said afterward, "are a fucking magician."

If there was a lasting legacy of my time at *Hockey Night in Canada*, it might just be *Hockey Day in Canada*. When we started that project, there was a real belief that it would turn into something special, an unofficial national holiday to reflect the passion and pride we take in hockey. But truly, the creation of the day was a bit of a fluke.

Originally, we had talked about an NHL triple-header involving all six (at the time) Canadian teams that would be preceded by a Canada vs. USA women's game. Coming off the exciting Olympic final between the two best women's teams in the world in Nagano in 1998 and the growing interest in the women's game, it made a ton of sense. However, while we owned the NHL rights and the Olympic rights, we did not own the television broadcast rights to any of Hockey Canada's properties. Those were held by TSN, who had become our biggest rival in the hockey domain. Once it was determined—and that happened quickly—that TSN would not give or sell us the rights for the single exhibition game between the two teams, we were back to a simple doubleheader format for a Saturday in February 2000.

I think we were all disappointed that we couldn't manage to get the four-game-day done, no one more than my boss Alan Clark, who was about to phone the network execs and give the programming time back. That's when it hit me that we could fill the time with a four-hour pregame show. Sounds crazy, right? Clark thought so, too, at first. But I thought we could do a show, starting at noon, to celebrate the game of hockey. Maybe even analyze or discuss how we can make the game better. Also, I figured that the network does a lot more than four hours of coverage on an election night. We had the resources, the people, so why not take advantage of that? Go to all ten provinces and the territories. Make the show about the game and our country. We were, after all, *Hockey Night in Canada*.

You could see the light go on in Alan's brain. That was the moment, with just the two of us in the room, that we felt we could do something special.

We enlisted people from the CBC News group to help facilitate the transmission. Chris Irwin, who had been our senior features producer, was assigned exclusively to work on content for *Hockey Day* and we were off to the races.

It wasn't to be about the NHL, but rather about the place the game has in small towns, big cities, and among English, French, Inuit, and First Nations. Selfishly, my son, Jake, was involved in minor hockey in our town, and even though I was on the periphery, I was feeling the empowerment of being a hockey parent. I felt there were obvious things that should change in the game, including the power and politics of the volunteers who ran minor hockey associations, leagues, and teams. *HDIC* was a perfect vehicle to dig deep into the roots of the game—its history—and the role it plays in Canada. In fact, we put rules in place to ensure that the stars of the show were the people who truly made the game great. This was to be about everyday Canadians who were driven by their love of the game, and not the money they made from it.

Hockey Day was about all of us: how we played the game, watched the game, coached the game, and about how we tried to make the game better, for everyone. It was about being Canadian.

On that first show, there were to be no mentions of the NHL in the first four hours. Just talk about the Trail Smoke Eaters, the Notre Dame Hounds, volunteers who were up at the crack of dawn to open the snack bar, rinks in Saskatchewan that still used natural ice, and pond hockey tournaments that went on for days.

That first *Hockey Day* was, and remains to this day, a source of great pride for all of us involved. There are *Hockey Days* all over the continent now, in cities and towns in both Canada and the United States. It has been so gratifying to see everyone loving the game the way we love the game.

Hockey Day has survived work stoppages, strikes, network shuffles, and weather of all types. We knew it was special, but we never envisioned it would last more than twenty years. But it has, and it will for twenty more. More than anything else I've done, it shows the power of hockey.

CONCLUSION

AS I GET OLDER, AND SO DO MY CONTEMPORARIES, I OFTEN GET ASKED WHEN I plan to stop doing what I'm doing. Quite frankly, I'm not sure I will ever want to stop, even though my body or brain might grow tired of the process. I've said it before: I have never really had a job. Or rather, my work has never felt like a job. It has always been a passion.

Making people happy, entertaining them, making them think, cheer, cry, and beg for more: that's the life I have led in broadcasting and sports. There is a true rush of adrenaline being the eyes at a game through which people watch, or the voice of reason (or not) that listeners can nod along to, whether they agree or not. It isn't so much a career as it is a journey. It has been a roller coaster of emotions, accomplishments, and embarrassments. But there has been so much to enjoy.

Born in the analog world and now living in a digital one, I went from being one of the youngest producers in the sports TV business to a grizzled old veteran announcer who, a few times, has lamented that the media world is changing so quickly it's hard to keep track. The difference from age twenty-two to sixty-two is the ability to compartmentalize your experiences—and control your emotions.

That being said, I was always able to stay above the fray of teams winning or losing. I understood that we had to do our best work answering on the air *why* something just occurred. Our pictures and sounds could not be blurred if our favourite team or player just scored. We needed to be at our best when the Stanley Cup was given out, or at Gretzky's last game, or when there was a catastrophic injury. Focused, deliberate, and comprehensive.

There's always an exception, though. That takes us to Salt Lake City, February 2002. I was one of two Canadians on a crew of seventy-five working for NBC. It was truly an honour, and particularly satisfying because just eighteen months earlier I was deemed not good enough to work for *Hockey Night in Canada*, but now I was directing for the National Broadcasting Company, in the host country of the 2002 Olympic Winter Games. Wayne Gretzky was running Canada's team, Bob Nicholson was part of the Canadian contingent as well, and the coach of the U.S. Olympic team was my old friend Herb Brooks, who had been brought back twenty-two years after the Miracle on Ice. It was part of the storybook Olympic legacy that American audiences loved to follow. After all, Brooks had been the last player cut prior to the 1960 Squaw Valley Olympics, which was also a gold-medal-winning team on American soil.

Now, it was Canada vs. USA for the gold medal. This was the year of the famous Canadian dollar coin embedded at centre ice, where Canada won its first Olympic gold medal in men's hockey in fifty years. It was a tremendous accomplishment for Gretzky, Coach Pat Quinn, and the players. It was an emotional moment for fans across Canada, and for me, too, but it wasn't my most emotional moment at those games.

That moment came three days earlier, on Thursday, when Canada's women's team won gold. It was not just that they won, or how they overcame about a dozen U.S. power plays to do so. It was the fact that as the clock was ticking down, my American coworkers took time to congratu-late me—*me*—on the victory. A victory I had nothing to do with. It is one of those events that have been engraved on my brain. You could see the tears streaming down the faces of the Canadian players behind their face shields. I could feel the emotions welling up inside me, as well. When they unfurled the Maple Leaf flag at centre ice and "O Canada" began, the tears streamed down my face, too.

There I was, directing the cameras, barely able to see through the cry-ing, probably barely able to speak—proudly Canadian in a foreign land.

I've covered thirty-two Stanley Cups, at last count, and with all the other great games, too, this was truly one of the most emotional high-lights of my career. It was difficult to keep composed. I'm not sure I did. It was draining. I had similar emotions when the men won the following Sunday, but nothing like the outpouring I had on that Thursday night.

Nearly two decades later, it was February 6, 2021. I was on an air-plane for the first time in eleven months. The pandemic has held us all hostage, although I'm fortunate I have been able to stay busy with a daily podcast with Bob McCown, as well as radio and television work across the country, and using Twitter to maintain connections in the sports and media world. My workload has kept me sane—or rather, sane enough.

I was on the way to Edmonton to be on a Sportsnet panel for three games in four days, for the Oilers' regional broadcasts. On the flight, I had Barack Obama's most recent book and was watching a four-part docudrama on former FBI director James Comey. I have always been a political junkie.

Canadian politics? Sure. American politics? Hell yes!

I had been working on this book and it occurred to me that I wasn't sure why anyone would read about a life in the TV business and find it anywhere near as compelling, entertaining, or influential as the lives of an Obama or Comey. But then I realized that what their stories truly drive home is not lessons about Trumpism, integrity, or transparency, but rather the importance of family.

Family is why I got into this business. Family is who I wanted to make proud. Family is who I wanted to support, and never wanted to embarrass (though I sometimes did).

My love of this business started when my older brother, Ross, sent away for a Columbia School of Broadcasting brochure, and then convinced our parents to buy a tape recorder to have fun with, to hear our own voices—to be the disc jockey or the sports announcer. My love of the business came from long nights listening to radio from all over Western Canada and the United States. It was magic that came beaming over the mountains, better when it was rainy and overcast, and announcers calling every sport possible. I remember those great voices so vividly.

Scully in Los Angeles calling baseball. Hearn in Los Angeles and Blackburn in Seattle calling basketball. King calling football in Oakland. Robson, McDonald, Hewitt, Gallivan, and Kelly calling hockey.

Radio brought us the world, and in our home we were encouraged to listen, to learn, to discuss, and to argue. Not just sports, but politics, space launches, the stock exchange—life.

As a young producer, long before I was married, I loved phoning home to my mom and dad, Cay and Bob, and saying hello from New York City, or Washington, or wherever I was. At that point, my dad, who travelled the world and spent time in Africa and Southeast Asia during World War II, would say, "Washington! That's great! I've never been to Washington. Is it as beautiful as the pictures?"

My parents were always proud of me. Not because I overcame having multiple surgeries for club feet. And not just because my brothers and I were always polite to friends and neighbours. They were proud that we had ventured outside the confines of our very small town to make a life. They never stopped being proud, even when I drove a brand-new car into a telephone pole, distracted by tuning the radio. They were still proud of me when after three weeks in Toronto, I asked to come home for Thanksgiving, so homesick and three thousand miles away (they said no, by the way, because they knew what was best for me). My parents wanted us to see the world. They had worked long and hard to ensure that my brothers and I were given every opportunity to succeed. They had worked long and hard to make sure their children had opinions. My gosh, we had to have opinions. We were always in bigger trouble if we said, "I don't know," as opposed to having a contrarian opinion. They wanted us to think, to learn, to believe, and to speak up. As children of the Great Depression and the war, they had given us the best chance to succeed.

Succeed we did. I am very proud of my brothers, Bob and Ross. They have lived their lives teaching and guiding, as our parents did, making people better. I've had bigger podiums than classrooms and gymnasiums, but I should be so lucky to have the influence they have had on the generations of students they've reached.

I grew up in the West. I believe in the West. My time running *Hockey Night in Canada* became in part about ensuring that the West receives its due as an important part of our audience. That's why the doubleheader was so important.

The West deserved our respect, with the Jets, Flames, Oilers, and Canucks. As did the Atlantic provinces, where so many fans stayed up late to watch the NHL—without having an NHL team. But they had players: Crosby, Gallant, MacKinnon, MacMillan, MacAdam, and so many more. It wasn't that I took Ontario and Quebec for granted, but those provinces dominated our audience. We needed to take time to give the East and the West their due. It's why *HNIC* has remained dominant for so long: small-town Canada, who via radio and then television lived vicariously with every shot on goal, every penalty, every triumph or loss of the Maple Leafs, Canadiens, and then the Jets (twice), Oilers, Canucks, Flames, and Senators. I should not forget the Nordiques. They had a fantastic fan base, and some very good hockey teams, but they were predominantly a team for our French TV network confrères at SRC and RDS (Société Radio-Canada and Réseau des sports). Our infrequent sojourns to Le Colisée were as a visitor, never the host.

Wayne Gretzky's Oilers, Trevor Linden's Canucks, Doug Gilmour's

Flames, and Dale Hawerchuk's Jets deserved our attention, but they had never really got it from a national television perspective, until playoffs or when the Maple Leafs or Canadiens travelled west. What we did in 1995 changed that. But while we paid respect to prime time in Manitoba, Saskatchewan, Alberta, and British Columbia, our greatest intention—and our greatest desire to pay respect to hockey fans in the West—may have backfired. In building the doubleheader, we actually increased the exposure of the Maple Leafs every Saturday. In previous years, without the doubleheader, not every Toronto game was seen nationally. Games in Winnipeg, Vancouver, Calgary, and Edmonton would be shown at the same time as the Toronto game. Now, in the doubleheader format, the early game was invariably a Maple Leaf game seen from coast to coast, while the game in Western Canada followed three hours later. The extra national exposure for the Maple Leafs defeated the purpose of the format change.

It was always my belief that *HNIC* needed, and succeeded because of, small-town Canada. Skating on the local pond, going to the local rink—these concepts are associated more with small towns than anywhere else.

It is why I have always loved what *Hockey Night in Canada* stood for. And always will, although it is not as influential as it once was. As a small-town boy, I think the show meant more to me than it did to those people in big cities, and with NHL teams. It was pure, iconic Canadiana.

If I were to choose between the NHL and *HNIC*, I would choose *Hockey Night*. It is ours—Canadian—and in my time on the show I was taught that the show was a "gatekeeper" for people north of the 49th parallel. I reinforced that idea throughout my career.

You see how quickly I jumped from family to *Hockey Night*—that is something I have never been able to avoid. It is my biggest strength, and greatest weakness. The show was like family to me. *Hockey Night* and hockey on television have been the ultimate distraction for me, and not always in the most positive way. The people that have paid the biggest price are my family: my wife, Mickee, my son, Jake, and my daughter,

Maja. Travelling overseas for Olympics, for sixty days at time, and every Saturday for decades, when I should have been home or at a local arena helping put skates on, probably took its toll. The tumult of witnessing my wife going through breast cancer, while I stayed too focused on my job running Canada's biggest sports show, certainly hurt our relationship. Going to work three days after she came home from the hospital—thinking that was justified or okay—was one of worst mistakes of my life. I regret it still.

But we survived that mistake and are still working through life's daily challenges. Supporting each other, arguing. Supporting our children, arguing with them, too. Making sure that our small family stays together and are always friends. My family has stayed loyal and done an amazing job at keeping me grounded—or as grounded as could be. They see the fire that burns inside me for sports, for hockey, for television. They tolerate it when I'm distracted, and revel in it when I succeed.

I can assure you, walking in the door of your home to tell your family that you have been suspended or fired or your contract hasn't been renewed, is an excruciating mental anguish. You can see it on their faces—they feel for you, but wonder what the future means for them. While their pride for you is strained, you continue to fight because their love never dies. I have never worried about being embarrassed for myself. That's life. I have always worried about embarrassing them, because it is something they can't control. I'm glad those moments have been relatively few, but the memories of disappointing them those five or so times, of their disappointment in me, and for me, never goes away.

I have rarely shared my own embarrassment or disappointment in myself with anyone, even my family or close friends. To me, it was always a sign of weakness. In the moment, I've always I felt I could manage it—whether for two minutes, or two weeks—by internalizing and talking it through myself. I feel blessed that my times of disappointment haven't worked their way into depression. I know I am very fortunate to be able to say that.

Self-reflection has always been a strength. Still, I do get emotional, I do get loud, I do get aggressive—but not about my own personal issues. I only get that way when our common goal of great television, great story-telling, fails. I always want people to be as passionate and committed as I am.

I am not a very good golfer, but as I grow older, I love the game even more. It is social, it is competitive, it is always a challenge. Invariably, I hit as many bad shots as I do good ones. But there has never been a time—*never*—that I have said to myself after a bad shot that I'm done, defeated. I have always looked at the trouble I created as a challenge I will meet with everything I have "in my bag." It's worth taking another shot and I always believe I can get myself out of the trouble. It is that same attitude that has driven my career. Believing in what I do, and believing I can always fix the problem, has kept me focused and in the game.

It has been, and continues to be, a wild ride. With all the bumps and bruises, I'm still around to talk about it, and gladly.

After all, we have to evolve, or we die.

ACKNOWLEDGEMENTS

I NEVER EXPECTED TO WRITE A BOOK. I ALWAYS THOUGHT IT WAS TOO MUCH WORK. My admiration for those people who do it for a living is high.

Well, it was work, but not as hard as I once believed it would be. In fact, during the pandemic, there were days that writing gave me a reason to get out of bed. And as most of you can relate to, during the lockdowns, there were times we needed something to give us focus. This book certainly did that.

To thank everyone responsible for this tome would be, well, redundant. The people who deserve the thanks have already been talked about extensively. I hope I have described all these people in a colourful and fair manner. They have impacted the path, or paths, I have had to travel through this crazy career. The good news is that most of those who have been written about are still talking to me, even after having a glimpse of the copy that pertains to them. Their friendship and loyalty are cornerstones to my journey.

There are many who did not get near enough credit in these pages who need to be given a nod. Karyn Savoia was my assistant in three jobs. She kept me in line, and conspired with my wife to keep me on time. Paul Graham, who I began working with in 1979, and remains one of my closest friends, and I have worked on countless projects together. We keep each other grounded in a fragile business and are each other's best critic. Others, like Greg Millen, Gord Cutler, Bob Nicholson, Scott Smith, and Don Metz, have been on many journeys with me, both personally and professionally. We have been there for each other through the toughest of times—some theirs, mostly mine. I'm proud to say our friendships continue to flourish, even though we don't work together anymore.

To the people at Simon and Schuster, thank you for pushing and reminding me that not everyone has the grasp of the inner workings of broadcasting and hockey that some of us might think we have. And it's important to ensure your readers don't need a broadcast degree to enjoy a book.

I grew up in a house focused on sports. My parents, who have passed, loved watching sports as much as my brothers and I did. Like sports, they taught us how to compete, to win, to lose, and to be the best teammate possible. My parents also taught me how to speak up, and lead, and always have an opinion. That has certainly helped me in the past decade, being on the air.

And finally, to my family, who have always made the sacrifices for me to gallivant across the world and the airwaves. I owe so much to my wife, Mickee, my son, Jake, and my daughter, Maja. They have learned to tolerate me when I get in "playoff mode." Even to this day, when the Stanley Cup Playoffs are on, and I have no direct influence on the games or the broadcasts, they understand that I will disappear for hours on end—daily, weekly, monthly—until Lord Stanley's Cup is handed out. They understand that I am fully committed to watching, dissecting, and commenting on every aspect of the game and the broadcasts. It has been that way for me for as long as I can remember. They know it will never change. Their tolerance is amazing.

INDEX